SCOUNDRELS

WHO MADE AMERICA GREAT

MARTIN HENLEY

abbott press

Abbott Press books may be ordered through booksellers or by contacting:

Abbott Press
1663 Liberty Drive
Bloomington, IN 47403
www.abbottpress.com
Phone: 1 (866) 697-5310

ISBN: 978-1-4582-1946-6 (sc)
ISBN: 978-1-4582-1947-3 (hc)
ISBN: 978-1-4582-1948-0 (e)

Library of Congress Control Number: 2015916141

Print information available on the last page.

Abbott Press rev. date: 08/26/2016

For Patricia

Contents

Introduction

On March 27, 1945 Ivy Millichamp had just begun to prepare afternoon tea when a German V-2 rocket dropped from the sky and detonated behind her house. It gouged out a crater 40 feet long and 20 feet deep. Sitting in their living room, her husband Eric recalled watching his wife put the teakettle on the stove seconds before the blast obliterated their kitchen. At age 34 Mrs. Millichamp suffered the unfortunate fate of being the last British civilian killed during World War II.

From 1944 through 1945, 3,000 German V-2 rockets spread terror and destruction among the populace of London, England, and Antwerp, Belgium. Travelling at the speed of sound, the V-2 carried a 2,200-pound warhead. Its unreliable guidance system made everyone in its range a potential victim. In late November 1944, a V-2 hit a Woolworth's department store in south London, killing 160 shoppers and injuring 108 others. There was no defense against the rocket, nor any way to alert civilians of its silent supersonic approach. During the final year of the war V-2s decimated large swathes of London, killing and maiming 9,277 men, women, and children. Citizens of Antwerp suffered a similar fate, with 6,236 casualties.

Construction of the deadly rockets took place in secret tunnels located in the Harz Mountains near Nordhausen, Germany. Slave laborers from the nearby Dora-Mittelbau concentration camp provided the workforce. The standard welcoming speech to new prisoners at Dora was: "You came in through that gate, and you'll leave through the chimney." German guards routinely forced half-naked workers to stand at attention in the bitter cold for hours. Prisoners were beaten, tortured, and used as guinea pigs for medical experiments. Those who resisted were hanged. Twenty thousand prisoners died; the V-2 is the only weapon to kill more people in production than in warfare. The man in charge of the design and production of Hitler's last-gasp "vengeance weapon" was a tall, aristocratic SS officer from Prussia. His name was Wernher von Braun.

At the conclusion of the war the United States and the Soviet Union engaged in a race to round up German scientists, technicians, and engineers. As a part of Operation Paperclip, von Braun and many of his colleagues were unobtrusively shipped to America. Once settled at White Sands Proving Ground in New Mexico, they took on the critical task of training military, industrial, and university personnel in the intricacies of rocket and guided missile design.

In 1950 von Braun resettled in Huntsville, Alabama. There his genius for rocketry and his lifelong commitment to space travel paved the way for an extraordinary career. A series of articles on space travel he wrote for *Collier's* magazine in 1952 put him in the national spotlight. Soon afterwards his enthusiastic presentations about rockets and space stations on the television show *Disneyland* enthralled a generation of postwar baby boomers. By the late 1950s the charismatic rocket engineer had become the media darling of the American space program. Stanley Kubrick featured von Braun's concept of a circular orbital space station in the film *2001: A Space Odyssey.*

In 1958 a Jupiter C rocket designed by von Braun and his team at the Development Operations Division of the U.S Army Ballistic Missile Agency in Huntsville launched the first American satellite, Explorer I, into orbit. A jubilant nation showered von Braun with accolades. Two years later he was elevated to the position of director of the newly formed Marshall Space Flight Center in Huntsville. On July 16, 1969, a Saturn V rocket designed by Marshall engineers launched Apollo 11 on an eight-day flight to the moon. With the successful moon landing von Braun achieved his most cherished dream.

Many among his contemporaries considered von Braun the father of the American space program. In 1977 the Carter administration awarded the Medal of Science to the dying von Braun. About von Braun, his biographer Michael J. Neufeld said, "The sum total of his accomplishments makes von Braun the most influential rocket engineer and spaceflight advocate of the twentieth century."

Regarding his wartime activities von Braun said, "I have very deep and sincere regret for the victims of the V-2 rockets, but there were victims on both sides.... A war is a war, and when my country is at war, my duty is to help win that war." His aloof comments regarding the V-2 program inspired musical satirist Tom Lehrer to pen the following lyric:

> Don't say he's hypocritical,
> Say rather that he's apolitical.
> "Once the rockets are up, who cares where they come down?
> That's not my department," says Wernher von Braun.

Collective hero worship is a longstanding American motif. What is often lost in the reverence for historical figures are the flaws that marked them as real people before they were anointed icons. Historian Michal Jan Rozbicki observed that underlying the adulation is the assumption that the "hero is essentially great, while his shortcomings are only scratches in the marble." Historical perspective is shaped not so much by deeds as by point of view. It is a convenience of American history to overlook the fact that the leaders of the rebellion were British subjects who, if caught, would have been hanged as traitors.

What can be said about our heroes can also be said about our villains. One person's traitor is another person's patriot. There is no one objective history, but many versions woven from different angles. When I was a schoolboy Christopher Columbus and George Custer were American icons; today their legacies are stained with the blood of indigenous peoples. Napoleon Bonaparte, who knew something about historical events, is reputed to have asked, "What is history but a fable agreed upon?" We like our heroes to wear white hats and our villains to wear black. Benedict Arnold is America's most infamous traitor. Yet the treachery of Charles Lee, Washington's second-in-command, earned him barely a footnote in American history. Unlike Lee, who was an arrogant underachiever, Arnold was one of the Revolution's most capable military leaders. In the cauldron of battle his courage and ingenuity were unparalleled. His accomplishments magnified his treachery.

Scoundrels Who Made America Great takes a fresh view on heroism. In this nonfiction narrative I use a central event in the life of each "scoundrel" to dramatize how infamous labels can obscure heroic deeds. Each of the five Americans described in this historical narration demonstrated courage and conviction during desperate times—Anne Hutchinson at her trials for heresy, Benedict Arnold at the Battle of Valcour Island, John Brown at his execution, Iva Toguri in Tokyo during World War II, and four time felon Clarence Gideon who challenged the Supreme Court from his prison cell, and won. I believe anyone who has an interest in American history will welcome a deeper understanding of how personal character and momentous events can converge to produce a scoundrel and a hero in one and the same person.

CHAPTER ONE

Anne Hutchinson

The Trials of the Puritan "Jezebel"

But for better or worse, her lot was cast in the seventeenth century, and her hand was to be felt in a theological tempest which shook the infant colony of Massachusetts to its very foundation.

Emory Battis, *Saints and Sectaries*

*N*o *woman made a more indelible mark on colonial history than Anne Hutchinson. In the Puritan, male-dominated society of 17th-century Massachusetts Bay Colony, Anne Hutchinson was a rebel. At a time when women were relegated to the role of producing babies (Hutchinson had 15 children), she demanded the right to express her opinions and her religious convictions. Branded as a heretic she was banished from Massachusetts Bay Colony. Hutchinson, her husband William, and their children settled in southern New England, where with Roger Williams she cofounded the colony of Rhode Island. Some historians consider her* *the first feminist, others call her a champion of religious freedom, and some simply herald her dedication to free speech.*

But the accomplishments of Anne Hutchinson defy niches and labels. Above all else, it was her indomitable will and uncompromising belief that being female did not limit her right to express her religious beliefs that is the hallmark of her legacy. In another era Anne Hutchinson would have been a suffragist, a minister, or a civil rights advocate. Instead, she was a time traveler—a 21st-century woman living in 17th-century New England.

Death came on the heels of barking dogs. Anne Hutchinson and her family were going about their daily chores at their farm at Pelham Bay, New Netherland, when she heard a commotion. Shielding her eyes against the bright August sun, she spotted the family's two big mongrels racing down the old Indian trail, headed straight for a group of Siwanoy warriors who were striding toward the farmhouse. Hutchinson called out to her son-in-law Will Collins to round up the dogs. The intrusion was not entirely unexpected. Neighbors had warned Hutchinson that the Siwanoy were on a vengeful spree. Over the previous few weeks warriors had attacked several homesteads in retribution for the massacring of 80 Siwanoy by Dutch soldiers. Despite the warriors' ominous painted faces, Hutchinson was confident that she and her family were safe. She trusted that God would protect them.

Most Puritans considered natives "savages," but Hutchinson believed that in God's eyes all people were one. As far as Hutchinson was concerned, the Siwanoy had no reason to harm her family, and she had no reason to fear them. She welcomed them as she would any guest visiting on a summer afternoon. When the sachem, Wampage, asked her to tie up the dogs, she complied. Once the dogs were restrained the warriors sprang into action. Brandishing hatchets and knives, they attacked Hutchinson, Collins, and her eight children. The unarmed settlers had no chance. After the bloodletting, the Siwanoy dragged their victims' mutilated bodies into the farmhouse and set it on fire.

Nine-year-old Susanna Hutchinson was picking blueberries in a meadow a short distance from the farmhouse when she heard the screams of her family and the bloodcurdling whoops of the warriors. Terrified, she hid in a crevice of an ancient granite rock in the center of the field. But it was too late; she had been spotted. A warrior yanked her out of the hiding place and threw her on the ground. She covered her eyes and waited for the end, but the deadly hatchet blow did not fall. Many of those who have researched and told her story believe she was saved by her red hair, for, rather than killing her, the Siwanoy took Susanna captive and renamed her "Autumn Leaf." Susanna assimilated into the tribe where she remained for several years until relatives in Boston ransomed her.

In Massachusetts Anne Hutchinson's enemies rejoiced at the news of her death. Her fate, they said, was just retribution for her sins. Concord pastor Peter Bulkeley spoke for many when he said, "Let her damned heresies, and the just vengeance of God, by which she perished, terrify all her seduced followers from having any more to do with her leaven." The Reverend Thomas Weld wrote from London, "Thus the Lord heard our groans to heaven, and freed us from this great and sore affliction." John Winthrop, governor of Massachusetts Bay Colony, delivered a pitiless epitaph: "Thus it has pleased the Lord to have compassion of his poor churches here, and to discover this great imposter, and instrument of Satan so fitted and trained to his service for interrupting the passage [of his] kingdom in this part of the world and poisoning the churches here...."

The depth of the scorn heaped on Hutchinson is at first glance puzzling. What misdeeds could a fervent Puritan wife of a successful textile merchant, and the mother of 15 children, possibly commit to reap such venom? There was no violence, enmity, or rancor in her heart. Rather, Anne Hutchinson was an outlier. In the male-dominated culture of Puritan Massachusetts Bay she spoke her mind freely, and she refused to bend to the will of the powerful men who governed the colony.

Anne Hutchinson's story actually began 57 years before her birth, with the establishment of the Church of England by Henry VIII. Henry's 24 years of marriage to Catherine of Aragon had produced a daughter, Mary, but no son. Determined to ensure the continuation of the Tudor dynasty, Henry petitioned Pope Clement VII to grant him an annulment. Henry contended that his marriage to Catherine was illicit because she was the widow of his deceased brother. The pope refused. Undaunted, Henry in quick succession secretly married Anne Boleyn, banished Catherine to More Castle in Hertfordshire, and established his own Protestant religion. In 1534 Parliament passed the Acts of Supremacy, establishing Henry as the "Protector and Only Supreme Head of the Church of England." But Henry, to whom Pope Leo X in 1521 had given the title "Defender of the Faith," was reluctant to dismiss all Catholic rituals. Throughout his reign the Church of England retained such Catholic ceremonies as the Mass and Holy Communion.

Henry was bitterly disappointed when on August 26, 1533, Anne Boleyn gave birth to a girl, Elizabeth. His limited patience strained, Henry accused Boleyn of adultery and plotting to assassinate him. On May 19, 1536, Boleyn was beheaded in the garden of the Tower of London. Two weeks after her execution, Henry continued his pattern of trading one wife for another. He married one of Anne Boleyn's ladies in waiting, Jane Seymour. In early October 1537, Seymour gave birth to a boy, the future Edward VI. Two weeks later she died from birthing complications. In the span of the next three years Henry married three more times. The first was a German princess, Anne of Cleves; after six months he had the marriage to a woman he called "The Mare of Flanders" annulled. His next queen, Catherine Howard, was executed for adultery. After Henry's death his last wife, Katherine Parr, served as Queen Regent until Edward was old enough to ascend the throne.

During his brief reign Edward VI accelerated the reformation begun by his father. He abolished clerical celibacy, eliminated the Mass, and changed church services from Latin to English. When Edward died at age 15, Mary the daughter of Henry and Catherine of Aragon, succeeded him. Mary strove to undo her father's and stepbrother's religious machinations by restoring Catholicism as the official religion of England. Her zeal launched England into a reign of terror. "Bloody Mary" executed hundreds of prominent Protestants, many burned at the stake. After Mary's death in 1558 her half-sister Elizabeth, the daughter of Henry and Anne Boleyn, restored the Anglican Church as the official Church of England.

Like her father, Elizabeth was reluctant to completely cut ties with the trappings of Catholicism. Ensuing theological disputes pitted Anglicans against each other. A conservative faction of the Anglican Church strived to "purify" the English church. Labeled "Puritans" by middle-of-the-road Anglicans, these orthodox followers of Calvinism jettisoned all vestiges of Catholic pomp and ornamentation from their church services. They scorned statues, stained-glass windows, and altars as "popish" artifacts. Their Sunday services supplanted the ornate liturgy of the Mass with fire-and-brimstone sermons measured in hours rather than minutes.

The stern Puritan theology dictated intense study of Scripture. Reading the Bible, meditating on its meanings, and searching for one's inner spirit was the Puritan way. Puritan social life was embedded in their religion. Hutchinson biographer and descendent Eva LaPlante noted, "Scripture gave them [Puritans] their laws, much of their culture and most of their understanding of human relationships and emotions." In an era when novels did not exist, studying Scripture, discussing sermons, and debating the finer points of God's revelations provided intellectual as well as spiritual stimulation.

Puritans followed the teachings of French theologian John Calvin. Calvin preached that God through his saving grace predestined salvation. Before a person's birth, the Almighty determined who would enjoy eternal bliss or suffer eternal damnation. According to Calvin, God selects those who will enter heaven, and He bestows on those chosen few His "covenant of grace." Calvin said, "God preordained, for his own glory and the display of His attributes of mercy and justice, a part of the human race, without any merit of their own, to eternal salvation, and another part, in just punishment of their sin, to eternal damnation." Living a moral life, behaving charitably toward others, and obeying the Commandments would not open the gates of heaven unless one was already among the elected. Puritans disparaged attempts to earn one's way into heaven, calling these futile attempts at salvation a "covenant of works." Only through rigid self-examination and faith in God's gift of grace ("covenant of grace") could one determine if he or she was among the chosen few.

One of the most outspoken of Puritan clerics was a charismatic preacher from Boston, in Lincolnshire—John Cotton. Cotton maintained that, rather than bringing one closer to God, mindless rituals such as rote prayers, genuflecting, and the taking of sacraments were impediments to direct revelation. Cotton's preaching set him apart from mainstream Anglicans. His sermons resounded with hopelessness for Anglicans who believed they could obtain salvation by obeying the commandments and living a charitable life. As his influence and nonconformist tendencies grew, Cotton attracted a larger congregation. Included among his followers was a successful Lincolnshire merchant, William Hutchinson, from nearby Alford, and his wife—Anne. But many mainstream clerics resented the dynamic preacher's influence. Chief among his critics was the powerful Anglican bishop William Laud of London.

Laud, who would become the archbishop of Canterbury in 1633 under the Catholic-leaning Charles I, strove for uniformity in church rituals and worship. Cotton's conservative teaching marked him as a religious dissident. In 1632 Bishop Laud summoned Cotton to the High Court of Commission—unwelcome news for the preacher. The synod of Anglican bishops had the power to excommunicate, mutilate (often by cropping ears), and imprison seditious clergy. Cotton was not interested in testing his chances in a tribunal administered by a prelate who sympathized with Catholicism. He decided to seek refuge across the Atlantic in the distant Puritan colony in New England—Massachusetts Bay. Cotton's hasty departure shocked his congregation. Many vowed to follow, including William and Anne Hutchinson. This was a momentous decision for the Hutchinson clan that would, in a short time, earn Anne admiration from some and scorn from many.

Anne Hutchinson, the daughter of a minister, Francis Marbury, was ardent in her devotion to Calvinism. Born during the Renaissance, she was a precocious and fortunate child. In an era when women rarely received a formal education, her Cambridge-educated father nurtured her intellectual development with a heavy dose of theological reading material. At age four she was reading passages from the Bible and the quintessential Puritan tome, Foxe's *Book of Martyrs: A History of the Lives, Suffering and Triumphant Deaths of the Early Christians and the Protestant Martyrs.* Anne's growth into young womanhood was marked by deep religious convictions sustained by her Bible reading and personal meditations. During one of her meditations she experienced a life-changing event: she claimed that she received a message from God. The Lord, she said, had spoken "by the voice of his own spirit to my soul."

Later she would insist that this direct contact with the Almighty had bestowed on her the ability to prophesize. The more immediate impact was the revelation that she was one of God's chosen. His absolute promise of salvation convinced her that one's relationship to the Almighty and one's place in the hereafter could be sealed only through direct revelation. Clerical interpretations of Scripture, according to Hutchinson, detracted from rather than sustained faith: assurance of salvation came not through sermons that preached the efficacy of human activities,

7

but only through a direct encounter with the Almighty, such as she had experienced. This was a precarious position to take in a country that was in the midst of religious turmoil and persecution. To some Puritans, her epiphany sounded dangerously close to the radical theology of the Dutch Protestant sect Familism (Family of Love). The Familists preached nonviolence, the equality of men and women, and the notion that free grace obviated the need to obey God's laws (antinomianism). The aura of anarchy that tinged Hutchinson's religious convictions would prove in time to be more a liability than her actual words and deeds.

By 1634, buffeted by Bishop Laud's persecutions, thousands of Puritans immigrated to New England. That summer the Hutchinson family joined the exodus. With servants, eight children, and building materials to construct a new home, they boarded the merchant ship *Griffin* in London, their destination the Puritan sanctuary—Massachusetts Bay Colony. There they planned to join their minister, John Cotton, in Boston Township, where they would be able to practice their religion without fear of reprisals. Moreover, their voyage had an economic motive. The English textile business was mired in a depression and colonists in New England were clamoring for manufactured cloth. Boston's natural harbor offered an ideal location for developing a transatlantic textile trading business. By working with partners on both sides of the Atlantic, William Hutchinson was certain he could build a profitable business in the new world.

One would be hard-pressed to conceive of a more miserable journey than crossing the North Atlantic on a 17th-century English merchant ship. From London to Boston, battling the Prevailing Westerlies, a typical 100-foot, square-rigged cargo ship would slide and dip through four-to-six-foot swells of endless gray sea for eight weeks or longer. Low-status passengers spent the majority of their day in the "tween deck," a tight space below the main deck and cargo holds. Five-foot-high walls forced adults to stoop each time they moved around the tight area. Meager ventilation came through small deck hatches that were sealed during foul weather. Adjacent to and below the passenger area, the holds reeked with livestock miasma. The noxious odors seeped into spaces already filled with the stench of vomit and chamber pots.

So that they would not interfere with the crew's work, below-deck passengers were allowed only a brief daily respite on deck. Daily fare consisted of rations of salt beef or pork, which usually turned rotten halfway through the voyage. In a matter of weeks, algae and insects spoiled fresh water stored in casks. Pirates, storms, and contagious diseases added to the hazards. Despite all this, 21,000 men, women, and children, including the Hutchinsons, sailed to New England during the "Great Migration" between 1620 and 1640.

After eight arduous weeks at sea, the *Griffin* dropped anchor in Boston Harbor, and Anne Hutchinson caught her first glimpse of her new home. The historian Michael Winship noted that the reality of life on the frontier of civilization did not always match expectations. "Perhaps Hutchinson had entertained hopes about Massachusetts as a promised land for God's chosen people such as herself. But what she saw as her boat pulled into Boston Harbor did not look like Zion. On a small peninsula, marshland and pastures filled with tree stumps surrounded three small hills on which sprawled a raw four-year-old town of eight hundred inhabitants...." For a woman accustomed to a life of prosperity, Massachusetts Bay was a shock. Hutchinson told one of her fellow travelers that, if God had not revealed to her that England would be destroyed, her heart would have sunk at the sight of Boston.

Yet the Hutchinsons adapted to their new surroundings, and in a short time they became respected members of the Boston colony's elite. William's textile business flourished, and Anne established herself as a nurse and midwife. They built a sturdy two-story, gabled house in the center of Boston Township, across the street from the home of the governor, John Winthrop. After some prodding from friends, Anne began hosting weekly conventicles, or "gossipings," popular gatherings that provided Puritan women with a forum to exchange social pleasantries and discuss Scripture.

Gradually the Hutchinson conventicles developed an adversarial tenor. Strongly influenced by John Cotton, now assistant minister to the Boston congregation, Hutchinson began detecting what she considered an overemphasis on good works as a sign one was among those chosen by God for salvation. Her gift-of-grace beliefs put her at odds with the prevalent view of colony ministers that redemption was signified through faith and a moral life. Puritans believed that God pardons a select few from the consequences of Original Sin (justification). As a result of the gift of God's free grace, the elected exhibit holiness in all their daily actions (sanctification). To emphasize the point, Puritans referred to each other as "saints." Colony ministers encouraged the faithful to demonstrate their sanctification through obedience to the laws of the colony.

As months passed Hutchinson's meetings morphed from gentle social conclaves to explicit critiques. She walked out on Sunday services and privately criticized ministers. As her public profile grew, attendance at her weekly meetings swelled, and soon men began to accompany their wives to listen to the teachings of the magnetic Mrs. Hutchinson. Perhaps most unsettling to the colony's status quo was her verve and audacity—unacceptable traits in a Puritan woman. While congregation members might argue points in Sunday's sermon with other "saints," in Massachusetts Bay one did not challenge clerical authority.

Resentment against her proceeded at a pace equal to her growing influence. Critics accused her of using her trusted midwife status to insinuate herself into the good graces of colony women. Minister Thomas Weld observed that "her custom was for her scholars to propound questions and she (gravely sitting in a chair) did make answers thereunto." LaPlante, Hutchinson's biographer, noted that, in Puritan culture, a woman sitting in a chair rather than on a bench "was especially grievous in a time when the single chair in every house was for the man alone."

The colony's governor, John Winthrop, lived across the road from the Hutchinson house. From his vantage he directly observed the growing popularity of the Hutchinson gatherings. He noted her "pretense was to repeat sermons, but when that was done, she would comment on the doctrines, interpret passages at her pleasure, and expound dark places of Scripture, and make it serve her turn..., going beyond wholesome truths to set forth her own stuff." But Winthrop had more than religious squabbles on his mind. A growing list of threats to the colony's survival did not need the addition of a discontented woman sowing seeds of dissension.

In the spring of 1637 a brief but bloody war with the Pequots underscored the threat posed by the indigenous population. In revenge for the murder of a colonist on Block Island, a joint force of colonists from Plymouth, Connecticut, and Boston attacked a Pequot village in Mystic. Several hundred Pequots—mostly women, children, and elders—put up a desperate defense of their palisaded village. (Most of the warriors had gone out on a raiding party.) Frustrated by their inability to claim a quick victory, militia Commanders Mason and Underhill ordered the village to be torched. In his journal John Underhill described the scene:

> Captaine Mason entring into a Wigwam, brought out a fire-brand, after hee had wounded many in the house, then hee set fire on the West-side where he entred, my selfe set fire on the South end with a traine of Powder, the fires of both meeting in the center of the Fort blazed most terribly, and burnt all in the space of halfe an houre; many couragious fellowes were unwilling to come out, and fought most desperately through the Palisadoes, so as they were scorched and burnt with the very flame, and were deprived of their armes, in regard the fire burnt their very bowstrings, and so perished valiantly: mercy

> they did deserve for their valour, could we have
> had opportunitie to have bestowed it; many
> were burnt in the Fort, both men, women, and
> children, others forced out, and came in troopes
> to the Indians, twentie, and thirtie at a time,
> which our souldiers received and entertained with
> the point of the sword; downe fell men, women,
> and children, those that scaped us, fell into the
> hands of the Indians, that were in the reere of us;
> it is reported by themselves, that there were about
> foure hundred soules in this Fort, and not above
> five of them escaped out of our hands.

When Governor Winthrop called on members of the Boston congregation to join the fight against the "savages," he was opposed by Hutchinson. Stating that we are all "One Indian," she persuaded men in the Boston congregation to refuse to join the militia. Her protest had a minimal effect on the final outcome; nevertheless, for a woman to contradict a call to arms was an assault on the social order of the colony and more significantly the authority of the powerful John Winthrop.

Puritan women were respected and even cherished as wives and mothers, but Hutchinson overstepped those boundaries when she undercut the governor's ability to raise a militia. Either Hutchinson was naive about the politics or she simply did not care. Time and again she ignored the political impact of her actions. Her apolitical stance gave her a false sense of security about the natives. She believed that respect coupled with God's grace would keep her out of harm's way. This would turn out to be a tragic error in judgment.

While conflicts with indigenous natives sparked sporadic conflicts, encroaching Europeans posed a more ominous threat. Dutch colonies spread across the Eastern seaboard from Delaware to New Amsterdam. In New York their settlements spread from

New Amsterdam at the mouth of the Hudson to Albany (i.e., Fort Orange). Beaver pelts, used in the manufacture of fashionable hats, were in high demand in Europe, and Dutch fur traders seeking new sources of the valuable fur penetrated New England territories. Enmity between Dutch and English settlers increased as each competed for a foothold in the lush and fertile Connecticut River region. In addition to challenges on the western boundaries of Massachusetts Bay Colony, the French, whose settlements stretched from the shores of Lake Huron to Newfoundland, coveted territory controlled by the Massachusetts Bay colony.

French trappers accompanied by Jesuit missionaries forged south from Canada into the Lake Champlain valley and eastern regions to the Atlantic. In the Maine territory of Massachusetts Bay Colony, French and English traders competed for the Abenaki tribe's beaver pelt trade. The competition turned deadly when the French killed two English traders from Plymouth and captured a small Puritan outpost in the Maine Penobscot homelands. In 1636, Massachusetts governor Henry Vane (who preceded Winthrop's second term as governor) received a menacing letter from French commander Charles d'Aulnay predicting a French invasion of Plymouth. The incursion never materialized, but it presaged enmity between the French and English that continued unabated for 130 years until the French withdrew from Canada at the conclusion of the French and Indian War.

Meanwhile in England the Catholic-leaning Charles I searched for a justification to withdraw the Massachusetts Bay Colony charter. Winthrop feared that, if left unchecked, Hutchinson's heterodox preaching would divide the colony and give Charles the excuse he needed to send a royal governor to wrest control from the Puritans. Survival required cohesiveness and an unquestioned compliance with the authority of the Massachusetts brand of Puritanism. In a colony whose survival was embedded in a shared faith and dedication to discipline and order, Hutchinson had become a dangerous woman.

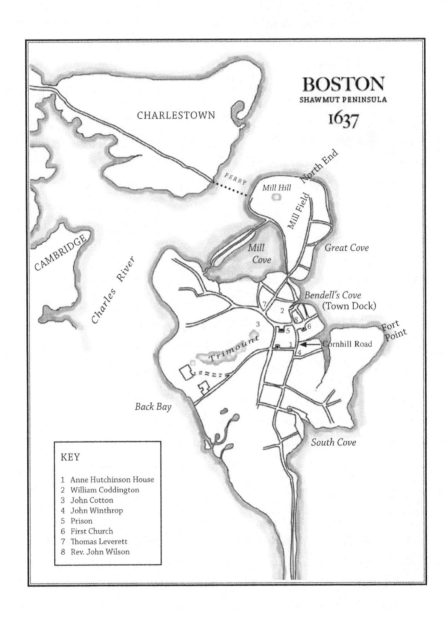

BOSTON
SHAWMUT PENINSULA
1637

CHARLESTOWN

FERRY

Mill Hill

North End

Mill Field

CAMBRIDGE

Charles River

Mill Cove

Great Cove

Bendell's Cove
(Town Dock)

7

2

8

6

Fort Point

3

5

Trimount

1

Cornhill Road

4

Back Bay

South Cove

KEY

1 Anne Hutchinson House
2 William Coddington
3 John Cotton
4 John Winthrop
5 Prison
6 First Church
7 Thomas Leverett
8 Rev. John Wilson

On a bitter cold November morning in 1637, Anne and her husband, William, awakened at dawn. After a breakfast of apples and corn mush they dressed quickly and set out on foot from their two-story gabled house on Cornhill Road in Boston to the Charlestown ferry. The mile walk to the North End took them past the homes of some of Massachusetts Bay Colony's leading citizens, including William Coddington, a surveyor and the richest man in Boston; her mentor, Reverend John Cotton; and church elder Thomas Leverett. The sturdy two-story timber and stone houses of the elite stood in stark contrast to the thatch-roofed shacks that sheltered the majority of the township's 800 residents.

The gray morning light barely made a dent in the bone-chilling fog that rolled in from the harbor. They passed the town prison and wended their way around ruts and slick icy patches that crisscrossed the rough road to the ferry landing at Mills Field. Waiting to join them was William's younger brother Edward. Once on board the three huddled together while the boatman struggled with the icy current of the Charles River. A week earlier a man in an open skiff had frozen to death making the same crossing.

They disembarked in Charlestown and began their four-mile trek to Newtowne (later renamed Cambridge). The road took them past wide virgin forests and small farm tracts. Straw-covered trenches lined with planks dotted the landscape. These primitive shelters provided some relief from the elements for indigent new arrivals to the colony. As they drew nearer to the township they passed several native huts sitting on a low rise. The smoke from their cooking fires mingled with the tangy scent of the salt marsh that ran along the southern bank of the Charles River. Traipsing through fields covered with ice and snow, the three travelers came to the town gate. They passed through the gate and along the cow common until, shortly ahead, they saw the distinctive profile of the timber-and-clay thatch-roofed meetinghouse.

Hutchinson did not keep a journal, so the content of her conversation with her husband and brother-in-law is unknown. But it is unlikely that on this dreary morning the three travelers were discussing the dismal weather. They had more serious matters to consider. The 46-year-old midwife and mother of 15 children had made the trek to Newtowne to stand trial before the Massachusetts General Court. The charge was sedition. Her accuser and chief adversary was Governor John Winthrop. Following English law, he would serve as chief prosecutor, judge, and jury.

The charge accused Hutchinson of slandering colony ministers by claiming they were preaching that deeds rather than Holy Spirit-bestowed grace led to salvation. This was a serious accusation, and her alleged criticisms were deeply resented by the majority of colony ministers. They viewed her accusations as tantamount to calling them "papists." The governor, colony ministers, and magistrates that ruled the 20 townships surrounding Boston were in no mood to tolerate challenges to Puritan religious authority. Deviation undercut the core values of obedience and discipline that unified the colony. The welfare and survival of the colony depended on accordance in religious and civic matters. Governor Winthrop believed that religion and government "unite the body politic as ligaments unify the human body" and that a colony splintered by religious schism would not survive. Although the formal charge against Hutchinson was sedition, many among her critics thought her a heretic, a crime punishable by death.

The politics of survival dictated a swift and decisive guilty verdict. In collaboration with colony ministers, the magistrates and the governor ruled the colony's 7,000 inhabitants. The only limit on a theocracy was the mandate that ministers were barred from government positions. According to LaPlante, "This court's vast power over the populace limited people's freedom to a degree that is unimaginable today. People were banned, for instance, from wearing any fur, lace or colorful cloth, and all citizens, whether or not they were church members, were required to attend church services." Earlier in the year minister John Wheelwright, Anne Hutchinson's like-minded brother-in-law, had been banished for sedition by the same tribunal that she was about to face. The prospect for an "innocent" verdict was as dim as the dreary morning.

Husband and wife entered the building through separate entrances—Anne through the women's door on the east side of the building, William and Edward through the west door. The building was jammed with spectators. All eyes turned to watch as Hutchinson made her way through the throng. Through the south "Door of Honor" 20 deputies and ministers of the Great and General Court of Massachusetts—dressed in greatcoats, leather gloves, and black felt hats—made their way to the dais at the front of the hall. They settled on benches, facing the congregation. Eight ministers, dressed in black robes with white skullcaps, followed the magistrates. These two groups comprised the most influential men in the colony; most of its wealth and power was concentrated among them. The magistrates would judge Hutchinson; the ministers would give testimony. Together they would determine Hutchinson's fate.

Last to enter was John Winthrop, chief judge and prosecutor of the Great and General Court of Massachusetts. Winthrop was a slender man, below average in height, with an angular face and a gray goatee. Over a white linen shirt, knickers, and thick stockings, he wore a greatcoat to ward off the chill of the dank day. A crisp, ruffled white collar encircled his neck. He walked to the center of the dais and took his seat on a cushioned chair behind a small desk.

John Winthrop was a man accustomed to wielding authority. Elected to office several times, Winthrop was more than the colony's governor: he was its founder and guardian. In June 1630, Winthrop, appointed governor of the Massachusetts Bay Company by Charles I, led a flotilla of 11 ships across the Atlantic to establish a Puritan colony in "New England." In addition to nearly 1,000 settlers, 240 head of cattle, and 60 horses, the ships carried bricks and nails to build their homes and muskets to defend their territory.

During the voyage Winthrop delivered a stirring sermon detailing his vision for Massachusetts Bay. Modeled after Christ's Sermon on the Mount, it exhorted Winthrop's fellow travelers to "knitt together in this work as one man." Knowing Charles I could cancel their charter at any time, Winthrop implored the congregation to "consider that wee shall be as a Citty upon a Hill, the eies of all people are uppon us...."

It took the voyagers almost two months to complete the hazardous journey across the north Atlantic. Their first port was the struggling colony of Salem established in 1626 at the mouth of the Naumkeag River by fishermen from Cape Ann. Shortly before landfall, Winthrop took the landing of a pigeon on the deck of his lead ship, the *Arbella*, as a blessing from the Holy Spirit. "Their came a smell off the shore like the smell of a garden," he exclaimed. His initial enthusiasm was quickly tempered by the reality of life in the harsh land. The winter before his arrival, 200 Salem settlers perished in meager shelters constructed of wood-covered holes in the ground. Determined to find a better site to erect his "City on a Hill" Winthrop ordered the ships to weigh anchor and head south.

They sailed parallel to the rugged coastline until they came to a natural harbor formed by the convergence of two rivers later named the Charles and the Mystic. At first Winthrop thought the site ideal; he named it Charlestown. But the marshy region lacked enough fresh water to sustain a large population. Within a few weeks "bloody flux," scurvy, and dysentery broke out in the crowded camp. Winthrop and the other leaders decided to disperse the company. By September the hardy settlers had established several towns along the coast, including Watertown, Roxbury, Dorchester, Medford, and Charlestown.

A half-mile south of Charlestown, a large peninsula jutted into the bay. Freshwater springs flowed through three prominent hills in the center of the peninsula. The Algonquin-speaking natives—the Wampanoag, Massachuset, and Pawtucket tribes—called the peninsula "nashauwamuk," meaning "he that goes by boat." The colonists called it "Shawmut." Winthrop dubbed the three hills Pemberton, Mount Vernon, and Beacon. He and other leaders of the expedition selected the peninsula as the site to construct the city he foresaw. They named their settlement after a town in Lincolnshire on the east coast of England: Boston.

Over the next few years, nearly half of the original thousand settlers died. Half of all newborns perished their first year. Despair dripped from the quill of one colonist: "The air is sharp, the rocks many, the trees innumerable, the grass little, the winter cold, the summer hot, the gnats in summer biting, the wolves at midnight howling." But Winthrop and the remaining colonists persevered against the elements, disease, and indigenous tribes. Now, six years later, he was not about to allow his vision to be disrupted by a 46-year-old midwife who claimed she received divine revelations.

Winthrop surveyed the crowded meetinghouse. His permanently arched eyebrows conveyed a haughty sense of authority. He was ready. Pausing for a moment to dramatize the magnitude of the situation, Winthrop beckoned Anne Hutchinson to approach the dais. Hutchinson walked to the front of the hall and stood before her accuser. There was nothing physically remarkable about the woman. In appearance she differed from none of the many Puritan women standing among the throng. Plain-looking, in her mid-forties, and of average height, she wore a long black dress, leather boots, a white linen smock, and a wool cloak. A white coif covered her head.

Standing no more than six feet apart, the two took the measure of each other. Despite Hutchinson's ordinary appearance, Winthrop detected something different about her, something that set her apart from others. It was her eyes. Not the color: the windowless Cambridge meetinghouse was too dimly lit to discern blue from brown or hazel. Hutchinson stood before him on trial for sedition, but he detected no trepidation in her gaze. Later Winthrop acknowledged that "Jezebel" was no ordinary woman. In his journal, he described Hutchinson as "a woman of haughty and fierce carriage, of a nimble wit and active spirit, and a very voluble tongue, more bold than a man." This was grudging respect from the man who held nothing but malice in his heart for the middle-aged midwife.

Then Winthrop spoke—loudly enough for all to hear in the crowded meetinghouse. "Mistress Hutchinson," he said. "You are called here as one of those that have troubled the peace of the commonwealth and the churches here.... You are known here to be a woman who hath a great share in the divulging of those opinions that are the cause of this trouble and to be nearly joined not only in affinity and affection with some of those the court had...passed censure upon"

He paused for effect and glanced around the crowded room. Hutchinson's husband, William, was seated near the front. The governor noted his worried look and continued, "But you have spoken divers things, as we have been informed, very prejudicial to the honour of the churches and ministers thereof, and you have maintained a meeting and an assembly in your house that hath been condemned by the general assembly as a thing not tolerable nor comely in the sight of God nor fitting for your sex, and notwithstanding that was cried down you have continued the same."

Winthrop concluded by warning her, "If you be obstinate in your course then the court may take such course that you may trouble us no further. Therefore I would intreat [sic] you to express whether you do assent and hold in practice to those opinions and factions that have been handled in court already, that is to say, whether you do justify Mr. Wheelwright's sermon and petition become his main objection."

Winthrop believed his terms were simple and direct: cease the weekly meetings and disavow the bent theology of her brother-in-law minister Wheelwright, and her transgressions would be forgiven. But Hutchinson didn't see it that way. Rather than an explanation for why she was being tried, she was hearing a diatribe against her beliefs and her sex. Winthrop was about to find out that authoritative reprimands linked to the threat of banishment would neither subdue nor cower the woman standing before him.

Hutchinson paused before replying. Perhaps in those fleeting moments she thought of her father, Francis Marbury, who 10 years before her birth stood before a similar court accused of a similar offense.

Francis Marbury was one of many reformist English ministers who railed against "popish" Anglican practices. Conservative Anglicans like Marbury wanted to purify the church Henry VIII had founded, and, when their denouncements earned them the derisive title "Puritans," they deeply resented the label. Marbury denounced the proliferation of priestly vestments, stained-glass windows, statues, and other Catholic ornamentations in English churches. From his pulpit in Northampton he preached passionate sermons about the misguided leadership of the clergy. He reserved his most vitriolic criticism for "dumb dog" ministers whose paltry education left them so ignorant that they were unable to intelligently preach or write sermons. The fault he laid at the feet of the Anglican bishops, who he said were more invested in advancing their careers than advancing an educated ministry.

For the most part, Puritan criticisms were tolerated by mainstream Anglicans, but Marbury pushed the limits when he began launching pulpit attacks on the Anglican clergy. The bishops, Marbury charged, were killing souls by ordaining clergy who lacked knowledge of the Bible and the zeal to inspire spiritual activism among their congregations. Brought before an ecclesiastical Court of High Commission at St. Paul's Cathedral in London for heresy, Marbury demonstrated the stalwart stock combined with lack of political acumen that his daughter would inherit. When the portly Bishop Aylmer asked Marbury where the money would come from to provide formal education for clergy, Marbury quipped, "A man might cut a good, large thong out of your hide, and it would not be missed." His wit and obstinacy came at a cost. The bishop denounced Marbury as "an overthwart Puritan knave" and sentenced him to two years in prison.

Nearly 50 years later his daughter stood before a different tribunal facing a similar charge: challenging the authority of the church. Her father's daughter did not back down. Her reply to the governor's accusations took the air out of whatever puffed-up expectations he might have had of a quick resolution: "I am called here to answer before you, but I hear no things laid to my charge." Her response set the tone for the rest of the morning, as Winthrop's attempts to build a case of sedition became tangled in a back-and-forth dispute about whether he had any case at all.

In one exchange Winthrop attempted to use her relationship with the discredited Wheelwright as proof of guilt by association.

> Winthrop: "So if you do countenance those that are transgressors of the law you are in the same fact."
>
> Hutchinson: "What law do they transgress?"
>
> Winthrop: "The law of church and state."
>
> Hutchinson: "In what particular?"
>
> Winthrop: "Why, in among the rest, whereas the Lord doth say honour thy father and thy mother" [i.e., church and state].

Hutchinson: "Ey Sir in the Lord."

Winthrop: "This honor you have broke in givin [sic] countenance to them."

Hutchinson: "What law have I broken?"

Winthrop: "Why, the fifth commandment: honour thy father and thy mother" [in this case, Puritan authority].

After several such exchanges, Winthrop grew increasingly agitated and switched his line of attack, saying: "We do not mean to discourse with those of your sex but only this you so adhere unto then and do endeavor to set forward this faction and so you do dishonor us."

With this statement Winthrop acknowledged what most troubled him. The woman's religious convictions were divisive, and Winthrop needed to protect the colony from splintering. All Puritans, Winthrop included, scrutinized the Bible for insight into their fate. He took inspiration from Luke 11: 14–26: "Every kingdom divided against itself is brought to desolation; and a house divided against a house falleth." This summarized the colony's vulnerability, and it provided a divine rationale for banishing Hutchinson. Survival required concerted actions. A clever woman who questioned Puritan teaching and criticized Puritan ministry presented an ominous threat to the colony's security. Massachusetts Bay Colony faced a precarious future. One way or another Governor Winthrop had to silence Anne Hutchinson.

She steadfastly refused to acknowledge any wrongdoing, and to make matters worse she was incrementally wresting control of the proceedings. Watching as their case against her floundered must have been an agonizing spectacle for the magistrates and ministers who had convicted her before she walked through the meetinghouse door.

Impatient with her impertinence, Deputy-Governor Dudley interrupted Hutchinson midway through one of her slippery rejoinders: "Mrs. Hutchinson, from the time she came hath made a disturbance, and some that came over with her in the ship did inform me what she was as soon as she landed." Dudley was referring to a series of angry exchanges between Hutchinson and the minister, Symmes, who had preached aboard the *Griffin*. Dudley, who clearly was in no mood to engage in a rhetorical debate, got right to the point: Hutchinson had "disparaged all our ministers in the land that they have preached a covenant of works."

There it was: the charge that had brought her to this place and time. Admission would prove her guilty of sedition. A denial would be hypocritical. Time and again in her meetings she had criticized colony ministers for preaching that good works, which included compliance to civic authority, demonstrated that one was among the chosen. Hutchinson stared at her accuser and replied, "Prove it."

Her retort brought on a spate of back-and-forth dialogue about whether she said the colony ministers had emphasized a covenant of works over a covenant of grace. Trying to regain the upper hand, the deputy-governor said, "I will make it plain that you did say that the ministers did preach of covenant or works." She replied, "I deny that." If someone asked her opinion in private she would answer truthfully, but as a Puritan woman she had no right to make public religious pronouncements.

Surely exasperated, the deputy-governor surrendered the prosecutor's rostrum to six ministers who in quick order concurred with the testimony of minister Hugh Peter, who stated that in a conversation she told him that he preached a covenant of works rather than a covenant of grace. The deputy-governor, perhaps sensing he had regained the upper hand, said, "I call these witnesses and you deny them. You see they have proved this and you deny this.… You say they preached a covenant of works and that they were not able ministers of the New Testament." Again she replied, "Prove that I said so."

As dusk descended over Newtowne, the governor ended the day's proceedings. The trial would resume in the morning. The magistrates filed out of the crowded meetinghouse, undoubtedly chagrined that they were unable to force an admission of guilt from the indomitable Mrs. Hutchinson.

Hutchinson and her husband stayed with a friend in Newtowne that evening. After supper, she reviewed a set of notes taken by minister John Wilson at a meeting in October 1636 between herself and six of the ministers who were giving testimony against her. Much of the prosecuting testimony up to this point had been based on statements Hutchinson had supposedly made at the meeting. They all testified that she had been critical of their preaching. Reverend Peter said, "She told me there was a wide and broad difference between our brother Mr. Cotton and ourselves. I desired to know the difference. She answered that he preaches the covenant of grace and you the covenant of works, and that you are not able ministers of the New Testament.…" According to Peter, he asked Hutchinson at their meeting what she thought of a minister who preached a covenant of works, she replied, "He had not the seal of the spirit." If in fact Hutchinson had said this, she meant such a minister was damned.

But Hutchinson found that the notes did not correspond to the testimony of Peter and the other ministers. Wilson's notes contained evidence that ministers had taken her comments regarding their preaching out of context. She had not accused them of preaching a covenant of works, she had merely said that they did not preach the covenant of grace as clearly as Cotton. Once the contradictions were revealed, the previous day's testimony would be inadmissible, and their complicity could lead to a charge of perjury. Hutchinson walked into the meetinghouse the next morning confident that she had devised a legal maneuver that would nullify the testimony against her. She would demand that each of the prosecuting witnesses take an oath attesting to the truthfulness of their statements. But her strategy withered when Winthrop denied her request. Oaths were unnecessary, he said, because this was not a jury trial. Then Winthrop addressed the audience: "Let those who are not satisfied in the court speak." This tactic backfired when many spoke out, "We are not satisfied." Perhaps sensing that Winthrop's uncharacteristic democratic gesture could be his undoing, the ministers continued to argue against the taking of an oath. Meanwhile, Hutchinson's contention that the testimonies given against her were untrue was ignored. The trial continued with Deputy-Governor Dudley calling for witnesses for the defense.

> Winthrop asked the first witness, John Coggeshall, a 46-year-old silk merchant, "Will you, Mr. Coggeshall, refute the previous [ministers'] testimonies?"
>
> Coggeshall replied, "Yes, I dare say that she did not say all that which they lay against her."
>
> Peter, one of the ministers, retorted, "How dare you look into the Court to make that statement?"
>
> The intimidation worked. Coggeshall replied meekly, "Mr. Peter takes it upon himself to forbid me to speak. I shall be silent."

The next witness, Thomas Leveret, remembered Hutchinson saying the ministers did not preach a covenant of grace as clearly as Mr. Cotton. Cotton believed that redemption rested on inner examination of the Holy Spirit's presence, while Wilson and the other more orthodox ministers believed assurance could be observed in one's actions.

Next Winthrop called John Cotton to testify. This was the moment everyone in the assembly had anticipated. Hutchinson revered Cotton. More than any other individual, the controversial minister had shaped her beliefs. A pudgy man with a round face, full lips, and long, curly brown hair, Cotton walked to the front of the meetinghouse and stood next to Hutchinson. Winthrop got right to the point: "Mr. Cotton, the court desires that you declare what you do remember of the conference that is now in question."

Cotton understood the gravity of his dilemma. Back Hutchinson, his most fervent follower, and his trial would be next; disclaim her position, and he would lose his credibility and the loyalty of his congregation. Pontius Pilate would have been proud of Cotton's cleansing statement: he said he was sorry that any comparisons had been made between himself and his brethren [fellow ministers]. On hearing this, Hutchinson must have felt betrayed. But the diplomatic minister was not finished. He concluded his testimony by saying, "And I must say that I did not find her saying that they [ministers] were under a covenant of works, nor that she said they did preach of covenant of works."

There it was, the testimony that could clear her of sedition. Yes, she had criticized the colony ministers, but only in a matter of degree, not in the damning way her accusers contended.

But Hutchinson's zeal overcame her good sense. Perhaps sensing her advantage, she decided to grasp the opportunity to teach her accusers. She described a revelation she had when the Lord visited her. "I bless the Lord, he hath let me see which was the clear ministry and which the wrong.... Now if you do condemn me for speaking what in my conscience I know to be truth I must commit myself unto the Lord."

Her accusers were stunned. Was she saying her views were infallible because they came directly from Jesus?" Deputy-Governor Dudley asked, "How, an immediate revelation?" Hutchinson responded by quoting Scripture and concluded by saying, "You have power over my body and the Lord Jesus hath power over my body and soul; and assure yourselves this much, you do as much as in you lies the Lord Jesus Christ from you, and if you go on this course you begin, you will bring a curse upon you and posterity, and the mouth of the Lord hath spoken it."

The meetinghouse broke out in a flurry of confusion and indignation. Did she just put a curse on the Court? Did she really believe the Lord had revealed himself directly to her? Winthrop tried to restore order. "I am persuaded," he said, "that the revelation she brings forth is delusion." Winthrop, Dudley, and her other enemies in the meetinghouse must have been elated. With her own words, she had just convicted herself.

Winthrop made his pronouncement: "The court hath already declared themselves satisfied concerning the things you hear, and concerning the troublesomeness of her spirit and the danger of her course amongst us, which is not to be suffered. Therefore if it be the mind of the court that Mrs. Hutchinson for these things that appear before us is unfit for our society, and if it be the mind of this court that she shall be banished out of our liberties and imprisoned til she be sent away, let them hold up their hands." All but three of the magistrates voted her guilty.

Satisfied that "Jezebel" was duly convicted, Winthrop addressed the defendant: "Mrs. Hutchinson, the sentence of the court you hear is that you are banished from out of our jurisdiction as being a woman not fit for our society, and are to be imprisoned till the court shall send you away." Hutchinson replied, "I desire to know wherefore I am banished." Winthrop replied, "Say no more. The court knows wherefore and is satisfied."

Based on her revelations, the court found her guilty of heresy and sedition. Winthrop gave Hutchinson a few days to wrap up her affairs. She was taken by armed wagon two miles south of Boston to Roxbury. There she was put under house arrest in the home of Joseph Weld, brother of one of her most ardent critics, minister Thomas Weld. Throughout an interminable winter that continued into April she was allowed only a few brief visits with her beloved husband and children. Her physical condition began to deteriorate. She was listless and fatigued. She was going through her 16th pregnancy, and as an experienced mother and midwife she knew this one did not feel right.

Moreover, her isolation did not bring relief from her enemies, who were not yet done with her. Colony ministers were intent on getting her to recant her odious statements regarding their ministry. If anything, she became more resolute, continually referring to her teacher and the man she considered her most ardent supporter: John Cotton. She proclaimed she shared the same beliefs as Mr. Cotton, and that she and Mr. Cotton were of one mind.

Although grudgingly respectful of Hutchinson's "nimble tongue," Winthrop also feared her. As a precaution he had 75 of her supporters disarmed. He was relieved at the banishment of Wheelwright and Hutchinson, but he was not about to allow any doubts about her heresy to fester. On March 15, 1638, Hutchinson faced another tribunal—a church trial. The purpose was clear: to strip Hutchinson of whatever lingering credibility she retained. Unwell, and pregnant, Hutchinson faced her accusers without her staunchest supporter—her husband.

In March, Will Hutchinson, along with William Coddington (the wealthiest merchant in Massachusetts Bay Colony) and 19 other dissidents, had sailed to Providence. Acting on an invitation from Roger Williams, they intended to establish a colony on Aquidneck Island (later renamed Rhode Island). Before they left Boston, Hutchinson and the other Massachusetts Bay men signed a declaration—the Portsmouth Compact. The document incorporated the signers into "a body politic" answerable only to "Lord Jesus Christ, the King of Kings, and Lord of Lords." The brief compact established the doctrine of religious tolerance for the first time in the New World. Historian Samuel Arnold observed that "their object was to lay the foundation for a Christian state, where all who bore the name might worship

God according to the dictates of conscience untrammeled by written articles of faith, and unawed by the civil power...." Ironically, Anne Hutchinson's decidedly intolerant criticism of Massachusetts Bay Puritanism lead to the establishment of religious freedom in Rhode Island.

On Thursday, March 15, unfettered by the civil trial necessity of proving guilt, Hutchinson's accusers conducted an inquisition, interrogating her for nine hours in the Boston meetinghouse. The ministers, led by her arch enemy, John Wilson, barraged Hutchinson with a fusillade of abstruse theological "errors," including her claim to infallible revelations, her seeming disdain for lawful behavior, and her assertion that the spirit and not the soul was immortal. Hutchinson defended herself as best she could, but her long confinement, separation from her family, and weakened physical condition had taken a toll. Her rejoinder— that she did not hold with every alleged "error" but that she had merely asked theological questions—received a biting reply from the Reverend Thomas Shepard: "The vilest errors that ever were brought into church were brought by way of questions."

This time there were no words of support from John Cotton. Perhaps sensing his own political vulnerability, her trusted mentor joined her critics and heaped on criticism that must have made her cringe. "Therefor, I doe Admonish you, and alsoe charge you in the name of Christ Jesus, in whose place I stand...that you would sadly consider the just hand of God agaynst you, the great hurt you have done to the Churches, the great Dishonour you have brought to Jesus Christ, and the Evell you have done to many a poore soule." When her son-in law Thomas Savage and her son Edward attempted to mount a defense, they were warned to remain silent or face similar accusations. Thomas Shepard made it clear that anyone who dissented with the tribunal was suspect. "If there be any of this congregation that do hold the same opinions [as Hutchinson], I advise them to take heed of it, for the hand of the Lord will find you out."

As the day went on, Cotton launched a cascade of invective. Seeming to relish his new role as her chief tormentor, he first addressed her son and son-in-law for attempting to support her: "You have proved vipers to eat through the very bowels of your mother—to her ruin...." To her female supporters he said, "Let not the good you have received from her in your spiritual estates make you receive all for good that comes for her. For you see she is but a woman." Then to the woman who had been his ardent follower since he preached from the pulpit in England, he said, "The dishonor you have brought unto God by these unsound tenets of yours is far greater than all the honor you have brought to Him. And the evil of your opinions doth outweigh all the good of your doings."

Not satisfied with limiting his admonishments to her deeds Cotton prophesied the sexual evils she would bring on the colony: promiscuity, the "filthy" coming together of unmarried men and women, unfaithfulness to husbands, and buggery. Sitting on a bench 10 feet away from Cotton, Hutchinson asked to speak. Begrudgingly, her former mentor allowed her a moment. She said: "All I would say is this, that I did not hold any of these [opinions] before my imprisonment." Unmoved by her simple declaration of innocence, Cotton and the other ministers continued to hammer away at her misdeeds for the duration of the day.

The following week, on the second and final day of her church trial, Hutchinson tried to negotiate a middle ground with her accusers. She admitted that she had spoken rashly and inadvisedly at her civil trial and repented her curse and prophesy of doom—but to no avail. If anything, it seemed her attempts at reconciliation angered the ministers even more. Questioning her sincerity, Thomas Shepard said, "I confess I am wholly unsatisfied in her expressions to some of these gross and damnable errors.... Any heretic may bring a sly interpretation upon any of these errors and yet hold them to their death." Reverend Hugh Peter of Salem rebuked her for overstepping her place as a woman: "You have rather been a husband than a wife; and a preacher than a hearer; and a magistrate than a subject." Her lack of humility was her gravest error, and for this there would be no forgiveness. The ministers concluded the proceedings by allowing that Hutchinson had modified some of her expressions, but her judgments remained unchanged.

Reverend Wilson delivered the final pronouncement of excommunication. Listing her principal errors of leading her followers astray and lying about divine revelations, he concluded, "Therefore, in the name of our Lord Jesus Christ and in the name of the church, I do not only pronounce you worthy to be cast out, but I do cast you out! And in the name of Christ, I do deliver you up to Satan, that you may learn no more to blaspheme, to seduce, and to lie." With these damning words the persecution of Anne Hutchinson concluded.

In April, Hutchinson was allowed to leave Massachusetts. Although snow still covered the roads, she chose to walk to Rhode Island rather than take the usual route of sailing around Cape Cod. Along with carts loaded with family possessions, she was accompanied by her daughter Bridget's family and nine of her other children. It took six days for the family to make the 56-mile journey to Portsmouth. Along the way they slept in hastily constructed wigwams. On the sixth day they reached the boundary of Massachusetts Bay Colony and entered into Providence Plantation, the settlement founded by another Puritan dissident, Roger Williams. From Providence, the clan traveled the final 16 miles south to Aquidneck by ship. After nearly six months of separation, husband and wife were reunited in the second week of April.

The settlement at Aquidneck resembled the early days of Massachusetts Bay, with recent arrivals sheltered in pits in the ground with bark-covered walls. The Hutchinsons selected a lot on the western shore of Great Cove and built a two-story structure with a large chimney and several windows facing the cove. Just as it appeared that the family was about to resume a normal life, tragedy struck. Rather than giving birth to her 16ᵗʰ child, the 46-year-old old mother had a miscarriage. The malformed fetus resembled nothing human: it was a hydatidiform mole, a mass of tubular growths caused by a blighted egg fertilized by one or two sperm cells. While miscarriages were common among women 40 and older, the news that Hutchinson had delivered a grotesque mass of tissue instead of a normal baby caused a sensation among her enemies. Her nemesis, John Winthrop, used the occasion to vent his enmity: "But see how the wisdom of God fitted this judgment to her sin in every way, for look—as she had vented misshapen opinions, so she must bring forth deformed monsters."

Anne knew her enemies would use the miscarriage to continue their campaign against her, but she also felt secure that she was beyond their reach in Portsmouth. Once the house was built they settled into the routine of farming, raising cattle, and tending the family. Anne resumed her practice of weekly religious meetings, and within a short time her gatherings attracted a bevy of followers. Meanwhile, in 1639, the environs that eventually would become the colony of Rhode Island continued to expand with the merging of Portsmouth and Newport. William Coddington was elected governor and Will Hutchinson assistant-governor. But wrangling among colonist leaders, including Samuel Groton, who opposed the increasingly autocratic Coddington, led to shifting political alliances. When rumors spread that Massachusetts Bay was planning a military expedition to annex Narragansett Bay, Anne and Will Hutchinson considered yet another move 130 miles south, to New Netherland. The Dutch haven would, once and for all, put the Hutchinsons outside the reach of her Puritan adversaries.

While the family was wrestling with the decision, Will, at age 55, died unexpectedly from unknown causes. The loss of her husband, combined with a visit from Massachusetts ministers intent on using her grief to leverage a disavowal of her beliefs, convinced Hutchinson, now a 51-year-old widow, to make the move. So in the summer of 1642, and for the third time in eight years, she uprooted her family to begin a new life. She was aware of sporadic conflicts between the Dutch and the Siwanoy in the region that is the present-day Bronx, but she trusted that God would protect her family. Living side by side with settlers who did not share her culture, religion, or language, she no longer lived with the dread of persecution. During her final days on earth, Anne Hutchinson experienced a period of tranquility she had not known since the fateful day the *Griffin* docked in Boston Harbor.

The legacy of historic figures often has less to do with their deeds than with the meaning ascribed to those deeds by future generations—and so it is with Anne Hutchinson. When John Winthrop, the governor of Massachusetts Bay Colony, sneered and called her "Jezebel," he could never have imagined that, a short walk from his mansion in Boston, she would one day be immortalized by a larger-than-life bronze statue. Located at the Massachusetts State House, the sculpture depicts Hutchinson, gazing toward the heavens, with her arm wrapped around a child. At the base of the stature a plaque reads: "In memory of Anne Marbury Hutchinson. Baptized at Alford, Lincolnshire, England 20 July 1591. Killed by the Indians at East Chester New York 1643. A courageous exponent of civil liberty and religious tolerance." In southern New York, a highway close to where she was murdered is named after her, as is a nearby river. In Rhode Island she is revered as the only woman to cofound a colony.

Demonized by her contemporaries and lionized by her admirers, Anne Hutchinson, in the words of historian Michael Winship, was "a prophet, a spiritual adviser, mother of 15, and an important participant in a fierce religious controversy that shook the infant Massachusetts Bay Colony from 1636 to 1638." Eleanor Roosevelt declared Hutchinson the first of America's foremothers.

Hutchinson exhibited a fierce spirit and a commitment to ideals untarnished by time or historical perspective. No woman in the early colonial history of America stood taller. Wampage, the Siwanoy warrior who killed her, recognized her power. Following the custom of his people he changed his name to "Anne Hoeck" to honor her memory. But it was the man of few words, her husband Will, who provided the most endearing epitaph. Approached by a group of ministers who beseeched him to convince his wife to recant, he replied, "I am more nearly tied to my wife than to the church. I do think her to be a dear saint and servant of God."

CHAPTER TWO

Benedict Arnold

The Battle of Valcour Island

The little American navy of Lake Champlain was wiped out, but never had any force, big or small, lived to a better purpose nor died more gloriously, for it had saved the Lake for that year.

Admiral Alfred Mahan,
War of American Independence

*I*n the summer of 1776 George Washington and the southern colonial army were in full retreat. In Canada, the British led by Sir Guy Carleton turned back an American invasion force decimated by smallpox and desertions. To observers on both sides it was obvious that an ill-equipped colonial army of farmers and merchants was no match against seasoned British regulars. With colonial forces in disarray, the British sensed an opportunity to quash the rebellion. They marshaled their forces to launch a two-pronged attack. A massive force from Canada led by Carleton would link up with General William Howe's British regulars in

Albany. The combined British armies would isolate New England from the rest of the colonies. Fractured lines of leadership, communication, and supplies would signal the death knell of the fragile Revolution.

The colonial situation was desperate, but one man had a plan: stymie the British northern invasion on Lake Champlain and buy time to build an adequately prepared colonial defense. The man was Benedict Arnold. This is the story of how Benedict Arnold led a ragtag American fleet against the most powerful navy in the world. Four years later he would be reviled as a traitor, but at Valcour Island, on October 11, 1776, Benedict Arnold saved the American Revolution.

North of Albany, about 50 miles south of the Adirondack high peaks, sits the bustling community of Saratoga Springs, New York. Renowned for its racetrack, spas, and mineral water, Saratoga vibrates with the tony electricity only money can buy. Eight miles southeast of the village, a bucolic national landmark stretches across a wide swathe of rolling hills, open fields, and woods. It was here in 1777 that one of the most crucial battles of the Revolutionary War was fought. In their first major victory of the war, the Battle of Saratoga, colonials defeated a large British invasion force from Canada. The unlikely victory blunted the British plan to quell the rebellion by seizing the Hudson River Valley and isolating New England from the rest of the colonies.

Tourists visiting the expansive battlefield encounter a puzzling monument at marker #7 on the nine-mile drive around the battleground. The four-foot-high marble display of a cannon, with an epaulet and a wreath sculpted above a horseman's boot, is dedicated to an unnamed hero. On the back an inscription reads: "In memory of the most brilliant soldier of the Continental Army who was desperately wounded on this spot, the sally port of BURGOYNE'S GREAT (WESTERN) REDOUBT winning for his countrymen the Decisive Battle of the American Revolution and for himself the rank of Major General."

The anonymous soldier had, in fact, been relieved of duty that day. But, in typical fashion, Benedict Arnold disobeyed General

Gates's orders to remain in his quarters. Instead he charged into the fray on the wide meadows of Bemis Heights. Ignoring intense enemy fire, Arnold rallied colonial troops to victory. After the battle an American soldier said of his commander, "He didn't care for nothing. He'd ride right in. It was 'come on boys,' not 'go boys'.... There wasn't any wasted timber in him." Three years after his valiant leadership at the Battle of Saratoga Arnold again made an indelible mark on the American Revolution, but not as a hero—as a traitor after he attempted to sell to the British documents describing the defensive fortifications of West Point.

While many Americans switched sides during the Revolution, none were more reviled than Benedict Arnold. The scope of his betrayal was magnified by his status as a hero of the rebellion. During the early years of the revolt in 1775, 1776, and 1777, Arnold was the most courageous and gifted officer under Washington's command. However, in post-Revolution America the condemnation of Arnold was so complete that his name became synonymous with the word "traitor." Ben Franklin's remark, that Judas betrayed one man but Arnold betrayed three million, succinctly captured a young country's revulsion toward its spurned warrior. Arnold was blackened in every conceivable way. He was hanged in effigy. His name was erased from the membership rolls of his Masonic lodge. His father and infant brother's grave markers were obliterated. Monuments celebrating his victorious battles were dedicated to others, and of course there is the empty boot. In pictures and print he was depicted in the company of Satan. A popular colonial child's verse warned mothers not to name their children "Arnold":

> *Mothers shall still their children and say—Arnold!—*
> *Arnold shall be the bugbear of their years,*
> *Arnold!—vile, treacherous, and leagued with Satan.*

Myths sprang up about a twisted childhood. Arnold was portrayed as a youngster who was cruel to animals, disdainful of authority, and a bully. Such undocumented tales were based on a conviction that his treachery was predetermined by a wayward childhood. However, there is not a shred of evidence that Arnold was anything more than an active and daring young man. His early life was difficult, but he lived during harsh times. Rather than being a prelude to self-destruction Arnold's childhood travails forged a resilient leader who, win or lose, was an inspiration to his men on the battlefield.

Benedict Arnold was born in Norwich, Connecticut, on January 14, 1741. His early years were typical of a well-to-do lad growing up in mid-18th-century New England. His mother, Hannah, was strict but loving. His father, Captain Benedict Arnold IV was a respected businessman. Young Benedict was an exuberant and active child. Several stories, some corroborated, others perhaps more fancy than fact, describe a daredevil. In one such tale the boy grasped a large mill water wheel with one hand and rode the wheel for an entire cycle. Another story, verified by a letter to his mother from his angry schoolmaster, groused that Benedict walked the ridgepole of a burning barn—a stunt that got him suspended from school.

In colonial America during the mid-18th century, 30 percent of children died before the age of 21 from such diseases as yellow fever, smallpox, and typhus. Even an infection from a small cut could be deadly. Arnold's sisters Elizabeth and Mary died of a mysterious illness the colonists called "throat distemper." The affliction started with a sore throat and eventually constricted the esophagus until the victim choked to death. Two of his brothers, Absalom and Benedict V, died of fever at a young age. (When children died it was common practice to name a newborn after a deceased sibling; his parents named Arnold, Benedict VI in honor of his dead brother.) Only one of his siblings survived to adulthood, his beloved sister Hannah.

In 1754, when Benedict was 13, French and English colonists clashed over control of the fertile Ohio Valley region. Known in America as the French and Indian War and in Europe as the Seven Years' War, the conflict had a devastating impact on colonial merchants. French naval blockades coupled with attacks by privateers dealt a series of hard blows to the Arnold family's shipping and trading business. Unable to pay his bills and hounded by creditors, Captain Arnold took solace in rum. His heavy drinking added to the family's problems, and within a short time the Arnolds faced financial ruin.

Barely 15 years old, Benedict found his world in turmoil. His parents could no longer afford schooling, debtors clamored for payment, and the family's status in the community spiraled downward. Historian Jim Murphy wrote, "Young Benedict's future was now entirely bleak. The business, which he would have normally taken over when older, was bankrupt; the formal education that would have been an immense advantage in his life was ended. He had seen his family go from the wealthiest and most respected in town to being humiliatingly poor and pitied."

Benedict's mother had two cousins who owned a successful apothecary and trading business in Norwich—Daniel and Joshua Lathrop. Like most pharmacies in colonial America, the Lathrop brothers' store was stocked with all manner of merchandise, from dried fruit to embalming fluid. The cousins agreed to accept Benedict as an apprentice. He moved into the Lathrop house, and within a short time demonstrated a precocious talent for business dealings. When his mother died in in 1759 and his father two years later, 20-year-old Benedict dedicated himself to repaying his family's debts and restoring honor to the Arnold name.

Buoyed by Arnold's knack for striking good deals, the Lathrops set him up in his own shop in New Haven. Much like his father 20 years earlier he quickly built a successful importing business. He made frequent trips to the West Indies aboard his sloop *Fortune* and traded manufactured goods with plantation owners for sugar, molasses, and rum. Where others saw obstacles Arnold saw opportunity. In his travels to New York he met traders from Canada. They told him that in the provinces good horses were hard to come by. The daunting Adirondack Mountains, covered with impenetrable woods, made travel to Canada by land virtually impossible. But Lake Champlain, tucked in between New York and the territory that would become Vermont, provided a 110-mile passageway to the Richelieu River and points north. The lake, with its northern current and frequent wind changes, was tricky to navigate, but Arnold's seamanship skills were ideally suited to the challenge. Within a short time he established a prosperous horse- trading business in Montreal.

Swarthy in complexion and five-feet-five inches tall, Arnold had piercing blue eyes, a hawkish nose, and the muscular physique of a lumberjack. He was a smart dresser, an accomplished horseman, and a crack shot. His energetic personality matched his bearing. Confident and quick-tempered, he tended to rub those he disagreed with the wrong way. Some thought him arrogant, but, among young men in New Haven, Arnold was on the rise. His admission into the Freemasons, a secret association that sought ways "to help all human beings unite and work together for the perfection of Humanity," could not have happened without the support of prominent citizens. On February 22, 1767, Arnold married Margaret Mansfield, the "hard working and prudent daughter" of Samuel Mansfield, the sheriff of New Haven. She would bear him three children, all boys—Benedict VII, Richard, and Henry.

While his business grew, his profit margins were shrinking due to a series of odious British taxes. The Sugar Act followed by the Revenue Act set a threepence duty on every gallon of imported molasses. An additional tax was levied on coffee, indigo, wine, and lumber. The Stamp Act of 1765 imposed a tax on virtually all important documents, including trade manifests, land deeds, newspapers, and wills. The Quartering Act passed in 1765 required public houses and inns to board British soldiers and supply them with provisions. Private property, including uninhabited houses, barns, and outhouses, were also included in the Quartering Act. The British Parliament considered colonial taxes fair payment for British protection and services. Irate colonists considered the taxes as nothing less than draconian dictates.

In order to avoid paying the disputed taxes many merchants, including Arnold, turned to smuggling. His illicit voyages to the West Indies gave him superb seamanship skills and a craftiness that would serve him well during his military career. He was on a trading trip to the West Indies when he heard that British soldiers had fired into a crowd of protesters in Boston, killing five and wounding six unarmed civilians. "Good God," he wrote in a letter to a friend on June 9, 1770. "Are the Americans all asleep & tamely giving up their glorious liberties or, are they all turned philosophers, that they don't take immediate vengeance on such miscreants: I am afraid of the latter."

In 1770, in response to heightened tensions within the colonies, Parliament repealed most of the taxes except for a tax on tea. Moreover, Parliament made it clear that it would continue to tax the colonies at any time and in any way it saw fit. Hostility toward "mother England" escalated as resistance to "taxation without representation" spread throughout the colonies. On December 16, 1773, members of the secret society "The Sons of Liberty" disguised themselves as Indians and dumped an entire shipment of East India Company tea into Boston Harbor. In retaliation Parliament passed the Coercive Acts. These "intolerable acts" stripped Massachusetts of self-government and closed the harbor to commerce. Anger turned to violence, and on April 14, 1775, British regulars and a hastily formed Massachusetts militia fought a running battle at Concord and Lexington.

When Arnold heard the news of the bloody exchange, he implored the town elders to relinquish the keys to the New Haven powder house. He intended to lead the local militia, officially named the Connecticut Governor's Foot Guard, to Massachusetts to support the rebel cause. The elders refused, saying they needed more information before taking action. Arnold, who had been elected captain by the militia, marched his men to the tavern where the elders were taking refuge. According to Edward Elias Atwater in *The History of New Haven,* he barked out, "[I]f the keys are not coming within five minutes, my men will break into the supply-house and help themselves. None but the Almighty God shall prevent me from marching." The elders handed over the keys. Now armed, Arnold and his unit of farmers and merchants, resplendent in their scarlet uniforms and bear hats, marched to Boston and into the throes of the American Revolution.

After taking heavy losses at Lexington and Concord, the British retreated to their stronghold in Boston. Although surrounded by thousands of colonials, Boston provided a safe haven. Open shipping lanes gave them access to the supplies they needed to wait out a siege. The colonials held the high ground surrounding the city, but they didn't have the artillery to take advantage of their strategic position. Dysentery, boredom, and desertions plagued the growing but unruly rebel encampment in Cambridge. Unless something was done to break the stalemate, the British could control the city of Boston and its valuable harbor indefinitely.

Upon his arrival at Cambridge, Arnold presented a plan to the Massachusetts Committee of Safety, the military arm of the Massachusetts Provincial Congress. Through his business travels, he was familiar with the Lake Champlain–Lake George region. He proposed to seize the lightly defended British fort at Ticonderoga and transport its extensive array of cannon to Boston. His plan approved, Arnold dispatched several officers to recruit a Massachusetts militia. Then he set off for Ticonderoga on horseback. Brash, fearless, and cunning, with a magnetic personality that both attracted and repulsed, Arnold was poised on the brink of a military career that would take more wayward turns than a broken compass.

When Arnold reached Castleton, 25 miles southeast of Ticonderoga, he encountered Ethan Allen and 200 of his Green Mountain Boys. Allen and his militia had their own plans to wrest Fort Ticonderoga from the British. The two strong-willed commanders argued over who had the legitimate right to lead the attack: Arnold had official orders, but Allen had armed men. A compromise was reached. The two agreed to share command—a shaky truce that didn't last long.

Shortly before dawn on May 10, 1775, Arnold, Allen, and the Green Mountain Boys attacked the remote outpost on the southern tip of Lake Champlain. After a brief skirmish, the British commander, Captain William Delaplace, surrendered. Allen's men ransacked the fort and commenced to drink all the rum they could get their hands on. The revelry lasted several days. When Arnold attempted to impose discipline, several of Allen's men threatened him with loaded muskets. Arnold stood his ground. The men lowered their muskets, but the standoff intensified the animosity between Arnold and Allen's entourage. Upon returning to Vermont, Allen and two of his officers—John Easton and Edward Mott—vilified Arnold in numerous letters to the Continental Congress and the Massachusetts Committee of Safety. The Congress put off censoring Arnold, but the cantankerous relationship with Ethan Allen and the Green Mountain Boys presaged a pattern of political squabbles that would haunt Arnold throughout his career.

With the gradual return of Allen's men to Vermont and the arrival of the Massachusetts militia, Arnold assumed command of Fort Ticonderoga. Built on a series of bluffs by the French in 1756, the fort had fallen into disrepair since the French and Indian War. Despite its poor condition, its strategic importance was obvious. The fort guarded the waterway that connected Lake Champlain to Lake George. If the British attempted an invasion from Canada they would have to sail directly under the array of cannon and mortars that lined the ramparts.

Arnold took official command of Fort Ticonderoga on May 14, 1775. He immediately set to work refurbishing the fortifications and artillery. The following January Henry Knox, a rotund Boston bookseller turned artillery officer, would haul on ox-drawn sleds 60 tons of Fort Ticonderoga cannons and howitzers 300 miles across the frozen wilderness of New York and Massachusetts to Boston; it was a remarkable logistical accomplishment. In March, three days of bombardment from the artillery Knox delivered to General Washington forced the British to evacuate Boston—an astonishing American victory, and Washington's last until the Battle of Trenton on December 26, 1776.

Confident that Fort Ticonderoga was secure, Arnold set sail to attack the British forts at Crown Point and St. John on the northern end of the lake. The forts were easily taken, and Arnold returned to Ticonderoga with military supplies, a British sloop, and five additional bateaux. His success received a mixed reaction among members of the Continental Congress in Philadelphia; some believed Arnold was exceeding his authority and undermining any chance of reconciliation with Britain. When news reached Arnold that the Congress was considering surrendering Ticonderoga to appease the British, he fired off a series of persuasive letters. In addition to emphasizing the value of Fort Ticonderoga in guarding against British access to Lake George and the Hudson River, he recommended that Congress consider a preemptive strike against the British in Canada.

Although his lack of tact offended some of the representatives, the letters achieved his goal. Congress decided to maintain control of Fort Ticonderoga and, after much debate, approved a Canadian invasion. However, the military leader they selected to lead the invasion was not Arnold but a patrician major general from New York, Phillip Schuyler. Meanwhile Arnold's political problems continued to escalate. Spurred on by malicious reports written by Green Mountain Boys Colonel James Easton and Lieutenant Colonel John Brown to the Massachusetts Committee on Safety and the Continental Congress in Philadelphia, Arnold's critics multiplied.

Dr. Benjamin Church, the chairman of the Committee on Safety, was especially vitriolic. Church, who would later be jailed as a British spy, maintained that the impetuous Arnold cared more for personal glory than for the welfare of the colonies, and that Arnold was dishonest in his accounting of funds expended in the taking of Fort Ticonderoga. The Continental Congress appointed a junior officer, Benjamin Hinman, as the new commander of the fort. Disgusted and humiliated, Arnold resigned his commission.

On his way home to New Haven, Arnold stopped at Albany to meet Schuyler. Despite Arnold's questionable reputation, Schuyler saw in him a competent leader. The two soldiers discussed a daring idea that had garnered support among some Revolutionary officers—an invasion of Canada. It was an enticing plan, but it had powerful detractors. The Declaration of Independence would not be signed for another year, and many in the Congress hoped their disagreements with Britain could still be resolved. It was one thing to seize forts at Ticonderoga and Crown Point in New York; it was quite another to attack Canada. Advocates of the plan hoped that, given the opportunity, French-Canadians who were unhappy with British rule would join the rebellion. Some dubbed Quebec the "14th colony." Opponents of the plan feared an invasion of Canada would unleash the full wrath of the mightiest army in the world.

A Canadian invasion was defensive as well as offensive strategy. If the British launched a successful attack down Lake Champlain, they would control the most strategic waterway in the colonies. During the French and Indian War and three other preceding colonial wars, the army that controlled the Lake Champlain-Lake George-Hudson River waterway was victorious. The Mohawks called the Champlain Valley "the great warpath." A preemptive strike into Canada would blunt a Canadian-British invasion of the colonies. After much political wrangling General Washington, with the approval of the Continental Congress, appointed General Schuyler to lead a force of 7,000 American troops up the Champlain Valley. Their objective was the British stronghold at Montreal.

During his trading expeditions to Canada, Arnold had learned a great deal about the readiness of the British forces commanded by the governor, Sir Guy Carleton. From Quebec to the Great Lakes, a mere 700 British regulars defended Canadian territory. Arnold believed Quebec City, guardian of the strategic St. Lawrence River, was vulnerable to an attack through Maine. No one had ever attempted to lead an army through the Maine wilderness before, but Arnold had acquired a 1761 map of trails, portages, and waterways that outlined a navigable route to Quebec City. Arnold convinced Schuyler that he could spring a surprise attack and defeat the sparsely defended British fortress. Schuyler agreed that Quebec City was a tempting target.

Arnold's political problems troubled Schuyler, but he also recognized Arnold's leadership ability. Schuyler asked him to be his adjutant. But Arnold was not interested in an assistant's job. He had his sights set on military glory. Schuyler recommended that Arnold travel to Cambridge and present his plan to General Washington. After Arnold departed, Schuyler wrote to Washington recommending Arnold and his plan. But he added a caveat: He asked Washington to make it absolutely clear to Arnold that he was subordinate to Schuyler in overall command of the northern army. Schuyler was not going to chance a repeat of the command bickering that had sullied the taking of Fort Ticonderoga.

While in Albany, Arnold received a letter from his sister Hannah. It conveyed dreadful news. His wife, Margaret, aged 30, had died of yellow fever. Over the past several years Margaret had become increasingly unhappy with Arnold's frequent trips away from home. Gradually, their romance withered, and she wrote less often. Despite their estrangement, Arnold was devastated. He rushed to New Haven to be with his sister and his boys. He visited his wife's grave with his children and then spent the next weeks contemplating his future. Always the astute businessman, he saw a potential mercantile bonanza. The Continental Army would need medicine, munitions, and horses. With his trading experience and military contacts, he could make a fortune.

But he also understood that a British victory would render short-term economic gains meaningless. A vengeful monarchy would undoubtedly implement new taxes, even more oppressive than the hated "Intolerable Acts." Those who served or profited from the rebellion would be hunted down and executed for treason. At Ticonderoga Arnold had thrown in his lot with the revolt. The future of his family and his business, not to mention his own neck, was tied to a colonial victory. He turned to his sister for help. Hannah moved into Arnold's home and took over the child-raising duties. She also had the business savvy to manage his assets. Confident that his boys and his commercial endeavors were in good hands, Arnold proceeded to Watertown, Massachusetts, to clear up his accounts with the Committee of Safety. He also intended to discuss his plan to invade Canada through Maine with the man who would become one of his greatest admirers—his commander, General Washington.

Arnold spent three long weeks wrangling with the Committee of Safety. Rather than reimbursing him for his personal expenses, the Committee, led by the irascible Dr. Church, accused Arnold of misusing funds and padding expenses. In response, Arnold provided a detailed accounting showing that the Massachusetts Congress actually owed him £400, four times the amount of money they had advanced him for the assault on Fort Ticonderoga.

Arnold was fighting a political battle he could not win. His friend Silas Deane, a Congressional delegate, urged him to back off his payment demands and instead forward his bill to the

Continental Congress. Arnold did so, and the Congress settled the dispute by awarding him twice the amount he requested. Although he was exonerated from the accusation of mishandling military funds, Arnold could not shake his reputation as an impetuous military leader. James L. Nelson's comment in *Benedict Arnold's Navy* summarizes Arnold's evolving political predicaments: "Arnold's preference for fighting over schmoozing would forever be a handicap to his career, and would play a big part in his eventual fall from grace."

With the unpleasant political wrangling behind him, Arnold proceeded to Cambridge to meet with Washington. Arnold had every reason to be confident of the outcome—he had a good plan, a surveyor's guide through the Maine wilderness, and a bold commander who did not shy from action.

In mid-August 1775, Arnold halted his horse on the road to Washington's headquarters. Dressed in a scarlet captain's uniform of the Second Connecticut Foot Guard and astride his favorite big bay, Arnold looked every bit a leader of men. Spread out before him was Cambridge, the nucleus of the American encampment. The rebel army stretched across a 10-mile arc from the Mystic River in the northeast to Roxbury in the south. Inside the arc 7,000 British regulars waited in Boston for Washington to attack. Arnold spurred his mount through a village that bustled with activity. The streets were crowded with carriages and riders on horseback. Shopkeepers hawked vegetables, pork, and fish. Taverns were doing a lively business. This was an army that would fight on full stomachs, supplemented with plenty of rum.

At the end of the main street Arnold reined in his horse at the entrance to the Harvard Common. He sat in his saddle and stared. Never before had he seen such a disorganized military camp. Slowly he weaved past overflowing latrines, dank lean-tos, and filthy sailcloth tents. This was the army of farmers, merchants, and fishermen George Washington had come to Cambridge to command. The chaos assaulted Arnold's sense of military discipline. Washington had made no secret of his disdain for the army of ragtag soldiers he was expected to lead, and Arnold could see why.

On a rise located a quarter of a mile from the river, he spotted the impressive gray mansion, previously owned by the Loyalist John Vassal, that now served as General Washington's headquarters. An aide greeted Arnold at the front door, took his riding coat and hat, and knocked softly on a mahogany door to the right of the small anteroom. After a moment, it opened, and George Washington, dressed in a blue and buff uniform, stood on the threshold. At six feet two inches he towered over Arnold. He had chestnut brown hair powdered and tied in a queue, gray-blue eyes, and a ruddy complexion. Pockmarks on his cheeks revealed a bout with smallpox contracted in Barbados when he was a young man.

Washington beckoned Arnold into the study that served as his office. Hundreds of books lined the floor-to-ceiling shelves on one wall; maps of Boston and surrounding towns covered another. Bright sunshine poured through three large windows providing a glimpse of the Charles River a quarter of a mile away. The general took a seat behind a small writing desk in front of the windows and motioned to Arnold to sit across from him.

Washington and Arnold exchanged views on a number of key concerns. They discussed the refurbished artillery at Fort Ticonderoga, the military significance of the Lake Champlain valley, and the details of the plan to lead an expedition through the Maine wilderness to Quebec. More than powder, muskets, and shot, Washington needed strong, disciplined officers. He believed that Arnold was such a man. After the meeting Washington deliberated for a few days. In an August letter he had said, "We are in a situation that requires us to run all risques." An attack on Montreal, coordinated with an assault on the walled city of Quebec City, was a daring plan. If successful, the pincer strategy could bring the province of Quebec into the rebellion as the 14th American colony.

On September 14, Washington officially sanctioned the invasion of Canada through the Maine wilderness, and he promoted Arnold to the rank of full colonel in the Continental Army. His orders to Arnold ended with the sentence, "You are intrusted [sic] with a command of the utmost consequence to the interests and liberties of America." Rumors spread quickly throughout the encampment that Arnold wanted volunteers for an arduous expedition against the British. Hoping to escape the tedium and squalor of the siege encampment, many volunteered. Arnold needed the toughest men he could muster for the daunting expedition, and within a few days he had selected 786 of the hardiest and most experienced woodsmen.

Arnold's plan required a forced march through a harsh, virtually unexplored landscape. The first stage involved navigating the swift currents of the Kennebec River. After the Kennebec their journey was dotted with a slew of obstacles. They would have to pole their 400-pound shallow-draft bateaux through rock-strewn streams and lakes. Numerous rapids, waterfalls, and rocky elevations would require dragging or carrying the heavy boats to the next navigable waterway. The second phase of the journey would take them through the "Great Carrying Place," a 12-mile portage to the "Height of Land," a section of the Appalachian Mountains that formed a natural boundary between Canada and Maine. There the expedition would have to cross the boggy Seven Mile Stream in order to reach the Chaudière River and Point Lévis. From there a short trip down the St. Lawrence River would take them to their objective—Quebec City.

To guide the expedition, Arnold used a map drawn by a British engineer, Lieutenant John Montresor. The British officer had made two trips through the Maine wilderness during the French and Indian War. Before the Kennebec leg of their march, Arnold asked Samuel Goodrich, a surveyor from Gardinerston, Maine, to revise the map. Unknown to Arnold, Goodrich was a Loyalist sympathizer. In his "revisions," Goodrich drafted incorrect routes and distances. Arnold left Gardinerston thinking the distance to Quebec was 180 miles; the actual distance was over 300 miles. On September 23, 1775, guided by a faulty map and provisions for only half the distance they would travel, Arnold's force set out for Quebec City.

Arnold divided his force of 786 men into two divisions under the command of Lieutenant Colonels Roger Enos and Christopher Greene. Joining the force at the last minute were 300 woodsmen from Virginia and Pennsylvania, headed by Daniel Morgan. Morgan had impressed Washington by leading his men on a forced march of 600 miles from Virginia to Cambridge in just three weeks. Morgan's woodsmen were not ordinary militia. In lieu of military dress they wore buckskin; rather than bayonets they carried tomahawks and scalping knives. They preferred long Pennsylvania rifles to muskets and bragged they could shoot a hole through a man's head half a mile away. This was not an idle boast. A British officer termed the Pennsylvania rifles "cursed twisted guns, the worst widow and orphan makers in the world."

The expedition set off up the Kennebec River with Morgan's men in the lead. Arnold assigned Morgan the difficult task of clearing trails. Almost immediately the stiff Kennebec current became a problem. The inexperienced oarsmen had difficulty navigating the bulky boats. When Arnold ordered the construction of several "bateaux," he expected to get 25-foot whaleboats, a craft common to Connecticut waters that was curved at both ends and had three-foot gunwales to keep out water sprays. What he got instead was the Maine version: ungainly flat-bottomed boats with narrow gunwales, which provided scant protection against the rough water Arnold's men were about to encounter.

To make matters worse, the hastily constructed boats were made from green wood.

After a few days on the river the wood began to warp, and the boats started leaking. Then the weather turned nasty. Cold, wintry rain buffeted the expedition. Supplies and munitions were soaked. Over a hundred men contracted dysentery from tainted drinking water. Then it began to snow. "Our fatigue seemed daily to increase, but what we most dreaded was the frost and cold from which we began to suffer considerably," lamented a soldier in his journal. In order to avoid bottlenecks at portage areas, Arnold divided the two divisions into four regiments of approximately 250 men each. While trail was cleared and difficult terrain traversed, supplies needed safeguarding. Arnold consigned the bulk of food and munitions to the rear regiment, commanded by Major Enos. Each day presented new difficulties.

On the third day the company encountered eight miles of surging rapids pitted with boulders and dead logs. They struggled over rocky outcrops, and through swamps, and gullies, none of which appeared on their maps. By the end of the first week it was obvious to Arnold that the maps were useless. A fierce winter storm combined with the leaking boats spoiled most of their cod, salt beef, cornmeal, and flour. Arnold sent a courier to Enos to bring forward fresh supplies with all possible speed. The messenger reported back two days later with the worst possible news: Convinced that the expedition was a failure, Major Enos and his officers had turned around and returned to Cambridge with all the supplies

The slog through the Maine wilderness was no longer a military expedition; it was a desolate journey with a single goal— survival. Arnold's remaining two regiments were starving. They ate their dogs, their leather cartridge boxes, their moccasins, and the bark off trees. The bodies of dead men were covered with snow and left behind. In a last-ditch effort to save his men Arnold pushed on ahead alone to find food. On the morning of

November 2 the struggling lead column witnessed a miraculous sight. In his journal Captain Thayer wrote,

> Discovered...some men and horses and cattle making toward us, at which sight Capt. Topham and myself shed tears of joy, in our happy delivery from the Grasping hand of Death. The Drover was sent toward us by Col. Arnold, in order to kill them [the cattle] for our support. Many of the starving men ate the butchered meat raw.

Finally, on November 8 Arnold and 650 of the original 1,000 men arrived at Point Lévis, a small spit of land on the banks of the St. Lawrence River. Weak and exhausted, the American troops stared across the St. Lawrence at their objective. Perched on a 200-foot cliff, like an immense medieval castle, the walled City of Quebec loomed in the distance.

While Arnold's men struggled through the Maine wilderness, the Montreal prong of the Canadian invasion fared better. After landing on the northern shore of Lake Champlain, the Americans laid siege to the British port of St. John. Suffering from a severe case of gout, American General Schuyler turned over his command to Brigadier General Richard Montgomery. After 42 days the British surrendered St. John. Emboldened by victory and replenished by captured artillery, Montgomery ordered an attack on Montreal. On November 11, Governor Sir Guy Carleton, hopelessly outgunned, fled Montreal with a small detachment of 200 British soldiers. With the surrender of Montreal, only Quebec stood between the American invaders and victory.

Unaware of events at St. John and Montreal, Arnold made preparations to attack the walled city. Quebec's defenses were meager. Only 170 British troops and a band of undisciplined Canadian militia defended the city. But Arnold's situation was not much better. While the Americans had superior numbers, they had only a few pieces of light artillery and no bayonets—a critical weapon in hand-to-hand combat. Many of the American muskets were either lost or ruined, along with most of their ammunition. Each man averaged a mere five rounds of musket balls. Undaunted, Arnold formulated an attack plan based more on bluff than on military superiority. He could not delay his attack. Winter was coming, and reports of men falling ill with smallpox increased daily.

Then fate intervened—in favor of the British. High winds, sleet, and a dearth of vessels to cross the river postponed Arnold's attack. While the Americans scoured the shoreline searching for canoes and bateaux, a relief detachment of 300 British soldiers, led by Lieutenant Allan Maclean, arrived to reinforce the city. Soon afterwards Governor Carleton, who had escaped Montgomery's pursuing troops, slipped into Quebec and took command of the city's defense. Arnold had no idea that, while he waited for the weather to clear, the balance of force had shifted to the British. His attack force numbered less than 600 men, many of them weakened by smallpox. Meanwhile, through conscription of Quebec citizens and the arrival of relief troops, the British now had 1,800 men under arms.

Thinking he had troop superiority, Arnold sent a message to the city's commander, Lieutenant-Governor Hector Cramahé, demanding that he surrender. To reinforce the message, a contingent of Americans crossed the river and let loose a flurry of musket and small-cannon fire at the Upper Town walls. When the defenders let loose with a barrage of superior firepower, Arnold knew he had lost his slim advantage. With no options left, he settled in for a winter siege. He moved his men to the nearby village of Pointe-aux-Trembles to await the arrival from Montreal of Brigadier General Montgomery with supplies and reinforcements.

Conditions in the camp were perilous. The frigid cold killed both men and spirit. Arnold sent out scouting parties to capture British troops so he could use their uniforms to clothe his men. The situation worsened when "camp fever," a combination of disease and dysentery, spread through the troops. In order to keep his men fed, Arnold used his personal credit to procure supplies from nearby villagers. Finally, on December 1, Brigadier General Richard Montgomery arrived from Montreal with supplies and an additional 460 men.

Despite the Spartan conditions, Arnold maintained military discipline. Shortly after arriving at Pointe-aux-Trembles, Montgomery wrote to General Schuyler, "I find Colonel Arnold's corps an exceedingly fine one, inured to fatigue, and well accustomed to cannon shot. There is a style of discipline among them, much superior to what I have been used to see this campaign. He himself is active, intelligent, and enterprising."

No longer able to delay—many enlistments were due to expire—Arnold and Montgomery launched their attack at midnight on December 30. In a howling blizzard, an American force of 1,100 men cast off the St. Lawrence shoreline in an armada of canoes and bateaux. Hidden by the swirling snow, they slipped past six British men-of-war anchored below the city. The Americans were divided into four detachments. The smaller two attacked the cliffs and walls of the Upper Town. These feints distracted the British defenders while Montgomery and Arnold led the main attack against the Lower Town, located on the more accessible river shoreline.

Arnold led an advance party of 25 volunteers he called the "forlorn hope" against the north side of the Lower Town. Their mission was to make a trail through the snow and eliminate any defenders outside the walls. Simultaneously, Montgomery attacked the Lower Town from the south. They planned to meet in the center of the Lower Town and then launch an all-out attack on the Upper Town. At first Arnold's men met little resistance. They fought their way through the city gate, and charged the first of two barricades that blocked their path. In the distance, they could hear warning bells ringing and the sound of musket fire. Montgomery's attack was underway.

Arnold paused briefly to wait for a six-pound cannon to blast a hole through a wooden barricade. As his men struggled with the artillery piece, a fusillade of musket fire erupted from behind the barricade. Fragments of a musket-ball ricochet punctured Arnold's left thigh and calf. His boot filled with blood, Arnold limped forward, urging his troops to follow, but he collapsed. Ignoring musket balls and grapeshot, Daniel Morgan made his way to his wounded commander. Despite Arnold's protests, Morgan ordered him to be taken on a litter to the camp field hospital. Then Morgan and his men continued the charge, but the British held. In the fray Morgan was knocked unconscious and captured. Leaderless, the remaining troops in Arnold's brigade retreated to their boats.

Meanwhile, on the south side of Lower Town, Montgomery and his men fought their way past two palisades. When they turned a corner they encountered a two-story blockhouse. Montgomery waved his sword and shouted to his men, "Come on, my good soldiers! Your general calls upon you!" Suddenly wooden portals sprang open and four cannon fired directly into the charging men. No more than 30 yards from the blockhouse, sword still in hand, Montgomery took a direct hit and slumped to the ground. British gunners firing at point blank range killed two other officers and six soldiers. The remaining American troops were taken prisoner.

Lying in a field hospital litter back at camp, Arnold received the battle report. Fifty-one Americans were dead, including Montgomery and several officers. Thirty-six others were wounded and two-thirds of his men captured. Arnold was devastated. But retreat was unthinkable. He had promised Washington and Schuyler a victory. The Americans and the British were at a stalemate. Arnold would not abandon his position, and the British were reluctant to leave the safety of their walled city to attack. With a siege his only option, Arnold set up a defensive line and waited for help.

Anytime during January, Carleton could have left the safety of the walled city and destroyed what was left of the American force. But each day Arnold repositioned his men, giving the impression that the Americans were still formidable. The ruse kept the cautious Carleton sealed inside the city while Arnold waited for reinforcements. Throughout February, small groups of Americans flowed into the camp, and, by March, the American force had increased to 2,500 men. On April 1, General David Wooster arrived from Montreal with additional troops. He also carried orders to relieve Arnold. Bitterly disappointed at leaving his men and the field of battle, Arnold complied.

Washington ordered Arnold to Montreal to recuperate. In recognition of his gallantry, the Continental Congress promoted him to brigadier general. Some were even calling him a military genius for his courageous march through Maine and for holding Quebec captive for five months. Among his admirers were Benjamin Franklin and John Carroll. Washington called Arnold a "brave friend" and said, "The merit of this gentleman is certainly great. I heartily wish that fortune may distinguish him as one of her favorites."

In a single year Arnold had led the raid on Fort Ticonderoga, secured the fort's artillery, marched an American force through the Maine wilderness, and laid siege to the Canadian capital. No one had done more in 1775 to demonstrate American fortitude and resilience. Up to this point, the British had underestimated the conviction and fervor of the small colonial rebellion. But that was about to change. The full fury of British military might was about to be unleashed on the Canadian invaders.

An infusion of 8,000 troops from England, led by a dashing young major general—"Gentleman Johnny" Burgoyne—decimated Wooster's siege force at Quebec. Wooster retreated to Deschambault, where his forces were again defeated. Six hundred Americans were killed or wounded. But Arnold was not about to give up all they had gained without a fight. He urged a counterattack at weakly defended Fort Anne to free American prisoners. But some of his officers, led by Colonel Moses Hazen, considered the plan foolish and reckless. Arnold and Hazen argued about strategy for three days. During the delay the outnumbered British suggested a cease-fire and prisoner exchange. The Battle of Fort Anne was averted, but in the process a new name, Moses Hazen, was added to the list of Arnold's political enemies.

In the meantime commander of the Canadian invasion force John Thomas, who had replaced Montgomery, died from smallpox during the retreat from Quebec. Washington appointed as his successor Major General John Sullivan. While the British marched on Montreal, Arnold and the inexperienced Sullivan differed over strategy. When American forces under the command of Sullivan were swept away at Trois-Rivières, Arnold knew that the only strategy left was retreat. He advised Sullivan, "There will be more honor in making a safe retreat than hazarding a battle against such superiority." And so, with the loss of Canada, Washington's hope of incorporating the massive "14th colony" into the rebel cause was dashed. (In 1776 Quebec Province stretched from the Atlantic Ocean to the Mississippi River. It included most of the Great Lakes and the present-day states of Ohio, Indiana, Minnesota, Illinois, Wisconsin and Michigan.)

The colonial force was in dismal condition. Half the troops had smallpox. Those who could fight lacked such basic necessities as tents, shoes, and shirts. They subsisted on raw pork and musty flour. Arnold's pleas for supplies fell on the deaf ears of a divided Continental Congress. The American campaign in Canada ended with the ignominious retreat of 2,000 militia from the last bastion in Canada—Isle aux Noix. Left behind were more than 3,000 comrades buried in shallow graves where they fell. While Sullivan led most of the Americans back to Fort Ticonderoga, Arnold and a small detachment lingered behind at Fort St. John to destroy any supplies and artillery that could be used by the British. With the enemy closing in, Arnold, the last American to leave Canada, set sail south on Lake Champlain to join what remained of the battered American force at Fort Ticonderoga.

Nestled between the Green Mountains of present-day Vermont and the Adirondack Mountains of New York State lies one of the largest freshwater lakes in North America—Lake Champlain. Formed by retreating glaciers 20,000 years ago, the lake is 110 miles long and 14 miles across at its widest point. Only the Great Lakes are bigger. Lake Champlain is the first link in a chain of waterways, including Lake George and the Hudson River, which form a nearly seamless waterway from Canada to New York City. The Iroquois named Lake Champlain "Caniaderi Guarante"—mouth of the country.

The lake was colonial North America's most vital economic waterway. Its straight-as-an-arrow north-south longitude eased navigation even during difficult weather. For over 200 years, the lake was the center of the lucrative beaver pelt trade. Furs purchased from native tribes in Canada were transported to New York in bateaux rigged with both sails and oars to accommodate the lake's variable wind conditions. Because the rugged Adirondack wilderness was nearly impassable by land, Lake Champlain offered the best possible route from Canada to the Atlantic for traders and invaders alike. British control of Lake Champlain during the French and Indian War was a key factor in defeating the French and driving them from Canada.

Emboldened by their victory in Canada the British prepared a massive invasion of the rebel colonies. Like a hound on the scent of a wounded rabbit, Sir Guy Carleton planned to pursue the Americans with a combined force of 13,000 British regulars, hundreds of Hessian mercenaries, and 400 Mohawk warriors. Carleton intended to clear Lake Champlain of all rebel resistance. Once the forts at Crown Point and Ticonderoga were seized, he would ferry his troops across Lake George and continue an overland march south through Saratoga to Albany. There his force would link up with General Howe and his army of 11,000 British regulars.

British control of the Lake Champlain-Hudson Valley corridor would separate New England from the rest of the colonies. Carleton's plan was based on the age-old military axiom: sever the head and the body will die. With complete control of eastern New York, the British would halt supply and troop movements between New England and the other colonies. Furthermore, New England Revolutionary leaders Samuel Adams, John Adams, and Silas Deane would be isolated and unable to coordinate with the Continental Congress. The combined British force would easily retake Boston and reclaim its strategic harbor.

The American situation was worse than desperate. Following his ignominious defeat at Long Island on August 27, 1776, Washington and his depleted army were on the run in the New Jersey wilderness. Militia were deserting in droves, and dissension among Continental Congress representatives was at its peak. If the British were successful in dividing the colonies, the fragile bonds that held the Continental Congress together would disintegrate. Revenge would be both sweet and swift. Carleton did not mince words in expressing his contempt for the American leaders: they were "rebels, traitors in arms against their king, rioters, disturbers of the public peace, plunderers, assassins, robbers, murderers." A British victory would end the rebellion, and the traitors Adams, Franklin, and Washington would hang.

The invasion force, led by Governor Carleton and his second-in-command, Captain Richard Pringle, was the most powerful British armada ever to sail on a freshwater lake. The pride of the fleet was the three-masted, 80-foot sloop *Inflexible*. It carried 16 nine-pound cannons and six three-pounders. Pringle's flagship, the schooner *Maria*, and its sister ship, the schooner *Carleton*, carried a combined arsenal of 26 six-pound cannons. The *Loyal Convert* was armed with seven nine-pounders.

Twenty-eight gunboats and three longboats accompanied the four large sea-going war ships. Each gunboat was armed with a single cannon in the bow. The gunboat cannons ranged in size from 12 to 24 pounds; each longboat carried two 24-pound cannons. Using their oars as "sweeps," the maneuverable gunboats and longboats were adept at fighting in tight quarters. The largest and most powerful of the British vessels was the 91-foot-long, two-masted radeau, appropriately named *Thunderer*. A radeau was a large, flat-bottomed sailing scow. True to its name, the 422-ton floating arsenal carried a massive array of six 24-pound cannons, over a dozen 18-pound cannons, and four eight-inch howitzers. Seasoned British crewmen sailed the vessels, and Hessian gunnery officers commanded the artillery. The warriors accompanied the fleet in massive birch-bark canoes.

The preparation of a British invasion armada was no secret. At Fort Ticonderoga, Arnold urged his superior, General Gates, to blunt the attack with a fleet of smaller craft more adept at shallow-water battle than the British sea-going behemoths. Gates agreed and, while Carleton was assembling his invasion fleet at St. John on the Richelieu River, Arnold feverishly supervised the building of a fleet of gunboats and row galleys at Skenesborough, a small village south of Fort Ticonderoga. Carpenters constructed four 72-foot-long row galleys rigged with lateen sails and equal-length masts, each carrying 10 cannons and 10 swivel guns. The cannons were capable of firing four-to-18-pound cannon balls. The gunboats were single-mast vessels measuring approximately 53 feet. They had oars to maneuver in tight spaces. To enhance the maneuverability of the gunboats Arnold copied the narrow bow and stern design of Italian gondolas. He called his modified gunboats "gundolas". Each was armed with eight swivel guns and three cannons.

Arnold had no illusions of defeating the superior British fleet, which had a four-to-one advantage in firepower. The British fleet carried 417 guns, while the Americans would bring no more than 91 guns into battle. Arnold planned to harry the British and in the process stall the invasion. Winter was fast approaching. Ice forming on Lake Champlain would stymie the British navy, and the untrammeled wilderness of the Adirondacks was impenetrable for a marching army. No roads or pathways from Canada south to Fort Ticonderoga existed along either shore. If the British invasion could be delayed until the following spring, it would buy the Americans time to rebuild the northern army.

As autumn approached, Arnold scoured Lake Champlain for the best site to engage the British fleet. He selected uninhabited Valcour Island, which was midway between St. John on the Richelieu River (present day Saint -Jean-sur-Richelieu), and Fort Ticonderoga on the southern end of Lake Champlain. Located several miles south of Cumberland Bay, the two-mile-long island offered the logistical advantage Arnold needed. Its oak-leaf shoreline provided several small inlets and coves suitable for sheltering his small fleet. The main lake channel, a three-mile expanse of water, flowed along the eastern side of the island, while the channel on the New York side was much smaller—a mile and a quarter at its widest point and a half-mile at its narrowest. The large British armada would likely sail past the island through the main channel. If Arnold could coax the British into the western channel the large ships would be unable to maneuver into the broadside positions they needed to fire their cannons.

Tall pine trees covered the hump-backed center of the Island. The rest was dotted with steep cliffs, rocky outcrops, and a few narrow beaches. Any ship sailing south in the main channel on the Vermont side of the island had an obstructed line of sight into the channel on the New York side. From a northern approach, the narrow stretch of water leading to the western side of the island appeared more like a river than a bay. Mooring his vessels in a cup-shaped inlet on the west, facing the New York shore, Arnold had the perfect site to spring an ambush. Sheltered by the island, he would wait for the British to sail past, Then his fleet would strike from behind. Arnold's small flotilla was about to fight the first American naval battle, and the outcome could determine the course of the Revolution.

On the afternoon of October 10, a cold southerly wind buffeted the small American flotilla anchored in the western bay of Valcour Island. The ships bobbed hull to hull in the tight inlet. For three weeks the fleet had weathered violent winds and turbulent, icy waters as they searched for signs of the British invasion force. The rough weather and lack of supplies had taken a toll. Some of the sailors were barefoot. Many were sick with fever and ague. Tattered breeches and tunics provided little relief from the penetrating cold. The cutter *Lee*, the two schooners *Royal Savage* and *Revenge,* and the sloop *Enterprise*, along with the row galleys *Congress, Trumbull,* and *Washington,* provided some shelter in their cabins and on their lower decks. Aboard the nine smaller gunboats the only relief from the relentless winds and icy lake sprays were the spruce-limb fascines Arnold had ordered his men to lash to the bulwarks as a barrier against musket shot and arrows.

As evening approached, the wind direction shifted from south to north. Arnold stood on the quarterdeck of his flagship, *Royal Savage,* his chin buried in a blue cape to ward off the raw Adirondack chill. With the favoring northerly wind, the British would soon be upon them, maybe as early as the next day. Deep in thought, he reviewed every detail of the upcoming battle. Around him, 60 seamen scurried about, preparing for the conflict. Sails and rigging were inspected, anchor cables tightened, cannon cleaned, gun carriages inspected for cracks. Sand was spread on the deck to provide traction when blood began to flow.

Their tasks completed, men huddled in small groups and chewed on their supper of salt pork and biscuits. Arnold inspected the crew's work. In battle, small mistakes multiplied rapidly. His fleet would not be defeated due to lack of preparation. Only a week earlier, in a dispatch to General Gates, Arnold had called his force of inexperienced seamen "a wretched motley crew." Few on the *Royal Savage* or on the other assorted galleys, schooners, and gunboats that made up the small armada had sea or battle experience. Ultimately, it didn't really matter. When cannon balls and grapeshot started flying, there would be no place to hide.

Arnold glanced down the line of his tightly packed fleet. It was dark now. Surprise was the backbone of his plan, so no light of any sort was allowed on the vessels lest it be spotted by British scouts. It is likely that doubts followed one another like whitecaps in the choppy channel. There were so many "ifs" to contend with. The plan might work *if* Pringle did not find out that the American fleet was hidden behind Valcour Island; *if* the wind stayed northerly so the British were forced to tack back to engage; *if* Arnold didn't run out of ammunition; and *if* his inexperienced artillerymen could shoot straight. His battle plan was good, but the only principle that holds true once the fighting begins is the law of unintended consequences. Even the best plan unravels with the failure of the first predicted outcome.

After one last tour around the deck of the *Royal Savage*, Arnold retired to his cabin. He woke at dawn and quickly ascended the short ladder to the quarterdeck. The early morning sun was burning off a mist that had shrouded the lake. A thin cloak of snow covered the Adirondack peaks. An early snow was his best ally: Arnold believed the British had neither the will nor the capability to fight a winter campaign. He ordered a gunboat into the main channel to look out for the approaching British fleet. Then he transferred his command flag from the *Royal Savage* to the more agile row galley *Congress*. This would turn out to be a providential decision.

To the north, Captain Thomas Pringle and Governor Carleton stood on the deck of the command ship HMS *Maria*, peering through the early morning mist that hovered over the rough black waters of Cumberland Bay. According to British spies this was where the American fleet was anchored. The British armada rounded Cumberland Head and moved into the bay. Seamen aboard the most powerful fleet ever to sail Lake Champlain primed, loaded, and aimed their cannons at—nothing. The bay was empty. In a letter to an unknown correspondent, Dr. Robert Knox, the Inspector General of Hospitals who was at the scene, described it:

> On the 10ᵗʰ in ye morning, we sailed, taking me with him and his brother Col Carlton ye Quarter Master Genl and his aid de Camps, we anchored that night at Isle au Motte, where Captn Carlton and a party of Savages and Canadian Volunteers were encamped, they received orders by sunrise to go thro the woods to ye other side of Cumberland Bay. We sailed from that at 7 o clock, first preparing our ship for battle, and about half after nine came in sight of the bay, but to our great mortification, we cou'd discover no ships....

Soon after, a single cannon shot reverberated off the steep cliffs of Valcour Island. The American guard boat had spotted the British fleet. Arnold winced: the British fleet was close at hand, and the shot had probably forewarned them of the American presence. Arnold ordered the captain to raise a white pennant, the signal for a council of war, and grimly limped along the deck to his aft cabin.

Fifteen minutes later Captains Waterbury, his second-in-command, and Wigglesworth, third-in-command, entered his cabin. Arnold spread out a map of Valcour Bay and revealed his plan of attack. The trees and hills of Valcour Island provided a shield from British lookouts. Once the enemy passed the island through the main channel the Americans would attack from behind. The strong northerly wind would make it difficult for Pringle to maneuver his fleet into firing position. Arnold read the orders issued by General Gates: The fleet was to provide a "resolute but judicious defense of the northern entrance" and was to retreat only after having "discovered the insufficiency of every effort to retard the enemies' progress" toward Ticonderoga.

When Arnold finished reading, Waterbury spoke up. He didn't like Arnold's plan. Waterbury feared the Americans would be trapped in the small bay and that the only hope for survival was to try to out-sail the British to Ticonderoga. Later, in a letter to John Hancock, Waterbury recalled the conversation: "I gave it as my opinion that the fleet ought to immediately come to sail, and fight them on a retreat in [the] main lake." Arnold was not a patient man, but he understood the importance of letting officers speak their minds. He let Waterbury finish, then replied that an engagement in the open water would give the British the opportunity to bring their entire fleet into action. The Americans would have no chance against their superior firepower.

Surprise, Arnold told his men, is the best weapon. If they could nullify the firepower of the *Inflexible*, the *Maria*, the *Loyal Convert,* the *Carleton*, and the *Thunderer*, they could delay the enemy's offensive. The British, Arnold said, had no stomach for a winter campaign. Although still skeptical, Waterbury assented to the plan. It was clear that Arnold had made up his mind: the time for talking was over.

Arnold commanded all the vessels to proceed from the inlet to their prearranged anchor buoys in the channel. They anchored side by side in an arc facing the south end of the bay. The crescent-shaped formation allowed for maximum firepower, which could be directed in a crossfire at multiple targets. Spring cables were wound around capstans. By cranking the cables the crew could maneuver the vessels to fire broadside volleys and then quickly swing back the bow-guns. The narrow bow-to-stern gunboat silhouette would present a difficult target for British artillery. Gun carriages were blocked, cannonballs stacked, and wet blankets spread over ammunition magazines to protect against fires. With preparations complete, the two schooners, single sloop, three row galleys, eight gunboats, and one cutter that constituted the American navy bobbed at anchor in the inlet and waited for the arrival of the British fleet.

At 11:00 a.m. under an azure sky the British armada, white canvas sails swelling in the northerly wind, sailed down the main channel past Valcour Island. On the other side of the island the American fleet waited in attack formation. When the entire British fleet materialized on the southern side of the island, it had sailed two miles past the American fleet. For his plan to work, Arnold needed to engage the larger fleet in the tight confines of the bay channel. The hook was ready; next, he needed to rig the bait.

Arnold ordered the two-masted schooner *Royal Savage* and the three row galleys *Trumbull, Washington,* and *Congress,* with himself in command, to weigh anchor and attack. Cannons blazing, the four American vessels sailed straight for the departing British fleet. An astonished Carleton ran to the stern of his command ship, the *Maria.* Arnold—the man Carleton called a "horse jockey"—was attacking him! He ordered the battle flag raised on the main mast, and slowly the British ships began the laborious maneuver of reversing direction. The brisk northerly wind that had eased their transport south was now their adversary. Just as Arnold predicted, the British were forced to tack against the wind—the larger the ship, the more difficult the maneuver. Arnold's plan was working. Only the smaller British gunboats, with oars to supplant sails, were making progress back to the Americans. While the larger British ships struggled against the wind, the three American galleys raised their lateen sails and quickly made their way back to the crescent formation in the bay. The schooner *Royal Savage,* however, was in trouble.

The *Savage* had a reputation as a difficult ship to handle. David Hawley, her captain, struggled to keep her on course against the stiff wind. On the lee side of the island the wind kept changing direction. From the deck of the *Congress* Arnold could see that the outcome was not promising. Sails flapping, the *Savage* fell behind the galleys. The wind was taking her into the boulders that lined the southern shore of the island. Like angry hornets, the nimble British gunboats swarmed toward the struggling schooner.

Cannonballs pounded her hull. Bar and chain shot shattered her mast and fouled her rigging. Arnold ordered a salvo fired at the gunboats, but they were outside the range of his smaller cannons. In desperation, Hawley ran his ship onto the rocks. Better to sink the *Savage* than allow it to fall into British hands.

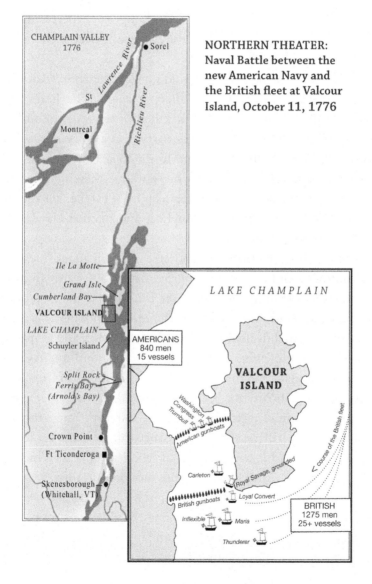

NORTHERN THEATER: Naval Battle between the new American Navy and the British fleet at Valcour Island, October 11, 1776

Seizing the opportunity, Lieutenant Edward Longcraft, captain of the *Loyal Convert*, adroitly maneuvered his way into the channel at the bay entrance. He ordered a boarding party into longboats, and they made for the *Savage*. His command lost, Hawley ordered the crew to abandon ship. Some escaped into the woods, but not all. Longcraft captured 20 of the American seamen. After he boarded the *Savage,* Longcraft ordered his men to fire the schooner's cannon at the American fleet anchored less than 500 yards away.

This was a mistake. On Arnold's order, the entire American fleet returned a murderous artillery barrage. The hunter was now the prey. With half his men killed or wounded, Longcraft and what was left of his boarding party beat a hasty retreat back to the safety of the *Loyal Convert*. In the meantime, Hawley and his men clambered over the rocky shoreline, making their way toward the American fleet. Captain John Thatcher on the row galley *Washington* launched a longboat and rescued Hawley and the remainder of his crew.

Meanwhile, the British gunboats set up their attack line across the southern end of the bay, approximately 300 yards from the American formation. For the next five hours, the steep cliffs of Valcour Island resonated with thunderous booms as cannons exchanged lethal fusillades of solid shot, bar shot, and grapeshot. Broad swathes of white smoke obscured the autumn sky. The crisp Adirondack air turned acrid with the stench of exploded gunpowder. Aboard the *Congress* Arnold repeatedly exposed himself to enemy fire as he strode back and forth across the deck directing his artillery. The small American fleet took a terrific pounding. Each hit sent shrapnel of wood and hot lead hurtling through the air. American casualties mounted steadily.

Midway through the battle, the black schooner *Carleton* under command of Lieutenant James Dacres worked its way past the eastern end of the British gunboats and into the channel 300 yards from the American battle line. Dacres ordered the crew to drop a spring anchor to compensate for the recoil of the *Carleton* cannons. Broadside to the American fleet, the British ship let loose a fusillade of six-pound cannon. In response, Arnold ordered his ships to concentrate fire on the *Carleton*. The combined firepower of the American fleet blasted one shot after another into the *Carleton's* hull. Lieutenant Dacres was knocked unconscious by flying debris. His second-in-command, Lieutenant Robert Brown, had his arm blown off. After an hour of sustained bombardment half the crew—some dead others wounded—littered the deck of the British schooner.

Its rigging cut and its hull repeatedly bored through with cannon balls, the *Carleton* was dead in the water. Midshipman Edward Pellow took command. With shot flying around him he climbed out on to the bowsprit to secure a jib sail and tow line. Lieutenant John Schank, commander of the British ship *Inflexible*, sent out two longboats to tow the *Carleton* to safety. Just as it seemed the rescue would be successful, American shot severed the towline. Again amidst a withering blast of American artillery Pellow shimmied out on to the bowsprit to attach a new towline, and this time the longboats managed to tow the *Carleton* to safety. Pellow's courage saved the only British ship to engage the Americans that day.

Fortunately for the Americans, none of the other British ships were able to effectively tack against the stiff wind. They got no closer to the American line than a mile. Some even furled their sails. Attempts at an artillery barrage were futile. Eighteen- and 24-pound cannonballs splashed short of the American line. This left the 28 British gunboats the task of engaging the Americans. Each gunboat carried 80 rounds of ammunition. Seven Hessian gunner's mates manned the single bow cannon in each gunboat.

With twice the firepower of the Americans, and commanded by veteran officers, the British gunboats were more than up to the task of demolishing the American fleet. The gunboats sat low in the water, and, with their bows directly facing the American line, they presented a narrow target to the inexperienced American gunners. Many of the American artillery shells flew harmlessly over their targets, but a few hit their mark. One Hessian-manned gunboat was blown out of the water by a direct hit on its powder magazine, and another, after absorbing multiple grape and cannon shots, sank in the cold Champlain waters.

Meanwhile, the incessant British bombardment was taking a toll on the Americans. The *Congress* was hulled by round shot several times, its mainmast damaged by bar shot. The gunboat *New York* was raked by enemy fire, and all its officers except Captain John Reed were killed. The gunboat *Philadelphia* took a fearful beating before it sank shortly before sundown. (It was raised in 1935 and is on exhibit in the Smithsonian Institution) Captain John Thatcher on the *Washington* was killed and his command assumed by Captain David Hawley, the officer Thatcher had rescued from the *Royal Savage* only a few hours earlier. The *Trumbull* took hits from several 12-pound shots. Her mast was splintered. Several crew were maimed and two killed by deadly projectiles of white oak fragments. Throughout the long afternoon, the sloop *Enterprise* served as a hospital ship. According to the journal of crewman Jahiel Stewart, "They brought the wounded abord of us the Dockters Cut of great many legs and arms and See Seven men threw overboard that died with their wounds."

In his report to General Gates Arnold summarized the battle toll:

> [T]he *Congress* & *Washington* have suffered greatly, the Latter Lost her first Lieut killed & Capt and Master wounded, the *New York* lost all her officers except her captain. The *Phila* was hulled in so many Places that She Sank, About one hour after the engagement was over, the whole killed and wounded amounts to abt Sixty, the enemy

Landed a large Number of Indians On the Island
and each Shore, who keep an incessant fire on
us, but did little Damage – the Enemy had the
Appearance Upwards of One Thousand Men in
Batteaus, prepared for boarding – We suffered
much want of Seamen and Gunners, I was obliged
myself to Point. Most of the Guns on board the
Congress which I believe did good execution – the
Congress received Seven Shott between Wind &
Water, was hulled a dozen times, had her Main
Mast Wounded in Two places & her Yard in One,
The *Washington* was hulled a Number of times,
her Main Mast Shot thro & must have a New one.
Both Vessells are very leaky & want repairing....

As the sun settled behind the high peaks, cannon fire from
both sides subsided. Gunners could not align their cannons in the
diminishing light. Soon an eerie stillness settled over the bay as
hostilities abruptly terminated. One by one the British gunboats
weighed anchor. Crews bent to their oars as they rowed through
the gathering gloom to join the larger ships anchored off the
southern tip of Valcour Island. Although the battle was a standoff,
the British had every reason to be confident of victory the next
day. The steady wind that hindered the advance of their big ships
was dying down. At dawn the British ships would navigate into
firing position and crush what was left of the American flotilla.

His fleet battered and his ammunition nearly spent, Arnold's
options were limited to surrendering or facing annihilation.
With his two top officers—David Waterbury and Edward
Wigglesworth—Arnold reviewed the situation. Ammunition was
low, and the battered American fleet could not absorb another
pounding by the enemy. The only resort, Arnold decided, was to
slip away during the night. British hubris had worked in his favor
before, and it might again.

Arnold laid out his plan. The fleet would arrange itself single file, with Wigglesworth on the row galley *Trumbull* leading the way. Each vessel in turn would raise a single sail to catch what was left of the dwindling north wind. No lanterns were allowed, except a single hooded lamp on the stern. One by one the battered gunboats and galleys would follow the stern light of the vessel ahead. Oars and oarlocks would be muffled and the wounded moved below decks to stifle their groans. The incessant daylong bombardment would hopefully have numbed British ears. Under the cover of darkness the fleet would sneak between the anchored British ships south of the island and the western New York shore. Arnold ordered his officers to alert the captains of the remaining seaworthy vessels to prepare to leave.

At half past eight, the *Trumbull* weighed anchor and got underway, its tattered foresail rustling in the fading wind. Following the lamp in the stern of the preceding boat, each vessel followed—some under sail, others propelled by oars. It was a moonless night. Fog limited visibility to a dozen feet. To the left a fog-shrouded, fuzzy red ball, the last remnants of the burning *Royal Savage*, flickered on the southern tip of Valcour Island. Slowly the convoy snaked along the western shore, at times so close to land that the crew members could hear waves breaking against rocks. Every unintended sound—a wounded man groaning or an oar creaking against a gunwale—compounded the tension.

Each man was keenly aware that, no more than a few hundred yards away on the New York shore, were camped hundreds of British regulars and Mohawk warriors. The entire convoy was within both arrow and musket range. In their swift birch-bark canoes the fierce Mohawks could be on the American decks in a matter of minutes, swinging deadly war clubs and bringing a bloody end to their escape. But, as Arnold predicted, British overconfidence contributed to their undoing. Pringle had moved his gunboats almost a mile from shore, and Carleton had given no order for the army to post sentinels. By midnight the small

American convoy passed through Valcour Island strait and into the central channel of Lake Champlain.

Overnight the north wind shifted to a friendly southern breeze. As the early morning fog melted away the British prepared to deliver the broadside salvos that would obliterate the paltry American fleet. Carleton had to give the "horse jockey" credit. Once again, though heavily outgunned, he had fought well. He was a cunning adversary. Carleton had heard rumors that Arnold was unhappy with Continental Congress politics; the same rumor mills hinted that he was in financial straits. If he could be taken alive, Arnold might be convinced that fighting for king and country was a far better alternative to hanging from a gallows with Franklin, Adams, and the rest of the rebel rabble. But when the morning lake mist faded the British saw that the Americans had vanished.

In his journal, British surgeon Robert Knox wrote, "[After the battle] the ships were ordered into their stations, and every man to remain at his quarters till morning when we would renew the fight, but to our utter astonishment, under the cover of ye night Mr. Arnold sailed thro' part of our fleet, and in the morning we saw them 3 leagues ahead of us going toward Crown Point...." How they had managed to avoid the entire British fleet was a mystery to be solved another day. Within an hour, on Carleton's orders, the British ships were underway, in pursuit of the Americans.

But in his haste to overtake the rebel fleet Carleton forgot to give orders to his infantry officers camped on the New York shore. Mortified, he turned the fleet around to rectify his error—his blunder gave the Americans a brief reprieve. Although Arnold had an eight-hour head start, his vessels were making slow progress against a growing southerly wind. Sleet and rain carried by headwinds raked the open decks. Choppy whitecaps broke over damaged bulwarks, soaking the crews and freezing their hands to their oars. Distances between the American vessels continued to grow as the more seaworthy vessels pulled ahead of their damaged counterparts. Fortunately for the Americans, the British were forced to tack against the same headwinds, which slowed their progress as well.

By dawn of Saturday October 12 the American fleet was strung out six to eight miles south of Valcour, but they were still more than 35 miles from Fort Ticonderoga. Arnold ordered the *Congress* and the gunboats to anchor off Schuyler Island. Though it was only 10 miles south of Valcour Island, the fleet took 12 hours to reach it. The exhausted crews needed respite and time to mend sails and rigging. Wigglesworth aboard the *Trumbull*, along with a couple of the gunboats, continued south to Ligonier Point to make repairs and wait for the rest of the fleet. Arnold delayed his departure from Schuyler Island to wait for the slower galley *Washington* to catch up. The *New Jersey* and the *Spitfire* were taking on water and floundering. Concerned that the British might capture the damaged vessels, Arnold ordered the two gunboats scuttled.

While attempting to drop anchor in the rough water, the *New Jersey* ran aground on submerged rocks. Arnold ordered it set on fire, but the gunboat was too waterlogged to burn. Finally, the row galley *Washington* arrived and dropped anchor. Seamen scurried about doing what they could to patch the shattered hull, but the damage to her sails and rigging was beyond repair. Listing to starboard, and with only minimal sails and oars to propel her, she was a doomed vessel. However, two of her cannons and five swivel guns were still operational. With the British no more than a few hours behind, Arnold decided to keep the *Washington* afloat as long as possible. When the British caught up he would need every artillery piece he could muster.

At approximately 2:00 p.m., British sails appeared on the horizon. The *New Haven, Providence, Boston,* and *Connecticut* weighed anchor and set out for Crown Point. The *Congress* and the *Washington* followed, their roughly stitched sails fluttering against the contrary southern wind. Once again, weary oarsmen aboard gunboats and row galleys pulled their sweeps. Distances between the American vessels increased as those with more intact rigging and sails outpaced others. And so, through another night without food or sleep, the weary crews inched their vessels south.

When Arnold took his bearings at dawn on Sunday he discovered that the *Congress* and the *Washington* had progressed a mere seven miles. They were still 30 miles from Fort Ticonderoga, and the distance between the faster American vessels led by Wigglesworth had widened. By mid-morning the vagaries of Lake Champlain's wind direction favored the British. The wind shifted to the north, filling the British sails, while the American vessels still struggled against a steady south wind. For every meter gained by the Americans, the British gained two.

Led by the *Maria*, the *Inflexible*, and the patched-up *Carleton*, the enemy ships closed in on the *Congress* and the *Washington*. With its rigging smashed and rapidly taking on water, the *Washington* was almost defenseless. Waterbury signaled Arnold and requested permission to run the *Washington* aground and blow it up. Arnold denied Waterbury's request. He needed every bit of cover the floundering row galley could provide. Its sails filled with jagged holes, the row galley continued to fall behind. The British ships closed in and, after a few merciless broadsides from 18- and 24-pounders, Waterbury struck his colors. With the *Washington*'s crew of 80 seamen taken captive, Carleton turned his full attention to the *Congress*.

Going in for the kill, three British ships converged on the vessel with cannons blazing. The *Carleton* and the *Maria* settled under the *Congress*'s stern, and the *Intrepid* moved starboard to maximize its broadside cannonade. Only a few hundred yards away, four American gunboats, their masts and rigging shot away, were unable to either escape or come to Arnold's defense. Like the *Washington*, they were easy prey for the enemy ships. Their only hope was that the *Congress* could shield them until they could row to a safe haven along the shore.

A fierce artillery duel raged for two hours. The reverberating echoes of the cannon fire could be heard 30 miles away at Fort Ticonderoga. The *Congress* was armed with eight cannons and 10 swivel guns, the latter virtually useless against the large British ships. The *Inflexible* carried 18 cannons, and the *Maria* and the *Carleton* were armed with 14 and 12 cannons respectively. Outgunned in firepower the *Congress* stood no chance.

Arnold dashed from one cannon to the other, urging his crew and lining up targets. Blast after blast of British cannon and grapeshot riddled the foundering row galley. Deadly wood splinters flew like spears across the deck. As its hull was hit again and again, the *Congress* listed to starboard. The deck angle made it impossible to aim the cannons accurately. Men struggled to keep cannon carriages moored. The *Congress* was a dying ship. Still Arnold refused to surrender. He had one more ace up his sleeve. He raced to the stern, grabbed the tiller and ordered his men to their sweeps. Then he signaled the four gunboats to follow the *Congress* into the shallow waters of the bay.

The British were startled by the sudden surge of the *Congress* past the *Intrepid*. Aboard the *Maria*, the British readied a broadside cannonade. Pringle ordered his helmsman to make a hard starboard turn, but by the time the *Maria* was in position the fleeing Americans were 100 yards off the beach. Unable to pursue them into the shallow waters, the British pummeled the beach with cannon fire. An 18-pounder made a direct hit on a nearby farmhouse; fortunately the owner, Squire Ferris, and his family were watching the battle from a safe distance in the woods.

When the five vessels touched the beach, Arnold told the marines to climb a 25-foot embankment and cover their retreat. Then he ordered the boats to be torched. With cannon and grapeshot raining down around them, the crews carried off the wounded and set short fuses to the powder magazines. Arnold was the last off the *Congress.* He ran up the embankment with the blasts from the exploding gunboats roaring in his ears. As he reached the crest, he turned and saw his flag ship engulfed in a sheet of flames, the Grand Union flag still fluttering in the wind. He had not struck his colors.

The British may have won the battle, but the Americans had not surrendered. When the flames reached the powder magazine, a thunderous explosion turned the *Congress* into a mass of debris, fire, and smoke. The detonation hurled a body high into the air. In the confusion, the gunner's mate responsible for seeing all the wounded off the Congress had overlooked a wounded officer, Lieutenant Goldsmith, lying on the deck. Arnold was outraged. Saber in hand, he stalked toward the gunner's mate. Crew members rushed to restrain him before he could run the man through on the spot.

During the battle, the galley *Trumbell*, schooner *Revenge*, sloop *Enterprise,* and gunboat *New York* escaped the distracted British fleet. With all possible speed, Wigglesworth headed his small contingent of remaining American vessels to Crown Point.

Although the British fleet was unable to enter the shallow bay, British troops and Mohawks traveling along the shore were close behind. Quickly Arnold organized his remaining crew of seamen, gunners, and marines for a forced march along the Vermont shoreline to Chimney Point. Meanwhile, the *Enterprise* reached Crown Point. Following General Gates's orders the Americans destroyed anything the British could use, including munitions, cannons, crops, and animals. They set the fort ablaze and departed for Fort Ticonderoga 12 miles further south. The *Enterprise* and the three other surviving vessels sailed the last few miles to the fort, and, when the British fleet arrived at Crown Point, there was nothing left to sustain or shelter their army through the approaching winter.

Arnold and his exhausted contingent reached Chimney Point on the evening of Saturday, October 13. Chimney Point on the eastern shore and Crown Point Peninsula on the New York side were opposite each another at one of the narrowest sections of Lake Champlain. Arnold recruited a local man to ferry him across the narrow waterway to a point south of the destroyed Crown Point Fort. From there he followed a trail to Fort Ticonderoga. The others continued south to the fort by trail on the eastern side of the lake. At 4:00 a.m. on October 14, Arnold arrived outside the gate of Fort Ticonderoga. The sentries were startled to see a bedraggled American officer appear out of the darkness and announce that he was General Arnold returned from Valcour Island. The rest of Arnold's entourage of 90 seamen, marines, and locals arrived safely at the fort that evening around dusk.

The Battle of Valcour Island was over. Eighty Americans were killed or wounded. Eleven ships were lost. The British lost three ships, with 40 combatants killed or wounded. The Americans salvaged the four vessels commanded by Wigglesworth—this small force was all that was left of the American navy. Still, the galley, two schooners, and one sloop had enough firepower to attack and sink British troop ships.

With winter approaching, Carleton's resolve wavered. It was clear that the Americans were going to put up a stiff resistance, and he was reluctant to lay siege to Fort Ticonderoga through the coming frigid months. Instead of pressing his advantage, the cautious Canadian governor turned his fleet around and sailed back to St. John to wait for spring. In a letter to Lord George Sackville Germaine, head of the King's Cabinet, Carleton explained, "[The] season is so far advanced that I cannot yet pretend to inform your lordship whether anything further can be done this year."

Arnold's plan had worked. He stopped the British invasion. In a letter to Gates, Arnold wrote:

> I was ordered to keep the enemy in check and I
> had done so; I had nearly destroyed his fleet; I had
> delayed him until we had an army at the head waters

of the Hudson.... We had built and sacrificed a few
wooden ships—and saved our frontier.

When Francis Scott Key Fitzgerald said, "Show me a hero and
I will write you a tragedy," he could very well have had Benedict
Arnold in mind. Arnold left Fort Ticonderoga a hero.

But, while his Quebec leg wound was mending back home
in New Haven, Arnold's political enemies set out to fracture his
reputation. Waterbury wrote to John Hancock blaming Arnold for
his surrender of the *Washington*. He claimed that Arnold sacrificed
the row galley to save his own skin. Old charges of mishandled
funds during the Quebec campaign resurfaced as his enemies took
advantage of Arnold's seclusion in New Haven to convince the
Continental Congress that he should be court-martialed.

Moreover, the British blockade had devastated Arnold's import
business. Congress owed him more than $3,000 reimbursement
for wages and supplies he had provided for his troops, but, instead
of paying him, some of the representatives accused him of trying to
swindle the government. The historian Jim Murphy summarized
Arnold's plight:

> In a matter of days Benedict's actions on Lake
> Champlain had been transformed from a heroic
> stand against superior odds into dangerous, useless
> self-aggrandizing glory hunting. Because Benedict
> wasn't there [in Philadelphia], and because he
> had few political supporters in Congress, the
> backstabbing went on unchecked, gathering
> momentum as the days went along.

Insult was added to injury when the Continental Congress
passed Arnold over for promotion in favor of five junior officers.
Believing that his character had been impugned and that the
Congress was riddled with petty politicians, the beleaguered

warrior began to have doubts about the Revolution and to wonder if he had merely traded one form of tyranny for another.

Still, Arnold had one powerful ally—George Washington. The commander advised Arnold not to overreact but to bide his time, and eventually the accusations against him would subside. In truth, Washington, also beleaguered by critics, was too busy fighting a losing war to take an active role in defending Arnold. When the disgruntled Arnold tendered his resignation to Congress, Washington ignored it. The British were amassing a major offensive. This was no time to lose a gallant American officer.

In early spring, true to Carleton's vow, the British resumed their drive to Albany. This British invasion force, led by General John Burgoyne, consisted of a force of 10,000 British regulars, 138 artillery pieces, and 500 Mohawk warriors. They easily captured the forts at Crown Point and Ticonderoga. But in the first of many bad decisions Burgoyne diminished his force by one-third to garrison the captured forts. Then he lost another 900 troops in an ill-advised attack on Bennington, Vermont. By the time Burgoyne set out for Albany, his force had shrunk by half to 5,000 troops.

The winter reprieve gave the Americans time to develop a new plan of defense: harry the British on their overland route past Fort Ticonderoga and make a stand at Saratoga. The spring thaw turned the southern Adirondack trail into a quagmire of mud, muck, and swamp. The summer provided no relief for the British, as a blizzard of vicious biting gnats, flies, and mosquitoes descended on the cavalcade. Overloaded with supply wagons, personal goods, and an entourage of officer wives, the best Burgoyne's troops could do was a mile a day.

The Americans added to the British distress by destroying bridges, felling trees across trails, and rolling huge boulders into fordable streams. The slow-moving British presented a turkey shoot to Daniel Morgan's Virginia sharpshooters. The long-rifle snipers picked off British officers and then melted into the wilderness. By the time Burgoyne's force reached the outskirts of Saratoga, most of the Mohawks, tired of British ineptitude, had simply walked away. Facing shortages of food and supplies, Burgoyne had no idea that south of Saratoga 6,500 American troops awaited, commanded by General Gates and his subordinate Benedict Arnold.

Through September and October 1777, the British and the Americans battled back and forth in the fields and hills near the small village of Stillwell, New York. Minor skirmishes were sandwiched around two major battles, one at Freeman's Farm on September 17 and the other on Bemis Heights on October 7. Confident of victory and wanting to insure his full measure of credit, Gates ordered Arnold to the rear of the battle. Arnold would have none of it. Each time the British made progress, Arnold appeared, rallying the American troops. Time after time, astride a black stallion and waving his sword, Arnold galloped into the teeth of the British battle line. It seemed that he was everywhere at once. On the third day, heedless of his own safety, Arnold led a charge against two British log fortifications. His horse was shot out under him and his femur was fractured in seven places by a musket ball, yet he refused medical attention until the battle was won. On October 17 General Burgoyne surrendered to General Gates in the hamlet of Saratoga. In what many historians consider the greatest American Revolutionary War victory, the British northern invasion and the attempt to split the colonies was defeated once and for all.

The defeat of a major British force sent shock waves through Europe. The American victory at Saratoga demonstrated that, rather than dealing with a disgruntled rabble of farmers and merchants, Britain was embroiled in a full-scale war with a formidable adversary. France and Spain agreed to lend money and supplies to the Americans. The European alliance spread, forcing the British to fight a two-front war. The morale of every colonial soldier, from General Washington to the lowliest infantryman, soared with the news of the decisive Saratoga victory. Naysayers among the members of the Continental Congress begrudgingly accepted the fact that a negotiated peace was now out of the question. The Revolution would continue for another six years, but the mystique of the impregnable British military was buried along with hundreds of British soldiers in the bucolic hills of northern New York State.

After Saratoga, Arnold, his left leg mangled, returned once again to New Haven to recuperate. Inactivity and a resurgence of criticism by jealous rivals put him in a dark mood. It seemed that the greater his contributions on the battle field, the more vicious the political attacks. General Gates, who had blundered through most of the Battle of Saratoga but blithely accepted victory accolades, demeaned Arnold's contributions, claiming that Arnold disobeyed orders and put American soldiers at risk with his frantic attacks on fortified British positions. Old charges of misuse of funds and self-promotion resurfaced. Arnold had left his family and his business to fight the British, but his most vicious enemies were actually on the American side.

Over the next months, Arnold was forced to endure a series of Congressional investigations. He was eventually found innocent of wrongdoing, but the findings did little to salve his wounded pride. Lame from his injuries, Arnold was no longer capable of commanding troops in the field. In 1778, in recognition of his service, Washington appointed Arnold commandant of Philadelphia. The home of the Continental Congress was a divided city where Loyalists and patriots lived side by side. Almost immediately, Arnold made an enemy of one of the most powerful men in Pennsylvania, Joseph Reed.

Reed, once a trusted aide to Washington, no longer supported the general, and he criticized Arnold's use of his commandant position to pursue personal business interests. The tension between the two was exacerbated when Reed led a movement to divest all Loyalist sympathizers of their property. Arnold viewed

Reed's attempted seizure of Loyalist property as nothing short of vigilantism. In turn, Reed accused Arnold of being a Loyalist sympathizer and using his position for financial gain. Reed demanded that the Congress remove Arnold from the position of commandant. Arnold fueled Reed's animosity when he married 18-year-old Peggy Shippen, the daughter of Edward Shippen, one of the most prestigious Loyalists in Philadelphia.

Despite his lofty status in Philadelphia, Arnold's future looked bleak. Debtors owed him more than £7,000, and the Congress owed him £4,800 in uncompensated military debts. Reed's harsh criticism of Arnold, along with old charges of misuse of military funds, culminated in a court-martial. Arnold was found innocent of all but two trivial accounting errors, but the public rebuke humiliated him.

While Arnold tussled with financial and political difficulties, the Revolution appeared to be on the brink of collapse. Soldiers were deserting in droves, and few were reenlisting. In 1775 the Continental Army had 27,500 troops; in 1778 the troop force was 3,000. Promised French support had not materialized, and many colonial leaders, including Reed, were insisting that Horatio Gates replace an ineffective George Washington as commander-in-chief of the army.

Then the British offered an olive branch. Parliament agreed to accede to all the original colonial demands except independence. Arnold thought the British offer a fair one, but few among Continental leaders shared his point of view. After years of recrimination instead of the honors he felt he deserved, Arnold was ready to shift allegiance. All he needed was the opportunity, and he found it in his own home.

During the British occupation of Philadelphia, and before she married Arnold, Peggy had frequently been escorted to social events by a dashing young 27-year-old British officer, Major John André. Soon after the British fled Philadelphia and returned to their stronghold in New York, André was appointed to General

Howe's staff. Arnold seized the opportunity to capitalize on his wife's friendship with André. In May 1779, Arnold made the most momentous decision of his life. He asked Joseph Stansbury, a Loyalist sympathizer, to take a message to Major André. For a sum of £10,000, Arnold would provide the British with American military intelligence.

Once the deal was negotiated, all that remained was for Arnold to gain access to information that would prove valuable to the British. The opportunity presented itself when Washington offered Arnold the position of commandant of West Point, a strategic series of redoubts and fort that guarded the Hudson River. Immediately upon his arrival, Arnold began weakening the defenses. He dispersed troops, sending them on trivial assignments. He neglected needed repairs to the fortifications, and he sent Washington confusing messages about the readiness of the men and defenses. Meanwhile, always the businessman, Arnold continued prolonged negotiations with British general Henry Clinton. Finally, Clinton agreed to pay Arnold £20,000 for the surrender of the fort and its 3,000 troops.

On September 25, 1780, a shocking packet of documents was delivered to General Washington at Robinson House, Benedict Arnold's headquarters two miles south of West Point. Washington and his entourage, including adjutants Henry Knox, Alexander Hamilton, and the Marquis de Lafayette, had arrived early that morning to inspect the West Point fortifications. Already in a bad mood because Arnold was not present to greet him, Washington opened the packet. Inside he found a detailed description of West Point garrison strength and cannon deployments, as well as the location of the great iron chain that formed a defensive barrier across the Hudson River—information invaluable to the enemy. The forts and redoubts of West Point sat on a steep bluff overlooking the river. British warships sailing north from New York City to Albany would have to pass directly beneath the West Point artillery. A note among the documents ordered safe passage through American checkpoints for John Anderson. The note was signed "General Benedict Arnold."

The previous day, outside the village of Tarrytown, three colonial militiamen had intercepted a civilian horseman. At first, the rider claimed he was returning from a business trip north of Tarrytown. But after a brief conversation the rider changed his story. Believing he had passed into British territory, "John Anderson" admitted he was a British officer on a secret mission. The Americans forced him to strip, and, when he removed his boots, they found the West Point documents in his stocking. An interrogation at musket point revealed the man's real name— Major John André, adjutant to British General Henry Clinton, the commander of his majesty's forces in New York City. André was a spy, and his collaborator was Benedict Arnold.

Arnold, the hero of Saratoga, Quebec, and Valcour Island—a traitor! The idea seemed preposterous, but the evidence was unmistakable. Washington was devastated. When discussing military matters, he always spoke in measured, unemotional tones. Not this time. When he realized what was in the packet, his words came like a fusillade of shrapnel: "Arnold has betrayed me. Whom can we trust now?"

Immediately after reading the treasonous documents, Washington ordered Hamilton to find and arrest Arnold, but it was too late. That morning, before Washington arrived, Arnold was eating breakfast with two of the general's advance aides when a courier delivered a message detailing the arrest of André. Knowing that Washington was due to arrive within the hour, Arnold calmly excused himself and went upstairs to his wife's bedroom to tell her that André had been captured and he had only moments to escape. Peggy Shippen Arnold understood the significance of her husband's plight—flee or hang.

Telling his breakfast guests that matters at West Point required his immediate attention, Arnold rushed into the courtyard, mounted his horse and galloped over the mile trail to the river where a boat stood ready to ferry him to West Point. He dismounted, lugged his saddle, sword, and pistols into the vessel, and ordered the astonished oarsmen to row not north to West Point, but south. He promised each two gallons of rum if they doubled their speed. An hour later Arnold boarded the British frigate *Vulture*. By late afternoon, he was in British-held New York City: he had made a clean escape.

That evening Arnold sent a message to Washington asking the general to protect Peggy and their infant son. Thanks to some elaborate theatrics on her part, which included wailing and tearing at her nightgown, Washington believed Peggy knew nothing of her husband's plot. Washington complied with Arnold's request and allowed his family to join him. Major André, however, was not so fortunate. A colonial military tribunal found him guilty of spying.

General Clinton sent a letter to Washington offering a prisoner exchange. The only trade Washington would consider was André for Arnold. If Clinton consented to Washington's terms, any other attempt he made to lure American officers to change sides would fail. His Faustian bargain with Arnold left Clinton powerless to save his favorite adjutant. On Sunday evening, October 1, André, who requested a soldier's execution by firing squad, was taken by military escort to a gallows on Tappan Hill in Tarrytown and hanged. His last words were, "I pray you bear witness that I met my fate like a brave man."

Meanwhile the British conferred on Arnold the rank of brigadier general. He received a lump sum of £6,000, a salary of £450, and an annual pension package of £360—hefty remuneration in the 18th century. How strange it must have been for Arnold to stand in front of a mirror for the first time in the scarlet "lobster back" uniform of a British officer. But the ever-adaptive Arnold wasted no time reflecting on the vagaries of fate. He led three British raids against the colonial cities of Richmond, Virginia, and New London and Groton, in Connecticut.

However, a change of uniform did not alter his lightning-rod personality. Embroiled in a number of political wrangles with other British officers, Arnold and his family moved to England, where he was feted by some and reviled by many. After the war he tried to establish a mercantile business in St. John and New Brunswick, Canada. His investments flourished for a while, but several unfavorable decisions in lawsuits he filed against debtors wiped him out. He returned to London in 1792, where he changed his family motto from *Mihi gloria sursum* (Through glory yielded to me) to a phrase that was a fitting epitaph: *Nil desperandum* (Never despair).

Arnold's battle wounds never healed properly, and a combination of other ailments including gout, dropsy, and insomnia slowly drained his vitality. He died at the age of 60 on June 14, 1801.

For many years it was rumored that on his deathbed Benedict Arnold said, "Let me die in this old uniform in which I fought my battles. May God forgive me for ever putting on another." Most historians doubt he made the unverified statement, but it would be nice to think he did.

CHAPTER THREE

John Brown

The Raid at Harpers Ferry

All through the conflict, up and down
Marched Uncle Tom and Old John Brown,
One ghost, one form ideal;
And which was false and which was true,
And which was mightier of the two,
The wisest sibyl never knew.
For both alike were real.

Oliver Wendell Holmes, *The World's Homage*

*O*n a gloomy October evening in 1859, John Brown led a small raiding party of 18 men across a train trestle spanning the Potomac River from Maryland to the tiny industrial village of Harpers Ferry, Virginia. Their target: 100,000 muskets, rifles, and pistols warehoused in the federal armory. Brown intended to seize the weapons and arm a slave revolt. The element of surprise allowed Brown and his men to briefly *control the town, but federal troops led by Colonel Robert E. Lee rushed to the scene and killed or captured most of his men.*

A Virginia court convicted Brown of treason and sentenced him to death by hanging. While pro-slavers in the South celebrated Brown's execution, abolitionists mourned his death. His raid at Harpers Ferry awoke a slumbering nation to the reality that the nightmare of four million humans held in bondage could no longer be tolerated. On April 2, 1861, Confederate artillery shelled Fort Sumter in Charlestown Harbor, South Carolina, launching the Civil War. As the war raged on, John Brown's legacy grew to mythic proportions. Some proclaimed him a madman, others called him a terrorist, and still others said he was a martyr. A final judgment about the enigmatic John Brown and his legacy continues to elude historians today.

December 2, 1859, was an unseasonably pleasant day in the Shenandoah Valley village of Charlestown, Virginia. The temperature was in the low 60s—Indian summer. Meadows and pastures surrounding the town had not yet exchanged their verdant luster for the dung-brown hue of winter. The Blue Ridge Mountains, framed by an azure sky, shimmered in the distance. On such a delightful day shops lining the main thoroughfare, George Street, should have been bustling with merchants and customers. Instead all main street shops were closed and shuttered.

On the day John Brown, the notorious abolitionist, was to hang, Charlestown was under martial law. Five days earlier General Taliaferro, commander of the Virginia militia, had issued a proclamation warning outsiders to stay out of the town on execution day. Women and children were ordered to remain indoors while male citizens of Charlestown were directed to arm themselves and guard their homes.

A month earlier the Virginia circuit court convicted John Brown of treason and sentenced him to death. Brown's bloody but unsuccessful raid on the federal armory in Harpers Ferry, five miles east of Charlestown, had sparked a firestorm of rage and fear throughout the South. As a precaution against reprisals, Virginia Governor Arthur Wise ordered 2,000 soldiers to Charlestown. He intended to make sure the execution would not be subverted by a mob lynching, but he was also concerned about radical abolitionists from the North. Rumors of an escape plot coincided with a spate of fires in local grain stacks, outbuildings, and barns—a common form of protest in antebellum Virginia. The governor was determined to insure that neither Southern retribution nor Northern scheming would supplant the rule of law.

But neither a proclamation nor a strong military presence deterred the vengeful, the remorseful, and the curious from swarming to Charlestown. By 10:00 a.m. Charlestown teemed with thousands of people clogging the narrow streets. They had begun arriving soon after daybreak—in carriages, on horseback, and afoot. Small groups of wary abolitionists from the North mixed uneasily with celebrating pro-slavers from Virginia and points south. Whiskey jugs were passed around. Cheers, jeers, and huzzahs accentuated the commotion.

Brown's raid, his capture, and his subsequent trial riveted the nation's attention on the burning issue of slavery. Journalists from North and South jammed the Charlestown telegraph office, feeding hungry readers with tidbits of news about the last day of the legendary abolitionist. In 1859 slavery was a cancer eating away at the Constitutional tendons that held a fragile Union together. John Brown's attempt at radical surgery alerted pro- and anti-slavers alike that violence might be the only cure.

The Jefferson County jail stood in the center of Charlestown. With its porticos and green shutters, the solid two-story red brick building seemed more a country inn than a jail. Virginia militia formed a quarter-mile cordon from the front portico to a 40-acre stubbled cornfield southeast of town. Fifteen hundred soldiers were stationed around the field perimeter. No civilian, Governor Wise ordered, was to be allowed near the execution. On a small rise in the center of the field loomed a single-trap-door gallows.

At 11:00 a.m., a light freight wagon with two white horses in harness backed up to the jail's front portico. In the back of the wagon a black coffin rested inside a large pine box. When the jail door opened, John Brown appeared in the doorway. His slim, angular build suggested a taller man than his five-foot-10-inch height. His face etched with deep lines, he appeared older than his 59 years. His straight gray hair hung below his neck, and a full white beard reached his chest. Most distinctive were his eyes. A witness that day, John Barry, later wrote, "His eyes were a dark hazel and burned with a peculiar light that gave promise of a quick temper and daring courage." Brown wore a wrinkled black suit over a white shirt. Faded red bedroom slippers covered his feet. His arms were tied to his sides above the elbows. A slouched black hat, its brim turned up, gave him a jaunty look, as if he were about to go for a pleasant ride in the country.

Brown paused in the doorway. With a quick glance he surveyed the soldiers, the street, and the wagon bearing his coffin. An 1881 painting by Thomas Hovenden depicted Brown stooping at that moment to kiss a black baby held in its mother's arms. No such event occurred. The security around Brown was so tight that no civilian, much less a black mother with a child, could get close to him. Nevertheless, the mythic kiss bolstered Brown's legend as the fearless protector of black youth.

With the jailer, Captain John Avis, on his left, and sheriff John Campbell on his right, Brown descended the stairs and climbed into the back of the wagon. As he sat on his coffin his beard billowed in a puff of spring-like air. Avis climbed into the wagon and sat next to him. Campbell followed in a carriage, accompanied by two medical officers. With a flick of the reins the town undertaker, George W. Sadler, slowly guided the horses toward the field, accompanied by a file of 300 armed soldiers.

Brown showed no emotion as the wagon trundled toward its destination. The undertaker turned and remarked, "Captain Brown, you are a game man." Brown replied, "Yes, I was so trained up; it was one of the lessons of my mother, but it is hard to part with friends, though newly made." As the wagon passed across the field Brown gazed at the undulating farmland and gentle hills surrounding the field. He turned to Sheriff Avis and said, "This is beautiful country. I have never had the pleasure of seeing it before."

For the next few minutes they rode in silence as troops in the field scurried to get into orderly formations. The field was a scene of controlled chaos, the pounding of cavalry horse hooves mingled with the tramping of boots. The harsh, discordant sounds of shouted orders, and soldiers rushing to their appointed stations, added to the tumult. Two howitzers manned by a detachment of Virginia Military Institute cadets dressed in red-flannel-shirt uniforms bracketed the gallows, commanded by Major Thomas J. Jackson. Two years later "Stonewall" Jackson would achieve Civil War fame as the staunch Confederate general at the First Battle of Bull Run. Embedded among the elite Richmond militia in a borrowed uniform, a handsome young Shakespearean actor, John Wilkes Booth, witnessed with satisfaction the unfolding events.

It took the wagon 10 minutes to travel the quarter-mile from the jail to the execution site. When it stopped in front of the gallows, Avis and Campbell helped Brown out of the wagon and walked him up the gallows steps. Avis placed a white hood over the condemned man's head. When directed to stand over the trapdoor Brown replied that he could not see to do so and asked Avis to guide him. Once he was in place, Campbell placed a cotton noose around Brown's neck. His executioners thought cotton a more appropriate noose for the abolitionist than hemp. No minister attended Brown's final minutes. Earlier in the day he had made it clear he would accept no blessing from Southern clergy. Avis asked Brown if he had anything to say. "I am ready," Brown replied, "but don't keep me waiting more than necessary."

But the troops were not yet settled. For 15 minutes officers barked orders, soldiers rushed to their positions, and Brown stood over the trapdoor. A Virginia officer, Colonel Preston, watched Brown from behind the gallows. Preston hoped to see signs of fear or cowardice. There were none. Once he thought he saw Brown's knees tremble, but it was only the wind blowing his loose trousers.

Then the clamor around the gallows melted into thin air, and an eerie silence covered the field. The only sounds heard were Campbell's footfalls as he descended the gallows steps. He walked behind the gallows, hefted a hatchet, and severed the rope that held the trap door in place. Brown dropped three feet. The noose jerked. He convulsed, then he went rigid. After a few minutes the body relaxed and swayed gently in the breeze. John Brown, leader of the ill-fated raid at Harpers Ferry, was dead. No one cheered. No one jeered. No one spoke. Then Colonel Preston's voice rang out: "So perish all such enemies of Virginia! All such enemies of the Union! All such foes of the human race!"

Pro-slavers believed the execution of John Brown was a powerful example for those who would attempt to cleave the cultural and economic fabric of the South. An editorial in the December 21ˢᵗ *Raleigh Register* affirmed the South's resolve.

> The affair at Harper's Ferry marks a new and most important era in our country's history. It will bring to an immediate solution the question as to whether the Union can be preserved, and the right of the South to hold property in slaves be maintained. This is the issue to be tried now. The trial can no longer be deferred. The issue has been forced upon the South, and let the result be what it may, her skirts will be clear of all responsibility. There has been one gratifying fact developed by the Harper's Ferry raid. The

promptness and ease with which large numbers
of troops were brought together from different
quarters of Virginia, and the alacrity with which
the call to arms was obeyed, will prove to the
Abolitionists at the North that although they
make an occasional foray into a Southern State,
and commit a few murders and arsons, they can
never maintain a foothold on Southern soil for
more than forty-eight hours.

In the defense of slavery there would be no shirking. The lines
had been drawn, and the Southern states stood as one.

The day John Brown died, the South was the fourth-largest
economy in the world. Since the days of the early white settlers,
tobacco had been the mainstay of Southern agriculture. Cotton
also showed promise as a profitable crop, but the preparation of
raw cotton balls into a product ready for textile mills was a time-
consuming task. In 1793, Eli Whitney's cotton gin accelerated a
difficult task: before his invention it took a single slave 10 hours
to separate a pound of cotton from seeds, but three slaves using a
cotton gin could produce 50 pounds of cotton a day.

Although Congress banned the importation of Africans as
slaves in 1808, the slave population continued to grow—from
80,000 the year the ban went into effect to four million held in
bondage in 1850. Cotton production increased to nearly three
million bales over the same period. The breeding and selling
of slaves provided plantations with the workforce they needed
to maintain their profitable financial position. A healthy male
aged 22 to 25 sold for $1,500, and a female suitable for breeding
sold for more. Families were split up, and runaway slaves were
hunted like prey. The back-breaking work of field hands started
at dawn, and continued well after dusk. Beatings, torture, and
lynching were routine. In 1900, an ex-slave, Egbert Lee, at a

memorial service in Springfield, Massachusetts, described his life in bondage:

> Our hours were as early as we could see and as late as we could see. We were limited in our food to three pounds of bacon and one peck of corn meal for a week and if that did not last, we had to go hungry until the next supply came along.... The overseers got so severe that after awhile the negroes turned on them. I have lived in Jasper and Morgan counties, and have seen them take a colored man and tie him before a fire and let him broil. I have seen them burn the bottoms of their feet and keep them so until their feet blistered so that they could not walk. I have seen them beaten so that they lost consciousness and called upon their masters to save them, never thinking it was their master who was beating them. I have seen both men and women run before the hounds all day....

From the time he was a young man, Brown's beliefs were cemented in an unbridled hatred of slavery. Bolstered by religion and framed by an uncompromising stubborn temperament, the sincere son of a Connecticut tanner was the most revered and feared abolitionist in antebellum America.

In 1805, when John was five years old, his father, Owen, moved his family of eight from Brown's birthplace in Torrington, Connecticut, to the Ohio town of Hudson in the Western Reserve. There Owen Brown's tannery prospered, and "Squire" Brown became a leader in the community. An ardent Calvinist, Owen Brown was a strict disciplinarian who dealt with misbehavior with the application of a beech switch he called the "limber persuader." Owen believed that in God's eyes all persons, black or white, were equal. As a child, he had befriended a slave named Sam who labored on a nearby farm. While he was plowing, Sam would let young Owen ride on his shoulders. When Sam suddenly died, young Owen grieved for his passing as much as he mourned his own deceased father.

Intermittent lessons from the limber persuader notwithstanding, the Browns were a close-knit family; the struggles of frontier life bonded them. Young John revered his father and mother, and he relished life in the wilderness. After finishing his chores, he roamed the nearby forests. He befriended a Seneca Indian youth who gave him a cherished gift, a vivid yellow marble. He captured a squirrel and kept it as a pet. He named it "Bob Tail." In later years the stoic Brown provided a rare glimpse into his feelings when he described his sadness when he lost the marble and the squirrel ran off. "You may laugh," he wrote, describing himself in the third person, "but these were sore trials to John, whose earthly treasures were very few and small."

In 1808 John's mother, Ruth, died giving birth to a stillborn infant. The family was devastated. Owen's business required frequent travel, and he needed someone to tend the children. A year after Ruth's death Brown married a local woman, Sally Root. The introduction of a stepmother into the family turned young John's grief to bitterness. His mother had taught him to read, and he found solace in books. By age eight he had read numerous classics. He pored over the Bible and committed himself to memorizing passages from Scripture.

His love of reading, however, did not transfer to formal schooling. John chafed against the dull routines. At age 10 he quit and went to work at his father's tannery. Trying to emulate his father's business success, he worked diligently to master the craft of curing and drying animal skins. He studied surveying and delighted in sprinkling conversations with Bible verses, a practice he continued throughout his life. Such verses such as Leviticus 24:20, "Fracture for fracture, eye for eye, tooth for tooth. The one who has inflicted the injury must suffer the same injury," provided the burgeoning abolitionist with moral justification for his future crusade against "the great sin of slavery."

At 12, Brown was the size of a grown man, and he took on a man's work, driving and selling cattle for his father. On occasion, he single-handedly drove livestock 100 miles to army outposts in Michigan. On one of these long drives he stayed overnight with a local sheriff who owned a young slave boy. Brown pitied the poorly clothed and malnourished youth, and he was appalled when the sheriff beat the youngster with an iron fire shovel. In later years Brown pointed to this incident as a driving force behind his fierce hatred of slavery.

A friend described the adolescent Brown as a sober young man who had no hobbies, no romances, and no way of letting off steam. He disliked frivolous talk, card playing, music, and dancing—in every sense he was an austere Calvinist. He taught Sunday school and, at 16, along with his 14-year-old brother, Salmon, he enrolled in a Plainfield, Massachusetts, preparatory school for the ministry, but his struggles with classical languages and his rapidly diminishing funds forced him to quit and return to Ohio. He resumed working in the family tannery. Each day he dedicated himself to doing every job, no matter how insignificant, to the best of his ability.

The verve he applied to his work, however, was conspicuously absent in his dealings with women. Painfully shy in female company, he struggled with his growing affection for Dianthe Lusk, the daughter of a woman his father hired to help with house chores. Dianthe was a plain and pious woman, a good match for the austere young man. His fumbling attempts at courtship led to their marriage, on June 25, 1821. John Jr., their first child, was born 13 months later.

In 1825 Brown moved his growing family of three sons to Randolph Township, a sparsely settled area in northwestern Pennsylvania. There he established a profitable tannery and cattle business. He was active in the small community, helping to establish a school, a church, and a post office. His reputation grew as an honest businessman and a religious zealot. Like his father before him, he rooted out the misdeeds of his children with the "limber persuader." However, the stern disciplinarian also had a gentle side. Historian Tony Horwitz noted:

> Despite his severity, Brown was beloved by his children, who also recalled his many acts of tenderness. He sang hymns to them at bedtime, recited maxims from Aesop and Benjamin Franklin ("Diligence is the mother of good luck"), cared for his "little folks" when they were ill, and was gentle with animals: he warmed frozen lambs in the family washtub.

In 1831 the hardscrabble frontier life took a toll on the Brown family. After bearing him six children in nine years, Dianthe died during labor at age 31. The child was stillborn. The deaths of his wife and child devastated Brown. Shortly afterwards he contracted ague, a malaria-type fever that weakened him so that he was unable to work. Debts began to pile up. Tending his children and keeping the tannery running became overwhelming. Less than a year after Dianthe's death, he married 16-year-old Mary Day. Mary was a big-boned, hardy woman with emotional resources that matched her physical stamina. She gave birth to 13 children, and over the ensuing years her courage and dedication sustained the Brown family during their darkest days.

After his marriage to Mary Day, Brown moved his family back to central Ohio. A national recession in 1837 triggered by speculative lending practices in the West and widespread bank failures stymied his efforts to gain a stable financial footing. The "Panic of 1837" lasted until the mid-1840s. During this period Brown's business enterprises continued to sink, while his abolitionist militancy grew more strident.

On November 7, 1837, in Alton, Illinois, a mob of pro-slavers, angered by editorials in an abolitionist newspaper, attacked editor Elijah Lovejoy. Lovejoy and a friend, Royal Weller, exchanged gunfire with the mob. Five shotgun slugs killed Lovejoy on the spot. The pro-slavers ransacked his newspaper office and threw the printing press into the Mississippi River. Throughout the North, abolitionists hailed Lovejoy as a martyr.

In Hudson, Brown and his father attended a Congregational Church meeting commemorating Lovejoy's sacrifice. Brown sat in the back of the church, listening to a number of stirring speeches. When the meeting was almost over, he stood, raised his right hand, and said, "Here before God, in the presence of these witnesses, from this time, I consecrate my life to the destruction of slavery." Brown's declaration reflected his deep reliance on Scripture in his personal war against slavery. Among Old Testament figures, he most admired Gideon, who blew his horn, raised his torch, and vanquished the Midianites. Inspired by Gideon, Brown hatched a plan to lead a small force of righteous fighters to destroy the wicked empire of slavery.

While his radicalism grew, his financial fortunes plummeted. His rigid and intense work ethic made him a difficult man to do business with. For Brown, negotiation was a weakness. His obstinacy cost him customers. There was only one way to do business—his way. The leather he tanned needed to dry completely before he would sell it: his business, he said, was selling leather, not water. Sometimes customers would travel distances of 10 or more miles over rough terrain only to be told to come back later because the leather was not completely dry. He could have discounted the leather or provided drying tips to keep his customers, but his inflexibility trumped his business sense.

He tried his hand at other trades, including raising sheep and surveying, but the outcome was always the same: creditors piled up and partners abandoned him. His poor money management skills compounded his financial difficulties, and in 1842 a federal court adjudged him bankrupt. His family was left with only the bare essentials needed for survival. It took several years of struggling for Brown, with his new partner, Colonel Simon Perkins, to make a slow ascension to solvency in the Akron, Ohio, wool trade.

At a wool traders' conference in 1846 Brown suggested a new approach to an old problem. The wool business was a buyer's market. Growers bargained with buyers on an individual basis. A buyer judged the graded quality of the wool and set the price. Because the buyers were in collusion, they had no competition, thus leaving growers with no leverage for negotiation. Brown suggested that the growers combine their wool stocks and establish an agency to bargain with the buyers as one. The agency would grade the wool and set the price, reversing the present practice. The traders enthusiastically endorsed Brown's plan, with the condition that he establish the enterprise in Springfield, Massachusetts, which was in close proximity to major textile manufacturers. Coincidentally, Springfield had a large population of free blacks and was a major stop on the Underground Railroad.

Perkins and Brown opened their warehouse at the corner of Watler and Railroad Streets. Perkins furnished the finances, and Brown supervised daily activities. He purchased a simple wooden frame house at 31 Franklin Street, which he shared with his two sons, John Jr. and Jason; soon after, his wife joined them. Scrupulous attention to detail earned Brown a reputation as a trustworthy man to do business with. He received praise for his timely correspondence and considerate managing of customers, but his shoddy bookkeeping raised eyebrows. He paid bills by check without tracking his balances. Consequently he was never sure if the business was running in the black or the red.

In 1846 Gerrit Smith, a leading social reformer, purchased 120,000 acres in North Elba, New York, and donated plots of land to black families. However, the rough Adirondack terrain stymied the inexperienced settlers' attempts to cultivate the land. Smith approached Brown and offered him a farm if, in return, Brown would assist the nascent farmers. Brown accepted, and for several years his family alternated between homes in North Elba and Springfield. Smith later joined five other financiers who pledged money to Brown. The so-called "Secret Six" were instrumental in backing his violent confrontations with pro-slavers.

By 1848 Brown's conversion from abolitionist to anti-slavery firebrand was nearly complete. Like his Bible hero Gideon, Brown yearned to lead an insurrection. But he had a singular problem: how to convince slaves, at the risk of their lives, to join him. Brown believed the support of the most famous black orator in America—Frederick Douglass—would provide the credibility he needed to persuade slaves to join his rebellion.

Born into slavery in Talbot County, Maryland, Douglass never knew his birth date. During his childhood he was traded from one Maryland plantation to another. Using purloined newspapers and magazines, the young slave taught himself to read and write. When he attempted to educate other slaves, he felt the bite of his master's lash. Several times, Douglass tried to escape bondage, and failed. Then, on September 3, 1838, disguised as a sailor, he successfully made his way to New York City and emancipation. In his autobiography he described the joy of being a free man:

> A new world had opened upon me. If life is more than breath, and the 'quick round of blood,' I lived more in one day than in a year of my slave life. It was a time of joyous excitement, which words can but tamely describe. In a letter written to a friend soon after reaching New York, I said:

> 'I felt as one might feel upon escape from a den
> of hungry lions.' Anguish and grief, like darkness
> and rain, may be depicted; but gladness and joy,
> like the rainbow, defy the skill of pen or pencil.

He settled in New Bedford, Massachusetts, where he capitalized on his oratorical skills as a preacher and fervent abolitionist. A handsome man with chiseled features and a thick mane of hair, Douglass was an imposing figure behind a lectern. In a rich baritone voice he captivated listeners with stories about his suffering in bondage. Within a short time he became a sought-after speaker who drew large audiences to his anti-slavery lectures. He also published an influential abolitionist newspaper, the *North Star.*

In November 1848, Douglass made a speaking appearance in Springfield. After the lecture Brown invited him to his home for dinner. Curious about the serious white man who spoke of slavery with "eyes full of light and fire," Douglass accepted. He was struck by the "Spartan" simplicity of the Brown household and even more by the easy manner of the family, whose nonchalant attitude about sharing their dinner with a black man struck Douglass as refreshing. Clearly he was not the first black person to break bread with the Browns.

After dinner Brown unveiled his plan to lead a slave insurrection. He brought out a map of the Allegheny Mountains, which ran from Pennsylvania deep into Virginia and points south. The caves that honeycombed the mountains would be ideal sites for launching guerrilla raids on plantations. Such swift attacks, Brown contended, would grow in force as newly freed slaves joined his freedom fighters.

Douglass doubted the practicality of Brown's plan. He told Brown slaves would consider fleeing from a plantation to join a guerrilla army to be dangerous and suicidal, and he expressed reservations about how Brown would continue to elude Southern posses over an extended period of time. Despite his doubts,

Douglass left that evening convinced he had met a compassionate white man who was dedicated to the elimination of slavery. Later, in the *North Star,* Douglass wrote that Brown "is in sympathy, a black man, and as deeply interested in our cause, as though his own soul had been pierced with the iron of slavery."

Gradually Brown's attention to business lost ground to his abolitionist fervor. The Springfield Underground Railroad was a vibrant system of secret routes and safe-houses that enabled hundreds of runaway slaves to escape to freedom in Canada. To counter the success of the Underground Railroad in Springfield and other abolitionist communities, Congress appeased Southern pro-slavers by passing the 1850 Fugitive Slave Act, which required law enforcement officials in slave and free states alike to pursue and arrest runaway slaves and return them to their masters. Anyone sheltering a runaway slave was subject to six months' imprisonment and a $1,000 fine. This was the tipping point in Brown's transition from rhetoric to action.

In 1851 he organized the U.S. branch of the Gileadites in Springfield. The purpose of the secret organization was to safeguard runaway slaves from slave catchers. At the initial meeting Brown publically declared his conversion to violence in opposition to slavery. As usual he drew his inspiration from the Old Testament. In Judges 12:4, the men of Gilead kill 42,000 Ephramites who are attempting to cross the Jordan. To Brown the slave chasers were the Ephramites, except that, instead of crossing the Jordan, they were invading the city of Springfield. At the first Gileadite meeting, Brown offered his "Words of Advice" to the 44 predominantly black Springfield citizens in attendance. After hearing Brown's speech, each pledged to protect runaway slaves and persecute slave chasers. Brown told them:

> A lasso might possibly be applied to a slave catcher
> for once with good effect. Hold on to your
> weapons, and never be persuaded to leave them,

part with them, or have them taken away from you. Stand by one another, and by your friends, while a drop of blood remains; and be hanged if you must, but tell not tales out of school. Make no confession…. Let no able-bodied man appear on the ground unequipped, or with his weapons exposed to view…. Your plans must be known only to yourself, and with the understanding that all traitors must die, whenever caught and proven to be guilty…. Let the first blow be the signal to all to engage, and when engaged do not do your work by halves; but make clean work with your enemies, and be sure you meddle not with any others.…

His words, meant to inspire the Gileadites, foreshadowed his own violent actions. When the wool market bottomed out, Brown closed his bankrupt business. This was his last foray into wool or any other entrepreneurial enterprise. His radicalism, fueled by the Fugitive Slave Act, had evolved to the point that he believed his mission in life was not to make money but to free the slaves. He saw himself as a messenger of God, doing God's work. At his trial several years later he made clear that all he had done, including the shedding of blood, his or others, was justified in the eyes of God:

I believe that to have interfered as I have done— as I have always freely admitted I have done— in behalf of His despised poor was not wrong, but right. Now, if it is deemed necessary that I should forfeit my life for the furtherance of the ends of justice, and mingle my blood further with the blood of my children and with the blood of millions in this slave country whose rights are disregarded by wicked, cruel, and unjust enactments—I submit; so let it be done!

Leaving Springfield, Brown took up permanent residence in North Elba and spent the next several years traveling throughout the country raising funds, speaking at abolitionist meetings, and guiding runaway slaves to freedom in Canada. With the backing of his "Secret Six" financiers, Brown continued to plan his mountain-based insurrection. But first there was work to be done on the Kansas frontier, where a life-and-death struggle was going on over whether the territory should be admitted into the union as a free or a slave state.

In May 1854, Congress passed the Kansas-Nebraska Act, which divided the Nebraska Territory into two parts. The smaller, southern section of the territory was named "Kansas" after the Kansa Indian word for "south wind people." Besides the Kansa, several indigenous tribes lived there, including the Kiowas, Pawnees, and Missouris. While much of Kansas consisted of grassy high plains, the eastern section encompassed a bountiful blend of woodlands, rivers, and fertile soil.

Congress intended the Kansas-Nebraska Act to be the first step toward statehood. For legislators, statehood for the Nebraska territory was a secondary consideration. The Kansas territory adjacent to the slave state Missouri was the immediate concern. The burning issue in the framing of the Kansas-Nebraska Act was slavery. The act provided for Kansas settlers to decide before entry into the union whether Kansas would be a slave or free state. After the act was passed, the "free soilers"—who advocated abolition—engaged in a bitter struggle with pro-slavers over control of Kansas. Free soilers from the North and pro-slavers from neighboring Missouri and Southern states poured into Kansas. Free-soilers were predominantly farmers and merchants from Ohio, Illinois, and New England—pioneers who made the arduous trek to Kansas to start a life anew in a territory they hoped would soon join the Union as a free state. But when violence broke out, their hoes and squirrel guns were no match against the marauding Missouri "Border Ruffians."

In 1855 President Franklin Pierce appointed Wilson Shannon, an Ohio Democrat with Southern sympathies, as territorial executive. Shortly after Shannon arrived in Kansas, a rigged election produced a pro-slavery legislature, which he supported. He immediately ordered federal troops to search out and arrest militant anti-slavers. Confrontations between anti- and pro-slavers escalated from intimidation to tar and feathers to murder. Both sides committed atrocities, but the pro-slaver raids were especially brutal. They burned homes, hanged runaway slaves, and murdered free-soilers in cold blood.

Into the maelstrom of "Bloody Kansas" entered John Brown. From Ohio he traveled by wagon to join five of his sons who had preceded him. Along the way Brown raised funds and purchased arms to support his Kansas anti-slave brethren. Once arrived in Kansas, the Browns settled in a small enclave near Osawatomie, where John rapidly established himself as an anti-slavery firebrand—a Bible-spouting, bigger-than-life abolitionist who preached that bullets were more persuasive than words. He organized a band of anti-slave vigilantes that he called the "Pottawatomie Rifles." Border Ruffians were winning through intimidation, but Brown intended to change that. In Ohio he had vowed to dedicate his life to abolishing slavery. Kansas would test his resolve

On May 21, 1856, pro-slavers raided and sacked the anti-slavery town of Lawrence, Kansas. Prior to the raid, deputy U.S. Marshall J.B. Donaldson warned the citizens of Lawrence not to interfere in his execution of a court order to arrest illegally elected anti-slavery legislators and instructed residents to put down their arms. Meanwhile, in the hills outside Lawrence, David Atchison, a former Missouri U.S. senator urged a band of 800 pro-slavers to destroy the town.

Draw your revolvers & bowie knives, & cool them in the heart's blood of all those damned dogs, that dare defend that breathing hole of hell, never to slacken or stop until every spark of the free-state, free speech, free niggers, or free in any shape is quenched out of Kansas!

Assuming they were abiding by a court order, Lawrence citizens surrendered the town without a struggle. When the notorious slave-hunting Sheriff S.J. Jones led a company of armed men down the main street, it was obvious that the legal order was a ruse. But it was too late. Pro-slavery raiders overran the town. They destroyed the *Herald Freedom* newspaper office, leveled the house of anti-slavery leader Charles Robinson with cannon fire, and burnt the Free State Hotel to the ground. Although the citizens' inaction sacrificed the town, they avoided bloodshed; no one was killed. After the sacking of Lawrence, Sheriff Jones is reputed to have said, "This is the happiest day of my life. I determined to make the fanatics bow before me in the dust, and kiss the territorial laws; and I have done it—by God, I have done it."

When the news of the raid reached Brown's encampment south of Lawrence he railed against the citizens who had done nothing to resist the pillaging of their town. He branded them cowards and vowed that pro-slaver violence would be answered in kind. As in many of his deliberations he leaned on Biblical verse for justification and "an eye for an eye" precisely fit his mood. He ignored the warning by his son John Brown Jr. not to do anything rash. Brown was set on revenge, and no argument would dissuade him. The response to the sacking of Lawrence, he said, must be swift and dramatic.

After a brief consultation with the members the Pottawatomie Rifles, Brown selected a small nearby settlement of pro-slavers in the town of Shermanville as his target. Shermanville inhabitants James Doyle and Allen Wilkerson did not own slaves themselves, but they were active pro-slavers who hunted and captured runaways. They also provided information used by the Border Ruffians to terrorize free-state people. Nearby, Dutch Henry ran a tavern where cheap liquor and prostitutes attracted a steady stream of pro-slavers and bounty hunters. According to Brown, killing Doyle, Wilkerson, and Henry would send a clear message to pro-slavers that violence against anti-slavers would be returned in kind.

On Thursday, May 23, 1856, John Brown; his sons Owen, Frederic, Oliver, and Salmon; and three local anti-slavers—Thomas Weiner, Henry Thompson, and James Townsley—set out by wagon on the south road along Pottawatomie Creek. Each was armed with a pistol and knife. Additionally, the men toted army surplus broadswords donated to Brown by supporters in Ohio. The swords had hollow bores filled with quicksilver. When brandished, the quicksilver slid from the handle to the blade adding force to a blow. They were cruel weapons designed to mutilate and maim. Brown thought them ideally suited to his purpose of striking terror into the hearts of pro-slavers.

The next night, as they neared the settlement, Brown ordered the men to leave the wagon and continue on foot. Clouds scudded across an evening sky illuminated by a three-quarter moon. In single file Brown and his seven accomplices followed a secluded trail to Shermanville. They moved quickly. There was no talk, only the sounds of the night and the crunching of their boots. Each man was alone with his own thoughts. None had killed before, but before the night was over all would have blood on their hands.

They waded across Mosquito Creek, a small tributary of Pottawatomie Creek, and climbed an embankment. Ahead of them, in a clearing, was James Doyle's cabin, near a frequently traveled wagon road. When they were 200 yards away Brown held up his hand. The small company halted and crouched in the shadows. Brown told Townsley and his son Frederick to stand guard by the road. Then he ordered Weiner and Thompson to reconnoiter in the direction of their next target—Allen Wilkinson. When all were in place Brown motioned to his three sons to follow him across the clearing. Suddenly a large dog sprang out of the brush, barking and snapping. Owen Brown swung his broadside and killed the animal with a single swipe across its neck.

The ruckus awakened Doyle, his wife, Mahala, and his three sons. Brown moved quickly to the door of the cabin and knocked. Doyle jumped from his bed and grabbed a poker from the fireplace. "Who is it?" he asked. Brown replied that he was lost and needed directions to the Wilkerson house. When Doyle cracked the door to get a glimpse of the stranger, Brown and his boys shoved the door open and forced their way inside. Brown pointed his pistol at Doyle and ordered him and his three sons outside. Mahala Doyle pleaded with Brown to release her youngest son, John, who was 14. Brown left the boy with his mother and marched Doyle and his two oldest sons—22-year-old William and 20-year-old Drury—down the road toward the Wilkerson house. When they were out of shouting range, Owen, Salmon, and Oliver attacked the Doyles with their swords. In a matter of minutes the settlers were hacked to death. James Doyle lay in a pool of blood, mortally wounded. Brown drew his pistol and shot him in the head.

After the slaughter Brown and his men headed down the road to the house of Allen Wilkerson. Brown knocked on the door and asked for directions to Dutch Henry's. This time the ruse didn't work; Wilkerson refused to open the door. Brown shouted that he was an officer in the anti-slave Northern Army. Either come out of the house, Brown said, or we will come in to get you. His wife sick with measles, Wilkerson wanted to avoid a confrontation in his home. He opened the door and walked into the gloom. A short distance from the cabin Weiner and Thompson dispatched him with broadswords.

Next, Brown and his men crossed the Pottawatomie and headed for Dutch Henry's tavern. Several men were inside, sleeping. At gunpoint Brown forced them outside and interrogated them about their pro-slavery activities. His primary target, Dutch Henry, was not among them. Earlier in the day Henry had ridden out onto the plains to search for lost cattle. Brown released all the men except William Sherman. They marched Sherman down to the creek, where Thompson and Wiener used their broadswords to split his skull.

After killing Sherman, Brown and his men confiscated the pistols, knives, and saddles they found in the tavern. They took several horses from Dutch Henry's stable and headed back to their encampment. Along the way they washed the blood and gore from their clothes in the Pottawatomie. Owen Brown wandered off a short distance and sobbed in the darkness. When they arrived at their camp he looked at Townsley with red-rimmed eyes and said, "There should be no more work such as that." Owen Brown's hope went unfulfilled.

John Brown predicted that the brutal retaliation for the sack of Lawrence at Pottawatomie Creek would "likely cause a restraining fear" among the Missouri Border Ruffians. He could not have been more wrong. Rather than checking pro-slave violence, the Pottawatomie Creek killings triggered immediate cries for vengeance. The pro-slave Missouri newspaper the *Border Times* urged readers to "Let Loose the Dogs of War!" The editorial predicted that "hundreds of the Free State men, who have committed no overt acts but who have only given countenance to those reckless murderers, assassins, and thieves, will of necessity share the same fate of their brethren. If civil war is to be the result of such a conflict, there cannot be, and will not be, any neutrals recognized."

Kansas governor Shannon feared that the territory was on the verge of war. In a letter to President Pierce, Shannon said that the Pottawatomie Creek murders "had produced an extraordinary state of excitement in southeastern Kansas." In an attempt to quell the violence the governor dispatched a company of federal

112

troops to the town of Osawatomie and another to Lawrence. Posses of Missouri Border Ruffians along with U.S. cavalry units scoured eastern Kansas searching for Brown. Not wanting to endanger his family, Brown, along with his sons Owen, Frederick, and Oliver, fled the family enclave and vanished into the wilderness.

Several days after the murders, James Redpath, a journalist from St. Louis, stumbled upon the Brown hideout. The previous evening a group of pro-slavers had accosted Redpath near Palmyra, Kansas. Recognizing him as an anti-slave sympathizer, they pulled him from his saddle and stole his horse. The next day, Redpath, disoriented and fearful for his life, was following a footpath that ran parallel to Ottawa Creek not far from Palmyra. He pushed through a thicket of brush and stopped short.

A heavily built man stood knee-deep in the creek holding a pail of water. He wore a coarse blue shirt and pantaloons tucked into calf-high boots. A thick brown leather belt held three pistols and a double-edged Arkansas bowie knife. The man's tangled hair and piercing eyes gave him a wild, ominous look. For a moment both men stood gaping at each another. Then the big man put down his pail and strode toward Redpath.

The journalist picked up a sturdy oak branch to defend himself. "Don't fear," said Frederick Brown. "I have seen you in Lawrence, and you are true." Redpath told Frederick he was searching for John Brown. His readers, Redpath said, wanted to learn more about the notorious abolitionist leader. He was delighted when Frederick offered to take him to their hideout. For an hour Brown led the journalist on a meandering trek through the woods and along the creek. Just as Redpath was beginning to wonder if the big man had lost his way, or his mind, they came to a clearing near a deep ravine. Redpath described the scene before him:

> A dozen horses were tied, all ready saddled for a
> ride for life, or a hunt after Southern invaders. A
> dozen rifles and sabres were stacked around the
> trees. In an open space, amid the shady and lofty
> woods, there was a blazing fire with a pot on it;
> a woman bareheaded, with an honest, sunburned
> face, was picking blackberries from the bushes;
> three or four armed men were lying on red and
> blue blankets on the grass; and two fine-looking
> youths were standing, leaning on guard nearby.
> [Brown] stood near the fire, with his shirt-sleeves
> rolled up, and large piece of pork in his hand....
> He was poorly clad, and his toes protruded from
> his boots.

John Brown welcomed the opportunity to get his intentions into print. During their talk he expounded on the evils of slavery and the qualities of a good soldier, but he refused to discuss the murders at Pottawatomie Creek. Redpath asked Brown how he could continue the free-slave fight against such overwhelming resistance from the Kansas governor, Missourians, and Southerners. Brown replied, "I would rather have smallpox, yellow fever, and cholera all together in my camp, than a man without principles. It's a mistake, sir, that our people make, when they think that bullies are the best fighters, or they are the men fit to oppose these Southerners. Give me men of good principles, God-fearing men, men who respect themselves, and with a dozen of them I will oppose any hundred such men as these ruffians."

Brown's rhetoric impressed Redpath, who later wrote of Brown's men, "They were not earnest, but earnestness incarnate." Redpath reserved his most glowing praise for Brown: "I left this sacred spot with a far higher respect for the Great Struggle than ever had I felt before.... I had seen the predestined leader of the second and holier American Revolution."

Four days after his interview with Redpath, Brown was presented with an opportunity to test his military convictions. A posse of approximately 60 Border Ruffians commanded by Colonel Henry C. Pate were combing the woods and ravines around Prairie City, searching for Brown. Captain Samuel Shore, commander of Prairie City's Free State Militia, tipped Brown off that Pate and his men were camped five miles east of the town. Settlers called the area "Black Jack" after the diminutive oak trees that proliferated along the banks of a wide stream. The enemy was at hand, and Brown was ready. Once again he drew inspiration from the Old Testament. He proclaimed that, like Gideon driving the Midianites across the Jordan, he would expel Pate and his slavers from Kansas.

Two days later at dawn Captain Shore, accompanied by 17 Prairie City volunteers and Brown's small band of nine men, dismounted their horses on the edge of the woods above Black Jack. Leaving his son Frederick to guard the horses, Brown ordered the troops to spread out and wend their way through a thicket of trees north of Pate's camp. They came out of the woods onto a plateau covered with tall prairie grass. Suddenly two shots rang out. Sentries had spotted the invaders. Alerted to an impending attack the pro-slavers set up a defensive line at the south edge of the plateau. Pate ordered his men to line up four wagons to protect their rear. Behind the wagons a ravine followed the meandering Black Jack stream. Shore's men were armed with Sharps rifles, a single-shot carbine deadly up to 500 yards. An experienced rifleman could get off eight to 10 shots in a minute. Pate's men also had Sharps, but Brown and his men had only muskets and pistols. Their weapons were useless at a range over 100 yards, and Pate's force was dug in several hundred yards away.

Throughout the morning the crack of rifle and musket fire reverberated across Black Jack. The combatants zigzagged through the prairie grass, finding cover where they could. Although his men killed several pro-slavers, Brown could not gain an advantage, and after three hours the anti-slavers began to run low on ammunition. As the stalemate continued, some of Shore's men decided they had dodged enough bullets. They sneaked back to their horses and rode off. Frustrated by the desertions and his inability to strike a decisive blow, Brown attempted to outflank Pate. Moving slowly through the thick brush he led several men into the eastern edge of the ravine. From their new vantage on Pate's right flank, they fired on the pro-slavers, who had taken cover behind their wagons. When six more Prairie City volunteers tried to abandon the fight, Brown confronted them. Kill the pro-slavers' horses and mules, he said, and we will cut off their ability to escape. The six followed Brown's orders. Soon the terrified cries of mortally wounded animals mingled with rifle fire and the moans of wounded men.

Brown's son Frederick was tending the horses on the far side of the woods. Throughout the Kansas campaign Brown had been concerned about Frederick's fragile emotional state. Despite his menacing appearance, Frederick did not have the stomach for bloodletting. On the rare instances that Frederick accompanied his father on a raid, Brown kept him away him from hostilities. Throughout the Kansas campaign Frederick had accepted his rear-guard status, but this day was different. For three hours he had been listening to the din of battle. Inexplicably, he mounted his father's horse and charged through the woods into the center of the fray. Waving a cutlass over his head he bellowed, "Father, we have them surrounded, and we have cut off their communication."

Believing that Frederick Brown was the vanguard of reinforcements, Pate panicked. He raised a white flag and sent a messenger to parley with Brown. Brown sent the man back and demanded that Pate come forward. The two leaders confronted each other in the center of the battlefield. Pate commanded Brown to surrender. He reminded Brown that he was a deputized U.S.

marshal. Brown cut him off and pointed a pistol at his chest. "I understand exactly what you are, and I do not wish to hear any more about it," Brown replied.

He told Pate if he didn't surrender unconditionally he would shoot him where he stood. Flabbergasted, Pate said, "You can't do this. I'm under a white flag. You're violating the articles of war." Brown simply stared at Pate and said, "You are my prisoner." Then he walked Pate back toward the Missourian's battle line with a pistol at his back. When they reached the wagons Brown raised his pistol to the back of Pate's head. No more words were necessary. Pate's men laid down their weapons.

Brown took 25 prisoners, along with food, ammunition, and guns, back to the Ottawa Creek camp. Several days after his release, which was brokered by federal troops, Pate said, "I went to take Old Brown, but Old Brown took me!" Over the next several years many bloody battles were fought over slavery. While Fort Sumter is generally considered the armed engagement that launched the Civil War, an argument can be made that the Civil War actually began on June 2, 1856, on an isolated Kansas plateau known as Black Jack.

Black Jack established Brown as a force to be reckoned with. Three months later, on August 30, at the Battle of Osawatomie, Brown proved that his victory at Black Jack was no fluke. Outnumbered 10 to one, his men fought valiantly to protect the town of Osawatomie against an attack from 400 Ruffians. The night before the battle Ruffian scouts killed Brown's son Frederick. During the battle Brown himself took a ball in the shoulder. Although the Ruffians, led by General John William Reid, eventually pillaged and burned the town, Brown's men inflicted many casualties on the banks of the Marais des Cygnes River.

News of Brown's courageous stand against a superior force of pro-slavers elevated him to legendary status among abolitionists. From that point on the gaunt, intense man who could not manage a business but who could inspire men to follow him into battle became known as Captain Brown, the hero of Osawatomie. But the final and most significant chapter of the legend of John Brown had yet to be written. That would occur three years later in a remote town in the Blue Ridge Mountains—Harpers Ferry, Virginia.

Harpers Ferry (part of West Virginia today) is located on a spit of flat land formed at the confluence of the Shenandoah and Potomac rivers 61 miles northwest of Washington, D.C. Early settlers found the small peninsula an ideal way station for river commerce. As the population increased, stone and brick houses ascended, like an Alpine village, up the shanks of a steep hill a stone's throw from the main commercial area. At the hill's pinnacle stood St. Peter's Church, its white steeple visible from miles around. For travelers from the east, Harpers Ferry served as a portal to the Shenandoah Valley and points west. Those headed eastward followed the path of the Potomac to Washington, Baltimore, and the Atlantic seaboard. Flanked by the Maryland Heights to the north and the verdant Blue Ridge mountains to the west, the picturesque meeting of land and water inspired Thomas Jefferson to write:

> The passage of the Patowmac through the Blue Ridge is perhaps one of the most stupendous scenes in Nature. You stand on a very high point of land. On your right comes up the Shenandoah, having ranged along the foot of the mountain a hundred miles to seek a vent. On your left approaches the Patowmac in quest of a passage also. In the moment of their junction they rush together against the mountain, rend it asunder and pass off to the sea.

Attracted by abundant waterpower for manufacturing arms, George Washington designated Harpers Ferry as a site for a federal armory. In 1859 the armory complex included 20 brick workshops and offices running in a double row for 600 yards parallel to the Potomac River. It employed more than 400 skilled and unskilled laborers. Yankee artisans, along with German and Irish day laborers, nudged the population to over three thousand. Approximately 300 blacks lived in Harpers Ferry, roughly half of them slaves. The total number of slaves in surrounding six counties totaled 23,000. Fewer than 6,000 were men between the ages of 15 and 59. Many slaves were house servants; others labored in modest-sized fields.

Jammed into the commercial area between the two rivers was an assortment of buildings, including the armory, an arsenal, the B&O railroad station, the Wager House Hotel, and the Gault Saloon. A covered train trestle crossed the Potomac from Maryland into the center of the commercial district. About a half-mile southwest of the commercial center, a toll bridge provided access across the Shenandoah River. The two main streets, Potomac and Shenandoah, intersected at the town center. Each ran parallel to the rivers for which they were named.

Over the years, as the armory and supporting businesses grew, the bucolic vista that charmed Thomas Jefferson morphed into one of the leading industrial towns south of the Mason-Dixon Line. It was a dingy, boisterous village plagued by the lack of sanitation common to 19th-century industrial towns. Manure and stagnant water often covered the streets. Hogs ran loose. Coal smoke from the armory and related industries polluted the air.

Despite its military importance, no special precautions were taken to protect the large stockpile of weapons. Accepted military thinking assumed that any attack on U.S. soil would come from a foreign enemy outside its borders. In late August, Secretary of War John B. Floyd received an anonymous letter stating that an association of violent abolitionists planned a raid on the federal armory in Maryland. The confiscated weapons could be used to arm a slave insurrection. The letter identified John Brown as the leader. Floyd thought the notion of a raid on a federal arsenal absurd. Besides, there was no federal arsenal in Maryland, so he ignored the letter.

On a drizzly, moonless night on Sunday, October 16, 1859, a bedraggled band of 18 men traipsed silently in pairs down a winding Maryland road that led to the Potomac River. A few were seasoned guerilla fighters from Kansas; the others had no previous fighting experience. They were farmers, artisans, lawyers, and merchants. Two were former slaves. A manumitted slave, Dangerfield Newby, was one of the only two raiders over the age of 30. His wife and several children were still enslaved in Virginia.

Each was armed with a knife, a pistol, and a Sharps rifle. Their destination, five miles away, was the covered B&O train trestle that crossed the river into Harpers Ferry. With gray shawls draped over their heads to keep out the chill, they trudged wraithlike through the mist. A farm wagon loaded with sledge hammers, crowbars, and pikes led the way. The men marched in silence. The only sound was the monotonous clip-clop of the horse's hooves pulling the wagon, with John Brown hunched over the reins. "You all know how dear life is to you," he had said just before they left their farmhouse hideout in Maryland, "and how dear your life is to your friends. Do not, therefore, take a life of anyone if you can possibly avoid it; but if it is necessary to take life in order to save your own, then make sure work of it."

Brown guided the wagon toward the flickering lights of Harpers Ferry on the far side of the Potomac. The village had something that he and his men wanted—guns, lots of them. Inside its red brick walls, the sprawling armory warehoused 100,000 muskets, rifles, and pistols. There is no record of Brown's thoughts during the two hours it took to descend the Maryland mountain to the B&O train trestle, but he had much to contemplate.

Two months earlier, at a secret meeting in a stone quarry outside Chambersburg, Pennsylvania, Brown had outlined his plan to the man he admired most, Frederick Douglass. Since their first meeting in Springfield, the two had become close friends. Douglass considered Brown the most fervent of white abolitionists, and he listened attentively while Brown described his plan to raid the armory at Harpers Ferry. Under the cover of darkness, he and his men would enter the village, cut the telegraph lines, take control of the B&O train trestle, and overwhelm the single watchman at the armory gate. While some of his men secured the armory and the nearby rifle factory, others would round up unsuspecting workmen, villagers, and plantation owners. Should they encounter resistance, they would use the hostages to barter their way out of the town. When the news spread of his successful raid, Brown was certain that slaves in Maryland and Virginia would flock to join his guerrilla army.

There were few men that Douglass respected more than John Brown, but he considered the plan ludicrous. An attack on a federal arsenal would trigger a massive military response and swing public sentiment toward slave owners. Bitterly disappointed with Douglass's rejection of his plan, Brown begged the abolitionist to reconsider and support him. "Remember the trumpets of Jericho?" Brown entreated. "Harpers Ferry will be mine. The news of its capture will be the trumpet blast that will rally the slaves to my standard from miles around. Join me, Frederick. Together we will bring slavery down…. The southern militia are cowards, and if they come to me they will be even less eager to fight in Virginia than they were in Kansas."

It was clear that Brown's unfettered commitment to freeing the slaves included sacrificing his own life if necessary. Later Douglass reported that he felt like the light of a taper next to a burning sun. While his respect for the fire-breathing abolitionist soared, it did not change his dim view of the Harpers Ferry plan. As they parted, Douglass said, "You forget, John, that I have some experience with the south. Virginia will blow you and your hostages sky-high rather than let you hold Harpers Ferry for an hour."

Brown wrapped his arms around his friend and made a last appeal: "Come with me, Douglass. When I strike the bees will begin to swarm, and I shall want you to hive them." The "bees" were the thousands of slaves in nearby plantations, whom Brown believed were ready to take up arms against their masters. Douglass was unmoved. He told Brown he was headed into a "perfect steel trap."

By the time the raiders approached the Potomac, Brown would have brushed away any lingering doubts. The time for contemplation was over: like Julius Caesar, he was about to cross his Rubicon. Straight ahead, the B&O trestle crossed the Potomac into the lower section of the village. The bridge had a tin roof and was a thousand feet long. A wagon path ran parallel to the tracks. The raiders were only minutes away from their target.

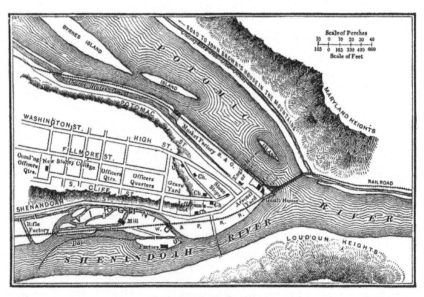

MAP OF HARPER'S FERRY.

Shortly before 11:00 p.m., B&O watchman Bill Williams was walking along the trestle wagon path, near the end of his

12-hour shift. The railroad paid him a dollar a day to monitor track switches and keep the tracks clear. Williams neared the Maryland end of the bridge and was about to reverse direction back to Harpers Ferry when he heard a horse's hooves and the creaking of a wagon. He raised his lantern and peered into the gloom. Suddenly the lantern was struck from his hand and three rifles were pointed at his chest. Brown's "Provisional Army of the United States" had taken its first prisoner.

The armory complex was located on a strip of land north of the B&O platform and the Wager House Hotel. A wrought iron fence ran along the south and west perimeter of the armory. The B&O tracks bordered the east perimeter. Beyond the tracks an embankment extended down to the Potomac. The main armory gate faced an open thoroughfare at the intersection of Potomac and Shenandoah Streets. Hall's rifle factory stood a half-mile south on a small island in the Shenandoah River. The Winchester and Potomac railroad tracks ran parallel to Shenandoah Street and converged with the B&O tracks at the train trestle.

At approximately 11:30 p.m., Daniel Whelan, the night armory watchman, finished his rounds. His primary responsibility was to make sure the forge fires in the armory's 20 buildings were properly extinguished. He was sitting at a desk in the fire engine house, a small brick building that doubled as a guard house, when he heard a commotion at the main gate. He walked outside and saw a group of men and a wagon emerge from the gloom. They called him over, and one of the strangers thrust his arm between the iron grates. He grabbed Whelan's coat lapels. "Open the gate!" he ordered. Behind the intruder a dozen or so men leveled their rifles at the astonished watchman.

Whelan later reported he was "nearly scared to death with so many guns about me." Despite his terror, he refused to comply and said he didn't have a key. The standoff lasted only a moment. One of the men grabbed a crowbar from the wagon and went to work on the lock. A few twists with the crowbar, and the raiders rushed into the courtyard.

Stunned, Whelan watched a wiry, bearded man wearing a battered straw hat climb down from the wagon: John Brown had arrived in Harpers Ferry. Brown surveyed the yard and nodded—so far, so good he seemed to say to himself. Then he ordered the two captives, Whelan and Williams, into the engine house, where he addressed them:

> I came here from Kansas, and this is a slave state;
> I want to free all the Negroes in this state; I have
> possession now of the United States armory, and
> if the citizens interfere with me I must only burn
> the town and have blood.

Once in control of the armory, Brown ordered his raiders to fan out across the town. Watson Brown and Stewart Taylor assumed sentry detail at the B&O trestle. Oliver Brown and Will Thompson secured the toll bridge that crossed the Shenandoah a half-mile from the center of the village. Charles Tidd and John Cook cut the telegraph lines. John Kagi, Aaron Stevens, Lewis Sheridan Leary, and his nephew John Anthony Copeland rushed down Shenandoah Street to seize the rifle factory. Albert Hazlett and Edwin Coppoc commandeered the unguarded arsenal outside the armory perimeter.

Satisfied that his main targets were secure, Brown dispatched six men to two nearby Jefferson County plantations. His orders were to take the plantation owners hostage and bring them to the engine house. First on the list was Colonel Lewis Washington, the area's most distinguished citizen. The 46-year-old widower was the great-grand-nephew of George Washington. His 670-acre estate was located five miles west of Harpers Ferry, just off the road to Charlestown, Virginia.

Colonel Washington was asleep when he heard a banging on his front door. He threw on a robe and rushed downstairs. At the bottom of the stairs six armed men greeted him. Aaron Stevens, the toughest and most experienced of the raiders, told Washington to get dressed and to order his carriage harnessed. Brown had heard that Washington possessed a pistol presented to his great-uncle by the Marquis de Lafayette and a sword that was a gift from Frederick the Great. Following Brown's orders Stevens took the heirlooms and gave them to one of the raiders, Osborne Anderson. Explaining the symbolic gesture, Brown told Stevens, "Anderson being a colored man, and colored men being only *things* in the South, it is proper that the South be taught a lesson on this point."

Meanwhile, on the B&O bridge, Brown and Taylor attempted to apprehend another watchman, Patrick Higgins, who had come to relieve Bill Williams. When two gray-shawled men armed with rifles emerged from the dark trestle, the startled Higgins took a swing at one of them and ran for his life. A rifle shot grazed his scalp. He dashed into the lobby of the Wager Hotel and bellowed, "Lock your doors—there are robbers on the bridge." William Throckmorton, the hotel clerk, rushed over to the railroad office to borrow the porter's pistol, and on the way back to the hotel he spotted the two armed men on the bridge. The eastbound express train from Wheeling to Baltimore was just pulling into the platform in front of the hotel. Breathless, Throckmorton hailed Andrew Phelps, the conductor, and told him there were armed men guarding the bridge. Phelps told the engineer and baggage master, Heyward Shepard, to investigate. Cinders crunching under their feet, the railroad men crossed the platform tracks and made their way into the black maw of the covered trestle. They were no more than 50 feet inside when a voice bellowed from the shadows: "Stand and deliver." Two men stepped out of the shadows, their rifles leveled at the two railroad men. One snatched the lantern from the engineer's hand and extinguished it. In the sudden darkness the startled men turned and sprinted back to the station.

A shot rang out and Shepard stumbled across the tracks. He had taken a bullet in the back. Two men bolted out of the hotel and helped him to the nearby railroad office, where they laid him on a plank between two chairs. A messenger from the hotel roused a local physician, Dr. Louis Starry, but there was little Starry could do; within an hour Heyward Shepard, the free black baggage-master, died. A black man, married and the father of several children, became the first casualty of the Harpers Ferry raid.

Not knowing the extent of the danger on the trestle, Phelps and the engineer determined that the best course of action was to sit tight. They tried to keep the passengers calm. A New York passenger gave the following account:

> Every light in the town had been previously ex-
> tinguished by the lawless mob. The train therefore
> remained stationary and the passengers, terribly
> affrighted [sic], remained in the cars all night.
> The hotels were closed and no entrance could be
> had into them. All the streets were in possession of
> the mob, and every road, lane and avenue leading
> to the town guarded or barricaded by them.

Standing by a window, the desk clerk, Throckmorton, saw one of the armed sentries walking across the town square toward the armory. He aimed the borrowed revolver and fired five shots. He missed his target, but the gunfire sent the jittery hotel guests into a near panic.

Phelps, Higgins, Throckmorton, hotel guests, passengers from the train—everybody had a theory about what was going on. Some thought the intruders were disgruntled armory employees, others said they were laid-off laborers from the nearby government dam project, or perhaps robbers intent on stealing the $15,000 in the armory paymaster's safe.

Dr. Starry determined to find out what was going on. He left the hotel and for the next few hours furtively made his way around town. He encountered one of Brown's sentries, who told him they had come to free the slaves. For the rest of the night Starry learned all he could about what was happening. He questioned sentinels on the bridge and armory gate. "Never mind," one of sentinels told him. "You will find out in a day or two." Shortly after dawn Starry had seen and heard enough. He sent a messenger to the Lutheran Church on Camp Hill overlooking the armory. Within minutes an alarm bell reverberated through the town. Then Starry mounted his horse and rode to Charlestown, eight miles away, to alert the militia.

Meanwhile, Aaron Stevens returned to the engine house around 5:30 a.m. with his hostages. He brought with him a dozen "liberated" slaves in a farm wagon and, in a carriage, Washington and another plantation owner, John Allstadt. By the time dawn approached, Brown's raiders had captured dozens of men. Some were armory and rifle works employees arriving early for work. The others were villagers who had the misfortune of being on the street at that early hour. Brown directed his men to herd the captives into the engine house and adjoining armory buildings.

He armed some of the plantation slaves with pikes and told them to guard the prisoners. In preparation for the raid Brown had a thousand six-foot-long pikes manufactured to his specifications. Most slaves had no experience handling firearms, but they would have no difficulty using the wicked-looking double-bladed weapons. Besides, Brown believed slaves armed with spears would present a fearsome sight to plantation owners. At 6:30 a.m. forge workers began to arrive at the armory gate to begin their shift. Brown quickly rounded them up at gunpoint; soon he held 39 hostages. With the intent to show that he meant no harm unless provoked, he sent a message to the Wager Hotel requesting "a good breakfast" for 45 men.

He also requested a parlay with the train conductor, Phelps. The conductor agreed. Covered by his men, Brown walked boldly across the street to the hotel and, in plain view of all, told Phelps that he had no quarrel with the people on the train and would allow it to leave. He wanted, he said, to serve notice that he had come to Harpers Ferry not to pillage and burn, but to free slaves. He informed Phelps that the train could continue on its journey to Baltimore, which it did. At 7:05 a.m. Phelps sent a telegram from Monocacy, Maryland: "Express train bound east, under my charge, was stopped this morning at Harpers Ferry by armed abolitionists. They say they have come to free the slaves and intend to do it at all hazards."

Phelps's alarm fit into Brown's plan. He needed the news of his raid to spread so that slaves from nearby plantations would join his rebellion. At the same time he was aware that an alert would bring militia from nearby towns. He counted on the slaves arriving first. His exit plan depended on having a force that could overwhelm local resistance. He was less concerned about federal troops. He believed they would take several days to mobilize; by then, his growing army would have disappeared into the surrounding wilderness.

At about the same time that Starry was riding to Charlestown, Thomas Boerly, a tavern owner and grocer, was opening his store. A neighbor told him that the armory had been captured and many townsfolk were being held hostage. Boerly grabbed his shotgun and started down Shenandoah Street toward the engine house. He spotted a sentry at the armory gate and fired. Dangerfield Newby returned fire with the more accurate Sharps rifle. A bullet to the belly delivered a mortal wound. Bleeding profusely, Boerly staggered into a nearby jeweler's store where, after receiving the last rites of the Catholic Church, the 45-year-old father of four children died.

News of Boerly's death spread quickly. The last thing Brown wanted was a shoot-out, but Boerly's death mobilized the villagers. Ironically, in a town that manufactured more than 100,000 weapons a year, the only ones available to citizens were their personal squirrel guns and pistols. However, a few weeks earlier a torrential rainstorm had threatened to flood part of the arsenal. As a precaution a cache of arms had been moved to a storeroom a half-mile behind Brown's position. Two townsmen gained access to the storeroom and carried off rifles, percussion caps, and bullet molds. Soon a steady barrage of sniper bullets was ricocheting off the brick fire engine house. Sporadic gunfire continued throughout the morning as the villagers and Brown's men engaged in random skirmishes.

Seeing that his position at the rifle factory was vulnerable, John Kagi sent a message to Brown requesting permission to withdraw. Brown told Kagi to hold his position—a fatal decision for Kagi and four other raiders. The first militia to reach the rifle factory, the Charlestown Jefferson Guards, advanced from the west down Shenandoah Street and mounted a fierce attack. Kagi and his men attempted to escape by leaping out the building's back window. The Guards, led by Captain Henry Medler, pursued them. An onlooker described the scene:

> They all ran for the river, and one who was unable to swim, was drowned. The other four swam out to the rocks in the middle of the Shenandoah River and fired upon the citizens and troops on both banks. This drew upon them the muskets of between two and three hundred men and not less than 400 shots were fired at them from Harper's Ferry, about 200 yards distant. One was finally shot dead. The second, a negro, attempted to jump over the dam but fell short, and was not seen afterward. The third was badly wounded and

the remaining one taken unharmed. The white insurgent wounded and captured, died a few moments afterwards. He was shot through the breast, arm and stomach. He declared there were only nineteen whites engaged in the insurrection.

Killed at the rifle factory were John Kagi, Brown's most trusted lieutenant; Lewis Sheridan Leary; and Jim, a local slave who threw in with the raiders to preserve his freedom. Copeland and Ben, another escaped slave, were taken into custody. Meanwhile, in the center of town, a contingent of Jefferson Guards outflanked Taylor, Newby, and Watson Brown at the B&O bridge. The raiders attempted to flee to the engine house.

One of the locals loaded a six-inch spike into his musket and fired at Newby. The missile slashed the ex-slave's throat from ear to ear. He died instantly. An angry mob beat the corpse with sticks, cut off his ears, and left his mutilated body lying in the gutter for the hogs. Newby had joined Brown's raiders to free his wife and children. In his pocket he carried a letter from his wife, pleading: "Oh dear Dangerfield, com this fall without fail monny or no monny. I want to see you so much that is the one bright hope I have before me." Before the raid Newby had set up a bank account to buy his wife and children's freedom. A few months after he was killed his widow was sold to a new master in Louisiana. She never saw a penny of the money. In her absence Newby's relatives claimed the $741 for themselves.

By noon Brown's situation had rapidly deteriorated. He was cut off from his men in the arsenal. Both bridges were in the hands of the militia, and the hillside above the armory offered snipers a clear shot at anyone who attempted to leave the engine house. The time to use his hostages to gain leverage had come. He sent Will Thompson out of the engine house, along with a hostage. Thompson carried a white flag of truce. Ignoring the flag, several men grabbed him and dragged him off to the Wager

Hotel. Brown tried again. This time he sent out two raiders—his son Watson Brown and Aaron Stevens. A.M. Kitzmiller, a hostage who was the armory's chief administrator, agreed to go along.

The three men were barely past the armory gates when shots rang out. Watson took a slug in the stomach. Mortally wounded, he crawled back to the engine house. Next Stevens fell after being hit by two slugs fired from the second floor window of the Galt House Saloon by a bartender, George Chambers. One of the hostages, Joseph Brau, ran out of the engine house and dragged Stevens to the Wager Hotel for medical attention. Then Brau, adhering to the Southern code of honor, returned to the engine house to resume has place as a hostage. Under cover of friendly fire, Kitzmiller made a successful dash to freedom.

One of the youngest raiders, 20-year old William Leeman, ran through the armory enclosure, crossed the railroad tracks, and clambered down the embankment to the Potomac. Amid a fusillade of bullets he began wading across the river to the woods on the Maryland side. He didn't make it. Desperate for cover, he ducked behind a large rock in the middle of the river. Several townsmen chased and cornered him; one of them pulled a pistol and at point blank range shot Leeman in the head. He slumped into the river, dead. A reporter the next day wrote, "His black hair may just be seen floating on the surface, waving with every ripple."

The death of the baggage handler, Heyward Shepard, infuriated Fontaine Beckham, his B&O employer and mayor of Harpers Ferry. Beckham had provided legal guardianship for Shepard so he could work in the town. Distraught, Beckham cautiously made his way along the train platform to a water tower about 30 yards from the engine house. Raider Edwin Coppoc, who was a Quaker, spotted him and fired two shots from behind the folding front door of the engine house. The second shot hit Beckham in the chest, and he dropped to the ground mortally wounded. Ironically, the bullet fired from a Quaker's gun freed five slaves: in his will Beckham had dictated that upon his death

Isaac Gilbert, his wife, and his three children were to be released from servitude.

Several men tried to retrieve Beckham's body, but a barrage of bullets from the engine house stopped them. The killing of the 69-year-old Beckham—one of the town's most respected citizens—enraged onlookers. Several townspeople rushed to the Wager Hotel to take their revenge on the prisoners Thompson and Stevens. Beckham's nephew described the scene:

> Mr. Beckham, who was my grand-uncle, was shot, I was much exasperated, and started with Mr. Chambers to the room where Thompson was confined, with the purpose of shooting him. We found several persons in the room, and had levelled our guns at him, when Mrs. Foulke's sister threw herself before him, and begged us to leave him to the laws. We then caught hold of him, and dragged him out by the throat, he saying: "Though you may take my life, 80,000,000 will rise up to avenge me, and carry out my purpose of giving liberty to the slaves." We carried him out to the bridge, and two of us, levelling our guns in this moment of wild exasperation, fired, and before he fell, a dozen or more balls were buried in him; we then threw his body off the tressel work, and returned to the bridge to bring out the prisoner, Stephens, and serve him in the same way; we found him suffering from his wounds, and probably dying; we concluded to spare him, and start after others, and shoot all we could find; I had just seen my loved uncle and best friend I ever had, shot down by those villainous Abolitionists, and felt justified in shooting any that I could find; I felt it my duty, and I have no regrets.

By Monday afternoon newspapers throughout the region were hawking exaggerated accounts of bedlam at Harpers Ferry. The Associated Press disseminated dispatches to newspapers announcing that a stampede of Negroes in Harpers Ferry had taken over the village. In fact, the opposite was true. Rather than inspiring a flood of rebellious slaves, the alarm mobilized local militias and federal troops. Brown had miscalculated the speed of an armed response to his raid. It would be his undoing.

In the midst of the maelstrom appeared 52-year-old Colonel Robert E. Lee with a contingent of 90 U.S. Marines. Following direct orders from President Buchanan, Lee took control of the situation. The future Confederate general presented Brown with a demand to surrender. Even with his son Watson bleeding to death at his feet, Brown refused. A file of Marines charged the engine house doors, but the thick wood withstood bayonets and sledgehammers. Under withering fire from the engine house, a double file of Marines battered the doors with a heavy ladder. The doors shattered, and they stormed the building, swinging swords and firing volleys into Brown and his men. Hand-to-hand combat and an exchange of pistol charges continued for a brief period.

One of the Marines, Private Quinn, was killed by a shot in the abdomen. Brown and his men attempted to take cover in the back of the small building between the fire wagons. An officer spotted Brown holding a rifle pointed at him. He rushed Brown and delivered a swift blow with his sword, gashing his neck. In his report he wrote:

> Instinctively as Brown fell I gave him a saber thrust to the left breast. The sword I carried was a light uniform weapon, and, not having a point or striking something hard in his accoutrements, did not penetrate. The blade bent double.

Other raiders were not so fortunate. Dauphin Thompson was run through and pinned to the rear wall by a bayonet. Jeremiah Anderson received a fatal bayonet strike as he attempted to hide under a wagon. Watson Brown died a day later. Shields Green and Edwin Coppoc surrendered. The raid ended with 15 people dead: nine of Brown's men, five townsfolk, one slave, and one Marine. None of the hostages were injured.

Although Brown's scheme for triggering a slave revolution failed, a new opportunity presented itself. His dramatic raid created a national sensation. Journalists flocked to Charlestown where Brown and his men were jailed. While Southern mobs clamored for retribution, Brown seized the moment to spread his message. The headline in the local newspaper, the *Independent Democrat,* proclaimed: "The Infernal Desperadoes Caught, and the Vengeance of an Outraged Community About to Be Appeased." Recovering from his injuries in a spacious jail cell shared with Aaron Stevens, Brown remained calm.

Throughout the rapid sequence of interrogation, hearing, and indictment, Brown stated his convictions with such authority that he impressed many among his captors. A Southern eyewitness to the raid and Brown's capture, Samuel Vanderlipp Leech, noted the piercing eyes and resolute demeanor of the raider:

> As Brown lay on the floor of the paymaster's office he was cool and courageous. Governor Henry A. Wise, U.S. Senator J.M. Mason of Virginia and Honorable Clement L. Vallandingham of Ohio plied him with questions. To all he gave intelligent and fearless replies. He refused to involve his Northern financiers and advisers. He took the entire responsibility on himself. He told Governor Wise that he, Brown, was simply 'An instrument in the Hands of Providence.' He said to some newspaper correspondents and others: 'I

wish to say that you had better—all the people of the South—prepare for the settlement of this question. You may dispose of me very easily. I am nearly disposed of now. But this question is yet to be settled—this negro question is yet to be settled—this negro question I mean. The end is not yet.'

To Governor Wise's comment to Brown that he had reddened by the blood of others the silver of his hair, and that he should stop casting blame on others and think upon eternity Brown replied:

Governor, I have, from all appearances, not more than fifteen or twenty years the start of you in the journey to that eternity of which you so kindly warn me; and whether my tenure here shall be fifteen months, or fifteen days, or fifteen hours, I am equally prepared to go. There is an eternity behind, and an eternity before, and the little speck in the center, however long, is but comparatively a minute. The difference between your tenure and mine is trifling and I want to therefore tell you to be prepared. I am prepared. You all have a heavy responsibility, and it behooves you to prepare more than it does me.

On October 27 Brown went on trial in the Jefferson County courthouse, located across the street from the Charlestown jail. The charges were treason, conspiring with slaves to rebel, and murder. The trials of the other captured raiders—Aaron Stevens, Edwin Coppoc, Shields Green, and John Copeland—would follow. The governor insisted that the trial be a quick to avoid more bloodshed. "There is a danger in one hand of a rescue by friends," he noted, "and on the other of Lynch-law from the indignant populace." The first day of his trial Brown appeared weak and haggard. His eyes were swollen from the wounds to his head, and he was unable to stand upright. He was carried into the courtroom on a cot, and he remained supine throughout the proceedings.

Judge Richard Parker, circuit court judge for Jefferson County, appointed Lawson Botts, who had taken part in the defense of Harpers Ferry, and Thomas C. Green, mayor of Charlestown, to defend Brown. Both owned slaves, and so did the judge. Outside the courthouse the Charlestown streets bustled with soldiers and curious citizens. Newsmen from both the North and the South added to the teeming crowd. In the courtroom spectators snacked on chestnuts and peanuts. A reporter from the *New York Herald* wrote: "The floor of the court, excepting a few feet by the Judge, was inches deep, in places, with nut shells, and the noise of people moving about was like that which would be made trampling on glass." His legs frequently propped on a table littered with books and legal documents, Judge Parker appeared more curious spectator than legal magistrate. Andrew Hunt, the prosecutor, was related by marriage to Fontaine Beckham, the murdered mayor of Harpers Ferry. Considered by many to be an able attorney, Hunt punctuated his remarks by spitting gobs of chewing tobacco into a spittoon.

No one doubted a guilty verdict was imminent. Brown had been arrested in a shoot-out, and he freely admitted his role in the raid. The looming question was whether his defense attorneys could save Brown from the gallows. The answer came on the first day of the trial when Botts read a letter to the court written by A.H. Lewis, a Brown supporter from Ohio:

> JB, leader of the insurrection at Harper's Ferry, and several of his family, have resided in this county for many years. Insanity is hereditary in that family. His mother's sister died with it, and a daughter of that sister has been two years

in a Lunatic Asylum. A son and daughter of his
mother's brother have also been confined in the
lunatic asylum, and another son of that brother is
now insane and under close restraint. These facts
can be conclusively proven by witnesses residing
here, who will doubtless attend the trial if desired.

When he finished, Botts paused for dramatic effect, put the
letter on the table and said to the court, "John Brown is innocent
of all charges due to insanity." One can imagine the shock waves
reverberating through the crowded courtroom. No one, not even
the most sanguine Brown supporter, considered the possibility
that Brown might escape the hangman's noose by claiming
insanity. Nevertheless, his reputation as a religious zealot, his
naive presumption that slaves would come flocking to Harpers
Ferry, and his belief that 19 men could successfully raid a federal
armory did not suggest the working of a rational mind.

However, the insanity plea did not sit well with his client.
Brown struggled to raise himself from his cot to address the judge:
"I look upon this as a miserable artifice and pretext of those who
ought to make a different course in regard to me. I am perfectly
unconscious of insanity, and I reject so far as I am capable, any
attempt to interfere on my behalf on that score." To the delight
of the courtroom observers, the judge agreed with Brown and
summarily rejected the insanity plea.

On the second day of the trial George Hoyt, a 21-year-old
attorney from Boston, arrived in Charlestown. Dissatisfied with
his defense, Brown discharged Botts and Green. This left only
the inexperienced Hoyt to present his defense. Hoyt argued that
Brown had treated the hostages well, and had ordered his men
not to shoot unarmed civilians. Brown claimed that the Harpers
Ferry shootings were in self-defense.

By the time two more experienced attorneys arrived—
Samuel Chilton of Washington, D.C., and Hiram Griswold of

Cleveland, Ohio—it was the last day of the trial. Having no time to hear witnesses or examine evidence, they attempted to build a defense based on a legal technicality. Brown, they said, attacked a federal arsenal. Therefore the state of Virginia did not have jurisdiction. Brown added that he should be tried as a prisoner of war rather than as a common criminal. Judge Parker rejected both of these points. On October 31 the attorneys made their closing arguments, and at 1:45 p.m. the trial concluded. Forty-five minutes later the jury returned with a verdict of guilty on all three counts. A journalist described the reaction:

> Not the slightest sound was heard in the vast crowd as this verdict was thus returned and read. Not the slightest expression of elation or triumph was uttered from the hundreds present, who a moment before, outside the court, joined in heaping threats and imprecations on his head; nor was this strange silence interrupted during the whole of the time occupied by the forms of the Court. Old Brown himself said not a word, but, as on previous days, turned to adjust his pallet, and then composedly stretched himself upon it.

Brown's execution was set for December 2. The jailer, John Avis, provided him with a spacious cell that included a writing table. For the next month Brown spent his time visiting and corresponding with supporters. When he caught wind of a plot to break him out of jail, he promptly dismissed the idea, convinced that hanging would do more to end the menace of slavery than anything he could achieve through militancy, Brown wrote in a letter to a young supporter,

> Tell your father that I am quite cheerful; that I do not feel myself in the least degraded by my

imprisonment, my chains, or the near prospect of the gallows. Men cannot imprison, or chain, or hang the soul. I go joyfully in behalf of the millions that "have no rights" that this great and glorious, the Christian Republic "is bound to respect." Strange change in morals, political as well as Christian, since 1776! I look forward to other changes to take place in God's good time, fully believing that "the fashion of this world passeth away...."

Brown was at peace with his fate. He did not fear death, and he embraced his role as martyr. A few hours before his execution he wrote this verse:

Not in vain is the lesson taught
A great soul's dream
Is a world's new thought
And a scaffold built
Is a throne ordained
For coming time.

Contrasted with Brown's messianic optimism is a letter written by George Mauzy, a Virginia slaveholder, shortly after the execution.

My dear Children:
Well the great agony is over. "Old Osawatomie Brown" was executed yesterday at noon—his wife came here the day before, & paid him a short visit, after which she returned here under an escort, where she and her company remained until the body came down from Charlestown, in

the evening, after which she took charge of it and went home.

This has been one of the most remarkable circumstances that ever occurred in this country, this old fanatic made no confession whatever, nor concession that he was wrong, but contended that he was right in everything he done, that he done great service to God, would not let a minister of any denomination come near or say anything to him, but what else could be expected from him, or anyone else who are imbued with "Freeloveism, Socialism, Spiritualism," and all the other isms that were ever devised by man or devil.

Mauzy's grudging respect for Brown was only partially right. It was dogmatism, not Mauzy's three "isms," that propelled Brown into the anti-slavery tumult. His self-righteous belief that he was doing God's work, no matter how violent his actions, marred his accomplishments and tainted his legacy. His commitment to emancipation was undeniable, but his actions eventually cost him the support of the person he respected the most, the black abolitionist Frederick Douglass.

Brown's inflexibility and unwillingness to compromise had always dogged both his political and his business decisions. His legacy is awash with contradictory opinions. Cofounder of the National Association for the Advancement of Colored People (NAACP) W.E. B. Dubois asked, "Was John Brown simply an episode or was he an eternal truth?" The answer is found in perspective rather than fact. Brown was a polarizing figure of mythic proportions whose actions raised the gnarly moral question: "Do the ends justify the means?"

Twenty-six men, including Brown, died as a result of the attack at Harpers Ferry, and five men were dragged out of their beds and hacked to death at Pottawatomie Creek by Brown and his men. But the day he was executed, black and white abolitionist churches throughout the North memorialized him as a martyr. Ralph Waldo Emerson waxed lyrical about Brown's glorious gallows fate. Union soldiers went into battle singing "John Brown's body lies a-mouldering in the grave, but his soul goes marching on." Julia Ward Howe added new words to the melody and gave us "The Battle Hymn of the Republic."

Was John Brown a martyr, a villain, or a madman? Whatever his defects in character or errors in judgment, his death inspired all who hated slavery, black and white alike. In his last letter before his execution he wrote, "I, John Brown, am now quite certain that the crimes of this guilty land will never be purged away but with Blood. I had as I now think vainly flattered myself that without very much bloodshed it might be done."

Brown anticipated that only a baptism of bloodshed would erase the stain of slavery. About this, he was right.

CHAPTER FOUR

Iva Toguri

"Tokyo Rose" and Zero Hour

"Hello out there, Enemies! How's tricks? This is Ann of Radio Tokyo, and we're just going to begin our regular program of music, news and Zero Hour *for our friends—I mean our enemies!—in Australia and in the South Pacific. So be on your guard, and mind the children don't hear! All set? OK! Here's the first blow to your morale—the Boston Pops playing 'Strike up the Band.'"*

Orphan Ann, 1945

*H*er name was Iva Toguri, but on the radio she called herself "Orphan Ann." However, to GIs throughout the Pacific she was "Tokyo Rose." Six nights a week Toguri hosted Zero Hour, a World War II Japanese propaganda broadcast beamed to American and Australian soldiers and sailors. Her orders were to play music, and demoralize the

142

enemy with insidious messages about lost battles on the front and lost lovers at home.

In collaboration with a swashbuckling Australian prisoner of war, Toguri subverted Japanese propaganda by turning Zero Hour *into a parody. Although she was one of several female broadcasters labeled "Tokyo Rose" by Allied troops, only Toguri was imprisoned and put on trial for treason. Oppressed by the Japanese military and persecuted by the FBI, she persisted in her conviction that she was a United States patriot. The ordeal of Iva Toguri is a remarkable tale of grit, loyalty, and final redemption.*

On an unseasonably warm Chicago afternoon on January 15, 2006, a small group of patrons sat down for lunch at Yoshi's Japanese Cafe. The diners were lured to the cozy eastside restaurant by more than sushi and sake. They had come to witness the culmination of one of the strangest sagas in American history. Convicted of treason in 1949 and pardoned by President Ford in 1977, Iva Toguri, known to many as the notorious "Tokyo Rose," was about to receive the 2006 Veterans Commission Edward J. Herlihy Medal for loyalty and honor to the United States.

All eyes riveted on the diminutive 89-year old Japanese-American woman as she stood to receive her award. Her steady gaze softened as James C. Roberts, president of the American Veterans Center, placed the red-white-and-blue ribbon with gold medallion around her neck. Faces wreathed in smiles, the small assembly burst into applause. Once and for all, the myth of the World War II traitor "Tokyo Rose" was dispelled, and in its place stood Iva Toguri—American patriot.

Toguri returned home that evening a happy woman. Her ordeal had finally ended. Many times over the past 65 years she had lamented the possibility that she would never rid herself of the brand "Tokyo Rose." Her redemption was now complete. In the eyes of those who mattered most to her, World War II veterans, she was not a traitor but a hero. Although there is no record of what Iva Toguri was thinking that evening as she climbed into bed, one can imagine her thoughts drifting back to that fateful summer day—July 5, 1941—when a good Samaritan mission took her to the wrong place, at the wrong time.

Seagulls wheeled in the sparkling California sky as the Japanese cargo liner *Arabia Maru* glided out of the San Pedro harbor. Its destination: Yokohama, Japan. Dressed in a white sharkskin suit, a slim 25-year-old woman leaned against the ship's port railing. Right hand shielding her eyes, Iva Toguri squinted against the harsh glare of sun and sea as she caught one last glimpse of her parents waving from the pier. How suddenly her life had changed! Instead of preparing for medical school, she was on her way to Tokyo to minister to her sick aunt Shizu. The young woman waved one more time. Then she turned and surveyed the mammoth vessel that would be her home for the next three weeks.

This was Toguri's first time at sea. It is likely she felt a pang of anxiety as she contemplated a 5,000-mile journey across the vast Pacific Ocean. Like thousands of novice seagoing voyagers before her, she might have stamped her foot on the gray metal deck, an irrational action intended to reassure a nervous imagination that the ship was indeed seaworthy. The *Arabia Maru* was no luxury liner. Built in 1918, the vessel was a hard-working cargo liner, more suited to transporting freight than passengers.

As it passed out of the harbor and into the open sea the ship began to rock gently. Testing her sea legs, Toguri took her first tentative steps toward her cabin. Skirting a cargo hatch, she passed beneath a complex arrangement of thick cables and towering booms. A dozen or so other passengers milled around the deck as they too sought to get their bearings. Meanwhile the crew scurried about stowing lines and shouting directions to each other in Japanese. At the top of the main mast a flag snapped in the breeze. The crimson circle stamped on a stark white background was recognized throughout the world as the iconic "Rising Sun" symbol of the mighty Japanese Empire.

As the ship cleared the harbor and picked up speed, the rolling expanse of cerulean sea stretched to the horizon. The chatter of the crew was a vivid reminder that Toguri was embarking on a journey to a world very different than the one she left behind. She was Nisei, second-generation Japanese, traveling to the land of her ancestors. She didn't speak Japanese, she couldn't use chopsticks, and she hated rice. Despite these drawbacks Toguri comforted herself with the thought that after a few months she would return home.

One issue nagged at her. Due to some bureaucratic delays before departure, she had not acquired a U.S. passport. Her father told her this was not a problem. The certificate of identification customs issued, he said, would validate her American citizenship. When she was ready to come home, she would have no difficulty booking passage. He could not have been more wrong.

Iva Toguri was born on the fourth of July 1916 in Los Angeles. The daughter of Japanese immigrants, Jun and Fumi Toguri, Iva was the second of four children. Her parents had immigrated to the United States from Japan in 1913. Both her younger sisters—June and Inez—were born in the United States; her older brother, Fred, was born in Japan. Her father was delighted when Iva was born in America on the fourth of July. According to Iva, "He was so proud of it! He wouldn't let me forget it." Although Jun ruled the household in traditional Japanese fashion, he was intent on "Americanizing" his children. While her parents often spoke to each other in Japanese, the children were allowed to speak only English. Forks replaced chopsticks, and potatoes supplanted rice.

When Jun's import business failed he moved the family from Los Angeles to the dusty border town of Calexico. He started a new business as a middleman trading cotton. The rural, small-town atmosphere was ideal for Iva, who loved to ride her bike, roller-skate, and play baseball. Unlike her demure sisters she preferred competitive games rather than domestic activities like cooking and sewing. Her passion was baseball, and she was a good first baseman. Jun tried to interest his daughter in fishing, but she said she would rather be doing something besides waiting for a silly fish to jump on her hook. Her sister June thought her a tomboy. One of her biographers, Frederick P. Close, described her as a restless youth:

> Over and over, as a child and as an adult, Iva Toguri displayed her love of action. She was not a contemplative. Hers was an exterior rather than an interior life. She preferred doing over thinking or talking, working over sitting or relaxing. Given a choice between board games and tree climbing, the youthful Toguri picked the tree every time.

Toguri's family attended a Methodist church. She was a Girl Scout, and she played on her high school tennis team. When she wasn't doing something more active, Iva loved to lie on the living room floor and listen to radio dramas. One of her favorite shows was *The Shadow*, which began every broadcast with the ominous warning: "Who knows what evil lurks in the heart of men? The Shadow knows." Another favorite was *Little Orphan Annie*. The popular broadcast chronicled the adventures of a young crime fighter, Orphan Annie, who was rescued from tight spots by her millionaire guardian, Daddy Warbucks, and his mysterious Sikh Indian companion, Punjab. The young Toguri had no way of knowing that a favorite fantasy about a lonely girl pitted against evil forces foreshadowed her own future struggles as Orphan Ann, propaganda radio broadcaster.

After high school she continued her education at Compton Junior College and then UCLA. She graduated from UCLA in

1941 with a bachelor's degree in zoology. She wanted to go to medical school, but a letter from Japan from her sick aunt, Shizu Hattori, changed her plan and ultimately her life. Unable to assist her sister because of her own medical complications, her mother Fumi asked Iva to take her place. In the Toguri household, duty to family superseded personal ambition. Reluctantly, she agreed to make the trip. The day after July 4, 1941, her 25th birthday, Toguri set sail for Japan.

At 3:00 in the afternoon on July 24, 1941, after 19 days at sea, the *Arabia Maru* docked in Yokohama harbor. During her first week on board, Toguri had suffered from a debilitating mix of seasickness and homesickness. Into the second week of her journey she became more comfortable and passed the time socializing with other passengers. But long sea voyages are tedious, and she welcomed the sight of the bustling harbor. Her joy at ending the voyage was short-lived. Japanese immigration officials did not accept her certificate of identification as a valid document. She had to wait another day for a temporary visa to be approved, and she was forced to spend yet another lonely night a gangplank away from dry land.

The next day, visa in hand, she disembarked and was greeted at the dock by her uncle, Hajime Hattori, and her cousin, Rinko. Aunt Shizu was too ill to make the trip. Hoping to make her feel at home, Uncle Hajime suggested lunch at a nearby United States-themed restaurant. Toguri was thrilled when she saw that the menu featured cheeseburgers and French fries.

After lunch the group boarded a train for the 17-mile trip to a Tokyo neighborhood, Setagaya. It was a steamy summer day, and Toguri sweltered in the humidity. The initial excitement at meeting her relatives dissipated as the reality of her situation began to sink in. Looking around the train, she saw only Japanese faces. Even though she shared their physical features, she felt out of place. She did not think of herself as Japanese; despite her appearance, she was American. In a 1948 interview Toguri described her feelings of alienation:

> Japan impressed me as very, very strange. All the customs were strange to me, the food was entirely different, wearing apparel different, houses different, people were stiff and formal to me.... I had no idea what the country was going to be like until I hit Yokohama.... I felt like a perfect stranger, and the Japanese considered me very queer.

As she settled into the routine of nursing her sick aunt, Toguri did her best to adapt to Japanese customs. She learned to take her shoes off before entering the house, to sit on a mat with her legs folded beneath her, and to eat with chopsticks. Privacy was minimal. The house was small, with paper-thin walls. Accustomed to rushing around, she had to learn to move carefully from one room to another, lest she disturb anyone. Even the bathroom was strange; there was no toilet, only a hole in the floor. Most troubling was her inability to understand what people were saying. Determined to fit in, she took a conversational Japanese class at the Japanese Language Culture School in the Shiba district of downtown Tokyo.

Her difficulty in acclimating to her temporary home was accentuated by the austerity of daily life. Japan was immersed in a brutal four-year war with China. Every aspect of life was affected. Food was parceled out with ration cards. The absence of fresh fruits and vegetables contributed to a rising incidence of beriberi and pellagra. Japan's militarism isolated it from other industrial countries, and imports dwindled. Common consumer goods such as cotton and wool could be obtained only on the black market. Civilians were expected to make whatever sacrifices necessary. Soldiers were billeted in private homes. Foreigners, particularly Westerners, were treated with suspicion. On several occasions Toguri saw neighbors whispering and pointing at her. Aunt Shizu cautioned her about speaking English and reading English-language newspapers in public.

Japanese authorities carefully monitored civilian political activity. Most feared were the Japanese Secret Police—Tokkō. Intimidated citizens called them "thought police." Like the Gestapo in Germany, the Tokkō were infamous for their indiscriminate arrests and brutal interrogation methods. Before Toguri's arrival more than 36,000 Japanese civilians detained by the feared agents vanished. Tokkō spies infiltrated all levels of society. One never knew if a colleague or neighbor would report a conversation to the secret police.

The day after Toguri arrived, Japanese military atrocities in China provoked President Roosevelt into freezing Japanese assets in the United States. Tensions between Japan and the United States, coupled with Toguri's obvious American ways, put her on the Tokkō watch list. Concerned about her safety and still homesick, she applied to the American consulate for a passport. They told her that there would be a prolonged wait while her application was forwarded to Washington for validation. The certificate of identification she had been issued in the United States was a worthless slip of paper.

As tensions between the United States and Japan accelerated, American visitors made plans to leave the country. On November 25, 1941, Toguri placed an international call to her father. She begged him to arrange passage to the States. On December 1, she received good news. Her father called and instructed her to book passage on the ocean liner *Tatsuta Maru*, which was departing for San Francisco the next day. Toguri rushed to the American consulate to check the status of her paperwork. She found that her application had been swept aside in a tsunami of red tape. The ship sailed without her.

Toguri was devastated and frightened. The Japanese propaganda machine was feeding its citizens a steady diet of anti-American misinformation: Nisei were American spies; America was preparing an invasion of Japan; President Roosevelt was a simple-minded cripple. On the U.S. side of the Pacific, American propaganda demonized Japanese: their women were insidious and their soldiers subhuman.

Five days later, at 7:48 on Sunday morning, December 7, six Japanese carriers under the command of Admiral Isoroku Yamamoto launched a sneak attack on military bases in Oahu, Hawaii. Three-hundred-fifty-three Japanese fighters, bombers, and torpedo planes pummeled military airfields and the Pearl Harbor naval base. Unprepared for an attack, American airmen and sailors never had a chance. Eighteen ships, including five battleships, were sunk or run aground. The battleship *Arizona* took an armor-piercing bomb in the ship's forward ammunition magazine. The explosion and fire killed 1,777 sailors. In total 2,403 Americans were killed and 1,278 wounded in the sneak attack President Roosevelt declared would "live in infamy."

Immediately after the attack, the *Tatsuta Maru* turned around and returned to Japan. World War II had begun and Toguri, along with 10,000 other Nisei, was marooned. Pearl Harbor changed Toguri's status from foreigner to enemy. Neighborhood children taunted her and neighbors called her "horyo." The phrase means "prisoner of war," but among her neighbors Toguri was branded a coward, one who surrendered rather than honorably dying in combat. Aunt Shizu warned her to avoid doing or saying anything that would draw attention to herself. "I went around in a daze," Toguri later recalled. "I could not believe war had broken out." A few days after Pearl Harbor, Tokkō agents interrogated her.

In the aftermath of Pearl Harbor, Japan was a dangerous place for Americans. Fearing for their lives many Nisei exchanged their American for Japanese citizenship. The Tokkō agents demanded that Toguri do the same. The switch was easily accomplished, they said, and her living conditions would improve. She would not have to make trips to the police station to register as an alien; she could apply for travel visas and ration cards, and—most important—Japanese citizenship would make it possible for her to find work. A lead agent, Mr. Fujiwara, told her, "If you keep your American citizenship there will be all kinds of trouble for you from now on." Toguri replied, "A person born and raised in the United States does not give up his citizenship for a piece of paper." She asked to be interred in a POW camp. The supercilious agents told Toguri she was no security threat. It would cost more money to feed her than she was worth. A more apt punishment would be to make her fend for herself.

On April 18, 1942, Army Lieutenant Colonel Jimmy Doolittle led 16 B-25 Mitchell medium bombers on a surprise raid over Tokyo. Toguri watched from a rooftop as the low-flying planes dropped their payload of 500-pound bombs. Damage was modest, but the 30-second raid bludgeoned Japanese pride and boosted American morale. Several years later Toguri told an interviewer, "People might think that I'm relating to you my feelings after the fact, but I was never so happy to see anything in my life. I felt like it's a baseball game when it is 8 to 1, and you think, what hope is there? Then all of a sudden, the home team loads the bases, someone hits a home run, and you wake up and think. 'There's life in this ballgame yet.'" Concerned for the safety of her relatives and with her financial resources dwindling, Toguri moved out of their home. Stranded in an enemy country and hounded by the secret police, she was now truly alone.

For three months she searched for employment. Her best opportunity would have been as an English translator, but she barely understood Japanese. At last she found a position as a typist in the Monitoring Division of the Domei News Agency. Her job required her to listen to English short-wave radio broadcasts from stations in San Francisco and transcribe "items of interest." Her pay was 130 yen a month—110 after taxes. The salary was barely enough to live on, but the job allowed her to follow the course of the war.

During the early days of June 1942, Japan and the United States engaged in one of history's great naval battles—Midway. Six months after the Japanese attack on Pearl Harbor, the two great armadas battled for control of the Central Pacific. Fighting was fierce, with neither side able to gain an advantage. The conflict swung the American way after two squadrons of American torpedo planes attacked the Japanese carrier force. Faulty torpedoes failed to detonate, and a lack of fighter support doomed the torpedo squadrons. Only one of 30 American pilots survived. But their sacrifices won the day. Overwhelmed Japanese carrier crews were unable to get their planes properly armed for the next attack. A wave of American dive-bombers struck with devastating accuracy. The enemy lost four aircraft carriers and one heavy cruiser—devastating losses from which the Japanese never recovered. The dramatic victory at Midway lifted Toguri's spirits. She believed a U.S. victory was imminent. But back in the States, unknown to Toguri, her family faced a desperate situation.

Pearl Harbor triggered an onslaught of anti-Japanese sentiment throughout the country. The majority of persons of Japanese ancestry who lived in California were industrious and loyal, but they carried the stigma of a reviled nation. On February 19, 1942, President Roosevelt signed Executive Order 9066 authorizing the immediate relocation of suspected saboteurs and spies to "exclusion zones." On May 3, General John Dewitt, California's military commander, ordered all individuals of Japanese ancestry, whether citizens or not, rounded up and shipped to relocation camps. Dewitt explained his decision to Congress, "A Jap's a Jap. I don't want any of them here. They are a dangerous element. There is no way to determine their loyalty. It makes no difference whether he is an American citizen, he is still a Japanese. We must worry about the Japanese all the time until he is wiped off the map."

Along with 110,000 other inhabitants of Japanese ancestry living on the Pacific coast, the entire Toguri family—father Jun and mother Fumi; brother Fred and his wife, Miyeko; and Iva's sisters, June and Inez—were ordered to a temporary assembly center in Tulare, California, to await transport to a permanent relocation camp. In her biography *Tokyo Rose: Orphan of the Pacific*, Masayo Duus described the primitive conditions of the so-called assembly centers scattered throughout the west:

> Within a few weeks they [individuals of Japanese ancestry] had been herded into jerry-built wooden barracks thrown up on racetracks, fairgrounds, or livestock pavilions. The barracks were crowded, flimsy and without any privacy. Even the toilets were communal.

With hundreds of other detainees the Toguri family arrived at Tulare assembly center on May 6, 1942. They were housed in a 10-by-20-foot horse stall with no windows, no fresh air. They slept on cots. Fifty-four year old Fumi, who was paralyzed on her right side from a stroke, grew weaker each day. On May 24 she died.

In early September the military moved the Toguris to the Gila River Relocation Center in Arizona. Despite strong objections voiced by the Gila River Indians, the federal government seized the Native-American reservation and turned it into an internment camp. Located on a barren stretch of desert approximately 30 miles southeast of Phoenix, the camp was designed to accommodate 10,000 detainees. But by December 2 more than 14,000 Japanese were interned there, making Gila River the fourth largest city in the state.

By internment camp standards, Gila River was one of the more humane. Residents lived in barracks specially built to ward off the desert heat. There were no watchtowers or barbed wire fences. No one was foolish enough to try to cross the harsh desert landscape on foot. The camp had playgrounds, a post office, stores, its own police force, and sundry other small-town services. All detainees were expected to work. Jun took a job at a supply store. Fred, who had studied law, worked as a butcher. June was a seamstress, and Inez worked in the mess hall.

Eleanor Roosevelt visited the Gila River Center in 1943. She surely must have had mixed feelings about what she saw. She praised the humanitarian conditions, but she also made it clear that she considered internment wrong.

> A Japanese American may be no more Japanese than a German-American is German, or an Italian-American is Italian, or of any other national background. All of these people, including the Japanese Americans, have men who are fighting today for the preservation of the democratic way of life and the ideas around which our nation was built.

Despite the unconstitutional internment program, 30,000 Japanese-Americans volunteered for military service. The army would not allow Japanese-Americans to fight alongside regular army troops, so a Nisei Regiment was created—the 442nd. The regiment fought valiantly in Italy, Germany, and southern France. Its distinguished battle record earned the 442nd eight Presidential Unit Citations. Regimental soldiers were awarded 52 Distinguished Service Medals, 588 Silver Stars, and 5,200 Bronze Stars. Twenty-one members of the regiment received America's highest award for bravery on the battlefield, the Congressional Medal of Honor. The regimental motto was "Go for Broke." Its nickname was "the Purple Heart Battalion." The 442nd Nisei Regiment is one of the most decorated infantry divisions in the history of the United States Army.

Despite the few rays of hope distant American victories gave her, Toguri's life was becoming more difficult. Her meager salary from Domei, coupled with whatever other part-time jobs she cobbled together working in various typing pools, barely provided enough money to live on. Moreover, her delight over Japanese defeats increased tensions between Toguri and her fellow employees at Domei, and her comments raised Tokkō suspicions that she was a spy. Then, suddenly and unexpectedly, amid all her troubles she found a silver lining. His name was Felipe d'Aquino. Part Japanese and part Portuguese, Felipe shared Toguri's American loyalty. His was a friendship she desperately needed to offset her escalating troubles.

However, a few fleeting moments of intimacy provided only a brief respite from the harsh realities of her life. Japan imported most of its food, and Allied embargoes created near-famine conditions within the island nation. In the early summer of 1943, worn out and emaciated, Toguri contracted beriberi. Those who could not procure ration cards were most vulnerable to the thiamine-deficiency disease. Beriberi means "I can't, I can't," and weight loss, fatigue, and lethargy are early symptoms. As the disease progresses, it causes severe neurological and muscular damage. Limbs swell and turn translucent. Fingers pressed against skin sink to the bone. Untreated, beriberi leads to a slow and painful death. When she began to develop symptoms Felipe urged Toguri to hospitalize herself. She reluctantly agreed. Ironically, it was a steady diet of polished white rice, the food she detested most, that had made her ill.

Toguri remained in the hospital for six months, and with no other options she borrowed money from d'Aquino and her landlady to pay her medical expenses. Shortly after her release, she was scanning help-wanted ads for additional employment when she saw an ad for a part-time typist at Radio Tokyo. She calculated that working at Radio Tokyo for two or three hours, six days a week, along with her Domei job, would double her income. She applied and gladly accepted the offered position. This would turn out to be the most momentous decision of her life. The forlorn American patriot was about to be thrust into the ignominious role of the infamous "Tokyo Rose."

During World War II, Germany had Axis Sally, and Japan had Tokyo Rose. Both were legendary female broadcasters who played music and spread propaganda. Their mission was to lower the morale of Allied troops by mixing devious half-truths about the course of the war with phony stories about depressing conditions back in the States. Axis Sally was Mildred Gillars, a German-American from Portland, Maine; Tokyo Rose was nobody and everybody. Axis Sally was a real person; Tokyo Rose was a generic name Allied troops gave to a score of female announcers who broadcast Japanese propaganda from Tokyo, Manila, and Jakarta.

The Tokyo Rose myth began in 1937 when construction workers listening to a short-wave radio in Samoa heard a female disc jockey broadcasting Japanese propaganda between musical selections. Incredibly, a rumor circulated that the broadcaster was the dashing American aviatrix Amelia Earhart, who had disappeared somewhere in the Pacific on July 2, 1937, in her failed attempt to be the first woman pilot to circumnavigate the world. According to Iva Toguri biographer Rex Gunn, the first military reference to a female propaganda voice was recorded by Chief Radioman J.M. Eckberg on December 11, 1941, aboard the submarine U.S.S. *Seawolf*. Four days after Pearl Harbor, Eckberg picked up a short-wave radio broadcast by a woman who called herself Madame Tojo. According to Eckberg, she crowed, in a phony Oxford accent, "Where is the U.S. fleet? I'll tell you where it is, boys. It's laying on the bottom of Pearl Harbor." Eckberg called her "Tokio Rose."

After the Pearl Harbor attack a score of females broadcast Japanese propaganda throughout the South Pacific. Most notable among these early versions of "Tokyo Rose" were Ruth

Hayakawa, who broadcast from Radio Tokyo; Myrtle Lipton in Manila; and the "Nanking Nightingale," June Suyama. Gradually the myth of a sexy and all-knowing "Tokyo Rose" grew to legendary proportions. Like Ulysses, who could not ignore the sirens' songs, Allied troops throughout the Pacific twirled the dials on their short-wave radios hoping to snatch a bit of entertainment and news from the sultry siren of the Pacific. The quality of short-wave reception was influenced by a number of factors, including equipment, time of day, and weather. Even with the best conditions, audio quality was spotty. For entertainment-starved troops, fighting bloody battles on one remote island after another, discriminating among female broadcasters was not a concern. It was simpler just to say, "Hey, I'm listening to Tokyo Rose."

The propaganda broadcasts alternated pop music selections with news about stateside disasters such as floods and train wrecks. To intensify the demoralizing effects, insidious comments about cheating wives and girlfriends were regular features. Most troubling were announcements about Allied troop movements and impending Japanese attacks. The August 20, 1943, issue of *Yank* magazine reported a Tokyo Rose claim that the "coward" "Butch" O'Hare, an ace American pilot and Medal of Honor winner, would soon die. On November 26, 1943, O'Hare's F6F Hellcat was shot down during a night raid on a Japanese aircraft carrier. Neither O'Hare's body nor his plane were recovered. Knowledge of pilot names, along with predictions of battle outcomes, lent a foreboding sense of danger to the Tokyo Rose persona.

In August 1943 Toguri started working part-time six days a week as an English typist at Radio Tokyo. Shortly before she began her new job, a career Japanese military man, Major Shigetsugu Tsuneishi, was appointed director of Radio Tokyo's propaganda division. One of his pet projects was a 20-minute, six-day-a-week broadcast called *Zero Hour*. The title was derived from the agile

157

and formidable Japanese Zero attack plane. The show mixed jazzy songs with messages meant to make U.S. servicemen—in Tsuneishi's flawed English—"homesicky." Lacking broadcast experience, Tsuneishi scoured POW camps to locate American and Australian POWs who had worked in radio.

Tsuneishi's prize discovery was an Australian major, Charles Cousens. Captured when Singapore fell to the Japanese, Cousens was a well-known radio personality in his homeland. Although threatened with torture, he had steadfastly refused Japanese orders to assist in propaganda broadcasts. In retaliation, he was put in solitary confinement and shipped to a heavy-labor camp in Burma. After several months of brutal treatment he was shipped back to Singapore, where an Australian POW colonel ordered him to cooperate with the Japanese. The colonel told Cousens that as a radio Tokyo announcer he would be in a position to transmit POW messages and solicit Red Cross aid.

He reluctantly acquiesced to the order. Ironically, he sailed from Singapore to Tokyo aboard the *Arabia Maru*, the ship Toguri had taken on her fateful voyage. After Pearl Harbor, it was refitted to transport Japanese troops and prisoners. At sea Cousens's daily ration was a cup of foul water, a ball of dirty rice, and seaweed soup. By the time the *Arabia Maru* docked in Yokohama, Cousens, wracked with dysentery, was a mere shadow of the debonair Australian major who had fought so gallantly at the Battle of Singapore. On October 18, 1944, the U.S. submarine *Bluegill* torpedoed and sank the *Arabia Maru*. Fortunately, no prisoners of war were aboard at the time, but 1,658 Japanese troops and 89 crewmen went down with the ship.

At Radio Tokyo, Major Tsuneishi was elated at the arrival of a polished professional announcer. He ordered Cousens to write *Zero Hour* scripts. Cousens refused. He told Tsuneishi, "Give me a pistol and a cartridge—that will save time for both of us." But Tsuneishi was not about to execute a valuable resource. A few days later Cousens reported to Tsuneishi's office. He was no stranger to Japanese brutality. During his forced march from Singapore to a Japanese labor camp Cousens had walked a road lined with heads of Chinese women impaled on sticks. Wayside ditches were scattered with the corpses of bayoneted babies. Cousens expected the worst.

Inside the office, dressed in full military regalia, Tsuneishi stood behind his desk. When Cousens entered the Major bellowed, "Attention!" Slowly and dramatically, he drew a two-handed samurai sword from its scabbard and placed it on the desk. The message was clear: cooperate or die. Sapped by months of constant abuse, his will to resist snapped like a stretched rubber band, and the next night Cousens sat in front of a microphone at Radio Tokyo and read a propaganda script. He accepted his temporary defeat, but he remained unbowed.

A few weeks later Tsuneishi ordered Cousens take over as producer of *Zero Hour*. At first Cousens resisted, but as he thought about it he began to sense an opportunity. Although Japanese censors understood English, they couldn't detect such nuances as sarcasm and double-entendres. Cousens slyly agreed to produce *Zero Hour*. Then he immediately set about to undercut Tsuneishi's plot to demoralize GIs by lampooning the scripts and in the process turning Zero Hour into a parody of Japanese propaganda.

He used subtle tactics to achieve his goal. He alternated his pace by reading scripts quickly and then slowly. He adopted an instrumental version of "Strike Up the Band" for the show's theme song. He mispronounced words and told stories that poked fun at Japanese hubris. One story detailed how a Japanese pilot shot down several American planes. As the pilot pursued the last plane, he ran out of ammunition so he grabbed a ball of rice from a lunch pail, opened the cockpit, and threw it at the American pilot. The startled American pilot crashed his plane into a palm tree. The Japanese loved the story, and so did the Allies. Another report described how 10 Japanese soldiers defeated a force of 400

American Marines without suffering a single casualty. Cousens hoped such outlandish tales would get by the censors and raise, rather than diminish Allied morale.

Meanwhile Cousens told Tsuneishi that the wild stories emphasized Japanese invincibility. While Cousens played on Tsueneishi's arrogance, *Zero Hour* gained in popularity among American servicemen. Soon two other POWs—an American, Wallace Ince, and a Filipino, Lieutenant Norman Reyes—joined Cousens on *Zero Hour*. Cousens wrote the scripts, and the three POWs took turns playing music and making announcements.

Toguri had been at Radio Tokyo only a few days when she spotted Cousens, Reyes, and Ince walking down a hallway. Their emaciated appearance startled her, but she was thrilled to encounter English-speaking soldiers. When the opportunity presented itself she struck up a conversation. At first the three POWs were suspicious. Many Nisei worked undercover for the Tokkō. As they chatted about baseball and news events back home, the POWs' suspicions gradually dissipated. After a few weeks Toguri agreed to smuggle them food and medicine. Providing aid to prisoners of war was punishable by death. Undeterred, Toguri hid contraband in her clothes, her handbag, and among documents. To the POWS such basic necessities as quinine, lemons, and aspirin were treasure. After work Toguri scrounged the Tokyo countryside for food. She bought whatever black market supplies she could afford. Despite the risks she was determined to do all she could to allay the suffering of her new friends.

By degrees *Zero Hour* increased in popularity. Major Tsuneishi decided to expand the time slot from 20 minutes to a full hour. He added two Nisei, who had traveled to Japan before the war to find employment, to the production team—George Mitsushio and Kenkichi Oki. Both were open supporters of Japan. Additionally, Tsuneishi insisted that a woman commentator be added to the program. This was bad news. The last thing Cousens wanted was a sultry-voiced Mata Hari-style announcer like June Suyama, "The Nightingale of Nanking," or sexy Myrtle "Little Margie" Lipton," to skewer his satire. Instead he selected the chatty Nisei typist, who had no radio experience and whose voice had all the charm of a scratched record—Iva Toguri.

Everyone connected to *Zero Hour* was astonished by Cousens's choice of Toguri. Ince said she had the voice of a crow. Mitsushio thought it was a joke. For Cousens, Toguri's voice was a perfect fit for his propaganda parody. He said, "With the idea I had in mind of making a complete burlesque of the program, her voice was just what I wanted—rough. I hope I can say this without offense—a voice that I have described as a gin-fog voice. It was rough, almost masculine, anything but a femininely seductive voice. It was a comedy voice that I needed for this particular job." It was a hard sell, but Cousens convinced Tsuneishi and Mitsushio that Iva Toguri was the best choice to host *Zero Hour*.

Promoting Toguri as the star of the show was one thing; getting her to accept was another. Convincing a woman who had endured intimidation, scorn, and malnutrition rather than relinquish her American citizenship, to become the female voice of a Japanese propaganda broadcast was a formidable task. When Cousens first broached the subject, Toguri flatly refused. She had access to news reports from the West, and she knew the tide of the war was in the Allies favor. The idea of participating in a Japanese propaganda effort was ludicrous. At first she laughed Cousens off, but he persisted, explaining that she would actually help the Allies by contributing to his parody. Cousens told Toguri that, if she didn't take the job, Tsuneishi would force him to use Ruth Hayakawa or another experienced Japanese propaganda voice. Although not fully sold on the idea, Toguri trusted Cousens, and, after many discussions she agreed to host *Zero Hour*—a life-changing decision that would brand the plucky American patriot as a traitor.

At 6:00 p.m. on November 13, 1943, Iva Toguri sat down in front of a microphone in Studio Five at Radio Tokyo. She made a few announcements and played four records. In 20 minutes she completed her segment of *Zero Hour*. Afterwards she confronted Cousens in the studio. "This is crazy," she said. "I'm no good at this." Cousens tried to humor her. "You are just what we want," he replied. "We want a Yankee voice with a certain personality in it—a little touch of WAC officer and a lot of cheer. I'll coach you to read scripts the way I want them, so don't worry."

A few days later Cousens told Toguri she needed a broadcast name. He took Ann from the first three letters in *announcer,* and combined it with "orphan," a term he thought GIs could identify with because many dubbed themselves "orphans of the Pacific." So Iva Toguri became "Orphan Ann," and an ironic twist was added to the life of the Nisei who, as a child, was beguiled by the Orphan Annie radio broadcast. Iva Toguri was a real-life Orphan Ann, but there was no Daddy Warbucks to save her. Immersed in the shadowy world of propaganda radio, Toguri and the three POWs walked a fine line between subversion and exposure. Under the noses of Japanese censors, the courageous efforts of Cousens, Toguri, Ince, and Reyes elevated rather than deflated Allied troop morale.

Zero Hour staff had no way of knowing that, even before Toguri made her first broadcast, the female voices Allied troops called "Tokyo Rose" were inadvertently foiling their own propaganda messages. A front-page story in the *New Castle* (Pennsylvania) *News* on September 17, 1943, ran an article that said Tokyo Rose was so uninformed in her war news announcements that she was boosting morale. Major John Canavan, recently returned from Guadalcanal, said that "Rose" could not get her story straight: "She was so wrong that the boys were vastly entertained. They began to look forward to her broadcasts for the laughs." In the October 5, 1943, the *Charleston* (West Virginia) *Gazette* wrote that troops complained about the scratchy, out-of-date records she played. Said one GI who had enjoyed Rose's broadcasts, "She's beginning to droop." These comments were documented more than a month before Toguri's first broadcast. To Allied troops who were winning the war, radio propaganda broadcasts that might have demoralized a losing side came across as a charade.

Typically, Toguri would introduce her music with some teasing remarks that Cousens hoped would be endear her to Allied troops. "Hello there, Enemies! How's tricks? This is Ann of Radio Tokyo, and we're just going to begin our regular program of music, news, and *Zero Hour* for our friends—I mean, our enemies!—in Australia and the South Pacific. So be on your guard, and mind the children don't hear! All set? OK! Here's the first blow to your morale—the Boston Pops."

One of Orphan Ann's ploys was to use the term "boneheads" when referring to Allied troops. Japanese censors had no way of knowing that the insulting-sounding word was actually Australian slang for "buddy." Fred Close, the Toguri biographer, described her on-air antics as a combination of cornball patter and Mitch Miller entreaties.

On August 2, 1944, the *Port Arthur* (Texas) *News* reported that Marines on Saipan favored Tokyo Rose over Bing Crosby, but they felt slighted because they were not included in her "bonehead" list of allied troops. The *Cumberland* (Maryland) *Evening Times*, on October 3, 1944, printed the banner headline "Tokyo Rose Broadcast Brings Hearty Laughs from Marines." The article featured a letter written from Saipan from Pfc Fred Theis to his parents. He said, "We like her music, and her attempts to make us homesick are funny.... Her broadcasts raise our morale.... Her inaccurate battle reports are a real laugh.... She said 50–60 planes raided Saipan about a week after we threw back their last desperate attack."

In mid-November 1943, while Toguri was making her broadcast debut, Major Tsuneishi supervised the construction of a secret concentration camp in the Kandu section of Tokyo. Its purpose was to house POWs with broadcasting experience. He selected a nondescript building that had served as a cultural center before the war. In the center of the camp was an ordinary-looking wooden structure built around an inner court. This was the prisoners' dormitory. The area was sealed off from the surrounding neighborhood by barbed wire. Armed guards in military uniforms kept gawkers away. A sign over the gate read "Sungadu Technical Research Center." To the outside world the compound looked harmless; a passerby would never have identified it as a concentration camp. On December 18, 1943, Major Cousens and Captain Ince were transferred there.

Living conditions were grim at Bunka Camp, nicknamed "Bunker Hill" by American POWs. Twenty-seven prisoners lived in a flimsy 40-by-60-foot dormitory room. There was no heat. Camp guards sold Red Cross medical supplies on the black market. A Dutch POW described the Bunka menu: "We got a ration of three cups of kaoliang (a grain often used as chicken feed) a day and three bowls of soup to get that down with. The bowls of soup were a little larger than the teacups. The soup consisted of daikon (radish)…, a little salt…, a little soy, to which water was added." Any stray dog or cat was a potential meal. Desperate POWs ate the buds off tree branches.

Prisoners were allowed to bathe every two weeks in a single tub of water after the guards washed their laundry. For three months, each morning, prisoners were forced to stand at attention in the courtyard as guards ranted about the fate of those who refused to participate in Radio Tokyo broadcasts. The treatment of Bunka prisoners was indicative of Japanese POW camps throughout Asia.

It was a dishonor for a Japanese soldier to be assigned prison guard duty; only the dregs of the Japanese military were posted to concentration camps. Guards took out their shame and frustration on their prisoners. Sadistic beatings and torture were daily events.

At the slightest provocation a guard would knock a prisoner senseless. Brutal conditions in Japanese concentration camps took a horrendous toll: 37 percent of captured Americans died. In comparison, 1 percent of POWs died in Nazi concentration camps. The average American prisoner of war lost 61 pounds during captivity. Men were crippled and disfigured from the constant beatings. Teeth were ruined, and many went blind from malnutrition. Beriberi was endemic, as were tuberculosis and dysentery. If the beatings didn't kill POWs, disease and starvation did.

When he arrived at Bunka Camp, Major Cousens was appalled at the conditions. As the ranking Allied officer, he demanded better treatment for the prisoners. His complaints were rebuffed with beatings. Prisoners suffering from beriberi, scurvy, and pellagra desperately needed medical attention. Cousens appealed to Toguri. She redoubled her smuggling efforts. She was no longer smuggling for three; now it was the entire camp of 27 prisoners who depended on her. She bought, bartered, and begged aspirin, quinine, and yeast pills. Friends contributed vegetables and fruits. She hid contraband in a tin mess can. She even managed to smuggle in a blanket for a sick POW.

In early 1944 Toguri accepted a part-time position as a secretary at the Danish legation. Her new job enabled her to add diplomatic rations of soap, sugar, and other scarce items to the supplies she smuggled to the Bunka POWs. Her friendship with Felipe d'Aquino evolved into a romance, and in May 1944 she moved to Felipe's mother's home. It was a two-and-a-half-hour commute to Tokyo, but Toguri was grateful for the opportunity to spend time in the countryside.

In the spring of 1944 a Bunka guard beat Ince mercilessly. His injuries were so severe that Tsuneishi removed him from the broadcast. In late June the 41-year-old Cousens suffered a heart attack. He was hospitalized and never returned to *Zero Hour*. Toguri faced a new challenge—she no longer had Cousens's direction in writing scripts. She began skipping broadcasts. Although her absences provoked Major Tsuneishi, "Orphan Ann" had become so popular with Allied soldiers that he was reluctant to replace her.

As Allied forces moved closer to Japan, it became clear even to the most ardent Japanese patriot that losing the war was not a matter of *if* but *when*. In an effort to keep the growing audience tuned in to *Zero Hour*, Major Tsuneishi minimized propaganda messages and increased music. Toguri was happy to comply. She encouraged her listeners to sing along with records, and she began referring to her boneheads as "you fighting GIs." Although still in charge, Major Tsuneishi stayed out of day-to-day operations. Overseeing production was left to the second-rate Japanese staffers who replaced Cousens and Ince. Lackadaisical censors didn't notice when Toguri played "Stars and Stripes Forever" after the American invasion of Saipan.

On November 1, 1944, a mammoth silver plane appeared in the sky above Tokyo. On its silver fuselage emblazoned in large red letters was the name "Tokyo Rose." The American B-29 Superfortress was the newest addition to the Allied war arsenal. Ninety-nine-feet long with a 141-foot wingspan, the B-29 was powered by four 2,200-horsepower Wright Double Cyclone engines. Its airspeed of 350 mph outpaced any other plane in the sky. The B-29's ability to fly at altitudes of up to 30,000 feet kept it well above anti-aircraft fire. Protected by four turrets, each equipped with two 50-caliber machine guns, the B-29 carried a 20,000-pound bomb load. In short, the B-29 Superfortress was the most deadly weapon of war in existence. Tokyo was defenseless. The first over-flight by the "Tokyo Rose" on November 1 was a reconnaissance; the following flights were lethal.

The first raid of 60 B-29s on November 24, 1944, hit the Nakajima airplane works at Kichijoji. The next attack obliterated the Yokohama-Tokyo industrial area. From that point on, Tokyo was subjected to the most destructive siege in the history of warfare. On November 29, 15,000 bombs were dropped on Tokyo. More than 2,000 civilian homes were reduced to rubble. But despite the success of the B-29 raids, Army Air Force General Curtis Lemay was not satisfied. Flying at 30,000 feet to avoid anti-aircraft fire made bombing accuracy a problem. Lemay decided to change tactics and ordered low-altitude attacks. Five-hundred-pound bombs were replaced with M-69 gasoline-jelly incendiary bombs that, upon impact, released 100-foot streams of fire. In order to inflict optimal devastation, the incendiary attacks required dry air and a good wind. With the proper weather conditions the M-69s, dubbed "Molotov fire baskets" by American flyers, created a firestorm with gale-force winds. Walls of fire sucked the oxygen out of the air. Some victims suffocated. Others died from seared lungs and smoke inhalation. Many were instantly incinerated.

The evenings of March 9 and 10 provided ideal conditions for a massive bombing raid. In the two nights, 289 B-29s dropped half a million M-69s on Tokyo. The main target was a patchwork of industrial buildings and workers' homes adjacent to the harbor. Fragile wooden buildings provided kindling, and the Tokyo harbor area was set ablaze. Robert Guillain, a French reporter, described the scene he witnessed on the evening of March 9:

> They set to work at once sowing the sky with fire. Bursts of light flashed everywhere in the darkness like Christmas trees lifting their decorations of flame high into the night, then fell back to earth in whistling bouquets of jagged flame. Barely a quarter of an hour after the raid started, the fire, whipped by the wind, began to scythe its way through the density of that wooden city.

Fire spouts leaped from one neighborhood to another. The most severe destruction took place in the Asakusa-Ku residential section of Tokyo, a densely populated area of 140,000 people that literally disappeared in a rain of fire. In all, 16 square miles of Tokyo were leveled. More than 100,000 men, women, and children perished. More people died during the March 8 and 9 American B-29 raids over Tokyo than were immediately killed by the atomic bomb blast over Hiroshima.

Since the end of October, Toguri, weary of the long commute from the d'Aquino house in the country, had taken up residence in a Tokyo boarding house. She faced her greatest peril as bombs delivered by her homeland rained destruction all around her. Afraid of being buried alive in a bomb shelter, she sat out the B-29 raids in a small, darkened room. She prayed the fragile building would be spared. When she peered out her window at the devastation, it looked like the whole world was on fire.

The firebombs did not leave behind the rubble typical of bomb-blasted European cities. Rather, the city resembled the aftermath of a massive forest fire. Fragile wooden homes were vaporized, while brick industrial buildings their interiors charred to ashes and their exteriors still intact, dotted the desolate landscape. All animal life—dogs, cats, squirrels, even birds—disappeared. Residents steeled themselves for the inevitable Allied invasion. Women and children trained to ward off invaders with bamboo spears. In April, amid the raids, Iva Toguri married Felipe d'Aquino. The only hitch in the festivities was a bombing raid that forced the wedding party to take refuge in a shelter.

On August 6, a single B-29, the *Enola Gay*, dropped an atomic bomb nicknamed "Little Boy" on the industrial city of Hiroshima. Three days later "Fat Man," a second atomic bomb, flattened Nagasaki. Anybody within a one-mile radius of each explosion was vaporized. Others burned to death, and still others succumbed to radiation sickness. In all, an estimated 300,000 Japanese, mostly civilians, were killed. Release of the most destructive weapon ever conceived had the desired effect. Emperor Hirohito declared that Japan must "endure the unendurable" and surrender. On September 2, 1945, Japanese officials signed a formal surrender document on the deck of the U.S.S. *Missouri* in Tokyo Bay. World War II was over.

Toguri was elated. Finally, she could return to America with her husband. The troubles of the last four years receded into the background as she and d'Aquino made plans for their future together. In the weeks following the Japanese surrender Tokyo swarmed with American correspondents looking for a scoop. There were three stories everybody wanted to get—an interview with General Hideki Tojo, a description of the Tokyo destruction, and an interview with Tokyo Rose. On August 31 a friend showed Toguri a newspaper story: two American correspondents were willing to pay $2,000 to interview "Tokyo Rose." In war-ravaged Tokyo this was a small fortune.

Toguri had first heard the name "Tokyo Rose" in the spring of 1944. Around Radio Tokyo opinions differed about which of several female broadcasters matched the GI nickname. Various descriptions of Tokyo Rose didn't fit one person. "She had a sultry voice"; "she broadcast on Sunday evening"; "she called herself Orphan Ann." The Orphan Ann moniker fit Iva Toguri, but she did not broadcast on Sunday evenings; that was Ruth Hayakawa's time slot. As for the voice, Toguri's was decidedly not sultry. June Suyama, the Nightingale of Nanking, had a sultry voice, but she did news rather than music. No one at Radio Tokyo fully understood the heavy baggage that went with the tag Tokyo Rose—least of all Toguri, who considered her broadcasts an entertaining diversion for GIs.

The cash-for-interview offer was stunning, but her husband was dubious. He felt there was something fishy about the offer. Why were correspondents offering such a huge sum of money to interview a female radio broadcaster? He told his wife that the money might be a lure to snare a propaganda broadcaster.

Maybe the American military did not view Tokyo Rose in the same favorable way Toguri thought of herself. Tokyo Rose was a melded personality made up of several different individuals. How could Toguri be sure that the reporters would accept her rather than June Suyama or Ruth Hayakawa?

Despite her husband's concerns, she was determined to do the interview and collect the money. There were other female announcers who could claim the title "Tokyo Rose." As far as Toguri was concerned, there was no risk. She and Major Cousens had molded Orphan Ann into a non-threatening buddy, who at worst teased GIs and at best boosted their morale.

Toguri was wrong, and her husband was right. To some, Tokyo Rose was a propaganda caricature. On August 7, 1945, the Navy had issued a tongue-in-cheek citation to Tokyo Rose for entertaining American troops—for consistently providing "excellent state-side music, laughter, and news about home." But for every positive opinion of Tokyo Rose there was a sinister point of view to counter it. Toguri had no way of knowing that the legend of Tokyo Rose had morphed into a bigger-than-life siren who slept with Prime Minister Tojo, predicted Allied troop movements, and broke the hearts of young GIs with stories of wayward girlfriends. American correspondents scouring Tokyo for Rose weren't searching for a wise-cracking comedian. They wanted a sexy firebrand who threw off sparks when she walked into a room.

Never the reflective sort, Toguri saw no danger, only the opportunity to start a new life in the States. Naiveté and impulsivity are a dangerous combination. Even though Toguri believed *Zero Hour* was harmless, she had been broadcasting enemy propaganda; somewhere deep inside, a caution light should have been blinking. But the hook was baited, and, suppressing any inner reservations, she contacted the two correspondents, Clark Lee and Harry Brundidge. A meeting was arranged at the swanky Imperial Hotel in Tokyo.

When the slight, decidedly unglamorous Iva Toguri walked into their hotel room, Brundidge and Lee were astonished. They were expecting a honey-voiced sexpot, and instead they got a chatterbox who wore her hair in pigtails. As Toguri said years later, "It should have been Ava Gardner, but instead it was me." Undaunted, the correspondents were not about to let disillusion spoil a good story. This was the scoop of a lifetime. Brundidge offered Toguri $2,000 for an exclusive Tokyo Rose interview. Toguri signed and spent the afternoon dictating her story. She talked about the subversive intent of *Zero Hour*, her smuggling of supplies to POWs, and her experiences with the Japanese secret police.

When Toguri left, Lee turned to Brundidge and said, "This story is a bunch of baloney." Nevertheless, the next day Lee cabled "Traitor's Pay—Tokyo Rose 100 Yen a Month—$6.60" to the *Los Angles Examiner*. The story caused a sensation in the States. The notorious Tokyo Rose had been found, and she was American!

Brundidge contacted his editor at *Cosmopolitan*. He told her he was writing a 5,000-word story about Tokyo Rose and asked for the $2,000 to pay Toguri. His editor wasn't interested in the story and refused. Stuck with a deal he couldn't keep, Brundidge contacted Eighth Army intelligence and told the commanding officer that he had the signed confession of the traitor Tokyo Rose. Toguri's husband had been right. By passing herself off as Tokyo Rose, she put herself squarely in the crosshairs of all those who sought retribution for war crimes real or imagined. She gambled and lost, and she never saw a dime of the promised interview payment.

Courtesy of the National Archives
Iva Toguri with reporters

The next day Toguri was arrested. Lacking evidence of a crime committed, the army released her, but the media would not let go of the story, and political pressure to prosecute Tokyo Rose increased. On October 18, 1945, the U.S. Justice Department ordered General MacArthur to take Toguri into custody on suspicion of treason. She was arrested and taken to Yokohama Prison. Six weeks later she was transferred to Sugamo Prison.

Sugamo Prison, an ominous fortress of barbed wire and concrete walls, spread over 12 acres of center-city Tokyo. Built by the Japanese in the 1920s to hold captive political enemies of the Empire, it had been untouched by Allied bombs. The U.S. Eighth Army took control of the prison and incarcerated some 5,000 Japanese war criminals. In total, 4,400 Sugamo prisoners were convicted of war crimes; of these, 984 were hanged, and 475 were given life sentences. Premier Hideko Tojo, the architect of Pearl Harbor, was hanged in Sugamo on December 23, 1948.

Toguri was kept in Blue Block, a special section designated for women criminals. For a year she lived in a six-by-nine-foot cell equipped with a toilet, a water basin, and a straw mat. She was allowed to bathe every three days. The army considered her a Japanese national; as a result, she could not send letters to her family in the United States. Her only luxury was the steam radiator in her cell that helped ward off the harsh Tokyo winter chill. During her incarceration, Toguri was denied the constitutional due process rights of a U.S. citizen: she was denied access to legal counsel, and she was held without an arraignment or bail.

Toguri kept telling herself it was all a mistake. She stubbornly clung to the belief that her Orphan Ann version of Tokyo Rose was a popular figure among American GIs. Her inability to grasp the severity of her situation led to some stupid mistakes. She signed autographs for prison guards "Iva Toguri/Tokyo Rose," and she was flippant with FBI interrogators. She had no way of knowing how the U.S. media was orchestrating the legend of an insidious Tokyo Rose. In the States, political cartoons, movies, and newspaper editorials embellished the myth of Tokyo Rose as a malevolent seductress who preyed on the loneliness of American fighting men. Her interview with Lee and Brundidge had sealed her fate. As far as the U.S. public was concerned, there was only one Tokyo Rose, and that was Iva Toguri.

Of the several females who broadcast Japanese propaganda, Myrtle (Little Margie) Lipton, whose radio shows emanated from Manila, came closest to the sultry stereotype. Myrtle was a hard-partying, fair-haired beauty with a voice that oozed sex. Sometimes she would show up for broadcasts drunk and entertain her listeners with Edith Piaf and Billie Holiday torch songs. She ad-libbed scripts and did not hesitate to rub in Allied losses. Her script writer, George Uno, described Little Margie to a reporter:

> This girl was a drinking girl, and sometimes she would come to the station at the last minute pretty well messed up, and she would say, "I can take care of myself"… and would give off

pretty much like a professional announcer, and all of a sudden she would lose control of herself and…well…she was reading something that was plain imagination…but anything she did was very effective. She painted horrible pictures of jungles, dropping bombs, and foxholes. Then she described "the good old days" back home, saying things like, "What a pity you fellows have to die in the jungles without even knowing what you are fighting for."

Cut off from the outside world, Toguri had no idea that the public perception of Orphan Ann overlapped with the well-publicized antics of Little Margie Lipton.

Time in prison dragged on. The only variations in her dreary routine were her husband's monthly visits and a series of interrogations by FBI agent James Tillman. For hours on end, Tillman grilled Toguri about her broadcasts. Did she predict troop movements? Did she tease Allied troops about the cheating women back home? Did she tell GIs that the Atabrine they were taking to ward off malaria would make them impotent? Did she gloat over Japanese victories?

Toguri was flabbergasted. She tried to explain to Tillman that the whole point of *Zero Hour* was to make fun of Japanese propaganda. Tillman concluded his interrogations unmoved by Toguri's protestation of innocence, but neither did he uncover any evidence of treason. He considered Toguri a naïve chatterbox. In an interview several years later, Tillman said of Toguri, "She wouldn't shut up. She was always cracking wise. I got tired of that."

Finally, after an exhaustive investigation, the U.S. Counter Intelligence Corps found no evidence that Toguri broadcast using the name "Tokyo Rose," or that she engaged in any activities that undermined troop morale. On October 25, 1946, a year after her arrest, she was released.

Toguri thought that her troubles were over. She and her husband made plans for their trip back to the States. But U.S. newspapers would not let go of the Tokyo Rose story. "Iva Toguri d'Aquino, one of four bedroom-voiced girl broadcasters the Allied soldiers called 'Tokyo Rose,' wants eventually to return to her native country, she said today," warned the August 1, 1947, *Long Beach* (California) *Press Telegram*. The November 6, 1947, *Cumberland Evening Times* stated, "Tokyo Rose, the wartime radio broadcaster who sank more fleets that America built, wants to go home to the U.S."

Meanwhile, Toguri continued to be stymied in her attempt to get a U.S. passport. She was trapped in a revolving bureaucratic paradox. Despite constant Tokkō harassment, she had refused to give up her American citizenship. When American authorities imprisoned her, their justification was suspicion of treason as a U.S. citizen. Yet her passport application was rebuffed because she could not prove her U.S. citizenship! Desperate, Toguri wrote a letter to the syndicated columnist Walter Winchell. She asked him to help with her passport application. When Winchell did not reply, Toguri believed she had run into another dead end. What she didn't know was that Winchell was hell-bent on getting Toguri returned to the States, but not in the way she imagined.

In 1947 Walter Winchell was one of the most powerful men in America. His newspaper columns, "On Broadway" and "Man About Town," mixed right-wing political opinion with snippets of juicy entertainment world gossip. His Sunday evening radio show, opened with the incessant tapping of a telegraph key and his trademark introduction, "Good evening, Mr. and Mrs. America, and all the ships at sea." At the height of his popularity he had a radio audience of 20 million. He was feared by politicians and admired by gangsters. President Roosevelt tried to stay on his good side. FBI director J. Edgar Hoover was one of his best friends. Winchell's favorite targets were liberals and communists, but what he loved best was a good crusade. After he read Toguri's letter, Winchell launched a mission of righteous indignation. He wanted her to return to the United States, but not to join her family. He wanted "Tokyo Rose" to stand trial for treason

On April 14, 1948, Winchell published an open letter to Tokyo Rose from Captain Frank Farrell, a veteran who had served in the Pacific with the 1st Marine Division. Saturated with sarcasm, the letter accused Tokyo Rose of broadcasting that the Atabrine tablets prescribed to treat malaria made them sterile. Many Marines died of malaria, said Farrell, because of Tokyo Rose.

The political pressure against Toguri gained steam when, in a public statement, James F. O'Neil, commander of the American Legion, demanded that the Justice Department prosecute her for treason. On June 9, 1948, Winchell claimed that Clark Lee had in his possession an 18-page document in which Toguri confessed to being Tokyo Rose. In later years the journalist Bill Kurtis described the campaign to prosecute Iva Toguri as the persecution of a person in order to exact revenge on a myth.

As far as the Department of Justice was concerned, the infamous Tokyo Rose and Iva Toguri were one and the same. On August 26, 1948, she was once again arrested for treason. Under military guard she was put aboard the U.S.S. *General Hodges* and transported to the United States to stand trial. Her husband was not allowed to leave Japan. Three weeks later, her odyssey complete, Toguri set foot on American soil. But instead of the homecoming with family and friends that she had yearned for, she was whisked to a San Francisco jail, where she was incarcerated for the duration of her trial.

The trial of Tokyo Rose was a national sensation. Only a few weeks earlier, a U.S. court convicted of treason American citizen Mildred Gillars, the Nazi propaganda broadcaster known as Axis Sally. Gillars was sentenced to a term of 10 to 30 years in a federal prison and fined $10,000. The prospect of the Tokyo Rose trial following the Axis Sally conviction had newspaper readers salivating. A grand jury charged Toguri with eight acts of treason. Prior to World War II, only two Americans had been convicted of treason: Thomas Wilson Dorr, who attacked a Rhode Island state arsenal in 1842, and John Brown, who raided the Federal armory in Harpers Ferry, Virginia, in 1859. Dorr was imprisoned, and Brown was executed.

Treason is defined in Article Three, Section Three of the Constitution: "Treason against the United States, shall consist only in levying War against them, or in adhering to their Enemies, giving them Aid and Comfort. No Person shall be convicted of Treason unless on the Testimony of two Witnesses to the same overt Act, or on Confession in open Court." If found guilty, Toguri faced death or imprisonment of not less than five years, loss of citizenship, and a fine of no less than $5,000. Eight years and one day after she set sail for Japan to tend to her ailing aunt, Toguri walked into a San Francisco courtroom to face her accusers. The trial lasted 13 weeks. It cost the government $750,000—the most expensive trial to date in American history.

On July 6, 1949, one of the strangest trials in the history of American jurisprudence commenced in a solemn, drab San Francisco courtroom. Roseate marble columns topped with cherubs supported the 40-foot ceiling. Dimly lit electric globes gave the space a gloomy aura. The jurors' box was located to the left of the judge's bench, the witness box to the right. Defense and prosecution tables were less than an arm's-length away from each other. Seats for 110 spectators were crammed into a small area just inside the large, gilded courtroom door.

The eight counts against Toguri were based on statements she allegedly made as an announcer on *Zero Hour*. The most serious was that she had gloated over the sinking of American ships at the Battle of Leyte. Following the battle, she was accused of making the following statement: "Now you fellows have lost all your ships. Now you are really orphans of the Pacific. How do you think you will ever get home?" Few outside the courtroom expected anything less than a guilty verdict. It was untenable for the government to have the alleged Tokyo Rose in hand and not follow through with a conviction.

The press hammered away at President Truman for being soft on war criminals. Walter Winchell's columns boiled with anti-Japanese outrage. Veteran groups and Gold Star Mothers, who lost sons or daughters in the war, joined the accusers' chorus. The *San Francisco Chronicle* promised its readers that the trial would be as exciting as a spy thriller. Newspaper accounts included reports that Toguri had predicted an attack on Saipan and concocted a tale about the Japanese sinking the battleship *Missouri*.

A slew of newspapers reported Toguri as saying, "Sure, I broadcast those radio shows. But I never said anything treasonable. I was just sitting on the fence as far as the war was concerned." However, none of the overdramatized newspaper accusations were included in the grand jury indictments. The newspapers energetically cultivated an image of Toguri as an Asian seductress. But when she entered the courtroom dressed in plaid skirt and an out-of-date jacket with overstuffed shoulders, and her hair pinned back in a bun, the pale young woman looked more librarian than sexpot.

The trial began with the government presenting first. The lead prosecutor Tom DeWolfe, special assistant to Attorney General William Clark, was the perfect choice to prosecute Toguri. The year before, he had successfully prosecuted two German propaganda broadcasters, Robert H. Best and Douglas Chandler. In his opening statement the tall and balding DeWolfe methodically outlined the prosecution's case. The grand jury had handed down eight indictments. Each alleged that Iva Toguri willfully participated in a Radio Tokyo propaganda broadcast between March 1, 1944, and July 31, 1945. With a smattering of a soft southern drawl, DeWolfe walked the jury through each count and then presented his summary. His entire presentation took 90 minutes.

De Wolfe concluded with the assertion that the government would prove that Iva Toguri did voluntarily and without duress broadcast Japanese propaganda with the intent to undermine the morale of U.S. troops in the Pacific. Stillness descended over the courtroom at the conclusion of the patrician De Wolfe's statement. It was an impressive show by a master trial attorney. De Wolfe sat down behind the prosecution table confident he had hit all his marks

Toguri's defense lawyer, Wayne Mortimer Collins, was a respected San Francisco civil rights attorney. His advocacy on behalf of Japanese-Americans was legendary within the Asian community. In 1945, Collins successfully halted, on constitutional grounds, a U.S. government attempt to force Japanese-Americans to renounce their citizenship. In the same year Collins blocked an attempt by the Peruvian and U.S. governments to exchange nearly 3,000 Japanese-Peruvian citizens for American POWs in Japan. Collins's defense strategy, he told the jury, was straightforward: he would disprove the government's contention that Toguri willingly tried to demoralize American troops.

For 13 weeks the two attorneys dueled over Toguri's motives. DeWolfe claimed that her broadcasts were voluntary, vicious, and demoralizing, while Collins countered that the broadcasts were under duress, friendly, and entertaining. DeWolfe, who several years later would commit suicide in a San Francisco hotel, knew he had a weak case. So much confusion existed among servicemen about who Tokyo Rose was and what she said that pinning guilt on a single individual was going to be difficult. For every serviceman who claimed Tokyo Rose demoralized his unit, another claimed Tokyo Rose was a morale booster.

DeWolfe was not about to lose his case for lack of preparation. Every night during the trial, he secluded himself in his hotel room, working late into the evening on his briefs. The government went to extraordinary lengths to round up witnesses for the prosecution. Nineteen Japanese citizens were flown from Japan and put up in San Francisco hotels. The government allotted each of them $10 a day for expenses. Collins insisted on equal government funding for the defense. His requests were denied. After the trial Collins fumed, "Every son of a bitch who ever set foot in Radio Tokyo was willing to testify against her for a free plane ride and ten dollars per diem."

DeWolfe's first witness was Richard J. Eisenhart, an army corporal and guard at Sugamo Prison. DeWolfe produced a one-yen note, which he identified as the one Toguri had autographed for him. Inscribed on the crumpled bill, in large cursive letters, was the signature "Iva Toguri." Beneath the signature in the same swooping style appeared the name "Tokyo Rose." To many observers in the courtroom the note was an admission by Toguri that she was indeed Tokyo Rose. After a few perfunctory questions that affirmed Toguri was the same person who autographed the yen, DeWolfe turned his witness over to Wayne Collins for cross-examination.

If the aristocratic DeWolfe was silk, hard-nosed Wayne Collins was sandpaper. Collins had a reputation as a tedious cross-examiner who hounded witnesses into submission. He went to work on the corporal. At the conclusion of his cross-examination, Collins had scraped the veneer off Eisenhart's testimony, one question at a time. Did guards have weapons? Did they carry clubs? Did he think a prison guard could intimidate a prisoner? Wasn't it true that Toguri refused his first request for an autograph? Wasn't it also true that for six straight days after her refusal the light bulb in her cell was kept on day and night? While DeWolfe's questions filled four pages of court transcripts; Collins's questions filled 20. By the time he finished with Eisenhart, witness and spectators alike were worn down. But Collins had made his point. An autograph given to a prison guard by an intimidated prisoner was not an admission of anything except fear.

As the trial continued, DeWolfe and Collins sparred over whether an assortment of documents could be introduced as evidence. DeWolfe then called his next witness to the stand, the personnel manager of Radio Tokyo. Whatever leverage DeWolfe gained with the jury was nullified by Collins's wheedling cross-examination, which coaxed one contradiction after another out of the witness. Collins's tactic of extended questions induced a somnolent state in almost everyone in the courtroom. DeWolfe needed a wake-up call—something dramatic to regain momentum.

His next witness opened eyelids and raised eyebrows. It was ex-Lieutenant Colonel Shigatsugu Tsuneishi, commandant of Bunka Camp and chief administrator of propaganda at Radio Tokyo. Courtroom observers took in a surreal moment as the dapper, trim Tsuneishi walked briskly through the courtroom to the witness stand. Only the day before, Mark Streeter, a defense witness and Bunka P.O.W., had accused Tsuneishi of being one of the worst of Japanese war criminals.

Why DeWolfe thought that an American jury would accept the testimony of an ex-Japanese army officer and alleged war criminal is a mystery. It was obvious to everyone in the courtroom that Tsuneishi would say whatever was necessary to save his own skin. The minimal advantage DeWolfe gained by the drama of bringing in Tsuneishi to testify was neutralized by Collins. DeWolfe could not have given Collins an easier pitch to hit, and the defense lawyer knocked it out of the park. Toguri's voluntary participation in Radio Tokyo broadcasts was central to the prosecution's case. Under cross-examination Tsuneishi acknowledged that he had instructed subordinates to tell Toguri that, if she did not participate in *Zero Hour*, she would be shipped off to a munitions factory or someplace worse. As the grilling by Collins continued, Tsuneishi also admitted that several other female broadcasters at Radio Tokyo fit the description of Tokyo Rose.

The next day the *San Francisco Chronicle* trumpeted: "Tokyo Roses bloomed all over Federal Court yesterday. It was a great day for the defense." DeWolfe's plan to convince the jury that Iva

Toguri was the one and only Tokyo Rose was unraveling. Like two poker players, DeWolfe and Collins raised the ante and called each other's bluff, and, as the trial entered its second week, chips were gradually accumulating on Collins's side of the table.

But DeWolfe held a trump card—Clark Lee. Tall, handsome, and suave, Lee had a distinguished record as a fearless war correspondent. Wherever there was action, Lee had been there. Before Pearl Harbor he reported on the Japanese invasions of Burma and China. He was with General MacArthur on Bataan, and he narrowly escaped capture when the Japanese invaded Corregidor. His reporting style mingled facts with chauvinism. During the war he wrote that he relished the day he could walk down the main street of Tokyo under a blanket of U.S. planes so thick they would hide the rising sun. Lee's jingoistic reporting endeared him to his readers. His marriage to a Hawaiian princess, Liliuokalani Kawana-Nakoa, burnished his celebrity status. The jury's attention sharpened as Lee took the stand.

The so-called "confession" culled from the Lee-Brundidge notes following the meeting at the Imperial Hotel was key prosecution evidence. In a little more than half an hour, DeWolfe walked Lee through the hotel room meeting. Lee testified that Toguri admitted she announced the sinking of American ships at the Battle of Leyte. This was a key point because it specifically matched paragraph VI of the indictment, "that on a day during October, 1944, the defendant did speak into a microphone concerning the loss of ships." Furthermore, Lee testified that Toguri identified herself as Tokyo Rose and signed a statement to that effect.

During his cross-examination Collins chose not to press the point that Brundidge had promised Toguri $2,000 for her story. Rather, Collins hammered away at a single point. Lee's notes did not verify that she had actually broadcast the message described in the paragraph VI allegation. Collins maintained that, although she was ordered to broadcast the sinking of American ships at Leyte, she refused. Another key prosecution strategy appeared to falter when Lee admitted that, as far back as 1942, a year before Toguri began working at Radio Tokyo, he had talked with servicemen about Tokyo Rose broadcasts.

Then Collins turned up the heat. He reminded Lee about a meeting Collins had had with Lee and Brundidge in a San Francisco hotel prior to the trial. Collins asked Lee about their discussion concerning a prosecution witness at the grand jury hearing—Hiromu Yagi. Wasn't it a fact that Yagi was Brundidge's friend? Didn't Brundidge coach Yagi on what to say to the grand jury? Collins reminded the jury that Brundidge had a significant financial interest in the Tokyo Rose case. If Toguri was convicted, Brundidge's notes would be worth thousands of dollars.

The closer Collins got to Brundidge's role in shaping the prosecution, the more vehemently DeWolfe objected. Judge Roche, who throughout the trial seemed intent on supporting the prosecution, ruled in favor of DeWolfe's objections. The judge told the jury to disregard Collins's questions regarding Yagi and Brundidge. At the conclusion of his testimony Lee's swashbuckling reputation won the day for the prosecution. Even Toguri later admitted that, if circumstances were different, she would like the affable Lee.

DeWolfe's last two prosecution witnesses were the two Nisei whom Major Tsuneishi put in charge of *Zero Hour*, Kenkichi Oki and George Mitsushio. Both men had grown up in California, and both had relinquished their American citizenship in Japan during the war. If they had not given up their citizenship, they would have been facing treason charges along with Toguri. The twisted nature of the situation—two Japanese collaborators testifying for the prosecution in a treason trial—was not lost on court observers. The *San Francisco Chronicle* described their testimony as "hokum" and "corn." Collins took advantage of the situation. Judge Roche allowed his scornful cross-examination of the two disloyal Americans despite multiple objections from the prosecution.

At one point Collins asked Mitsushio, a former Boy Scout and ROTC student, to repeat the Pledge of Allegiance. Toguri, who usually sat at the defense table with downcast eyes, stared straight at her former supervisor, awaiting his reply. Sweat beaded on Mitsushio's face and in a trembling voice he whispered, "I pledge allegiance...to the flag...of the United States of America...and to the republic for which it stands...one nation...indivisible..." Then he mumbled, "I don't remember the rest." Judge Roche finished it for him.

For a conviction the prosecution needed two witnesses to an overt act of treason. Both Oki and Mitsushio swore they heard Toguri announce after the Battle of Leyte that the Americans were "orphans of the Pacific" who would never get home because all their ships were lost. But it appeared the testimony would count for little with the jury. Throughout the courtroom there was a palpable sense of dislike for the two witnesses. As Mitsushio left the stand, Judge Roche whispered to Frank Hennessy, one of DeWolfe's assistants, "Where did you get those witnesses?"

In fact Oki and Mitsushio had been prepped for their testimony by correspondent Brundidge. He was peddling his notes to various publishers as the Tokyo Rose "confession." Without a conviction the notes were worthless; with a conviction Brundidge had a marketable commodity. Leading up to the trial, he had proved to be a valuable source of information for the FBI. But DeWolfe knew that Brundidge, the man who had the most to gain from Toguri's conviction, would be taken apart by Collins on the witness stand. When Toguri's trial began, Brundidge quietly slipped out of town and was never called as a witness.

The basis of the treason indictment was radio propaganda, yet no one in the courtroom had heard a Toguri broadcast. After four weeks, the jury was finally instructed to put on their earphones. This was the moment everyone had been waiting for—the hard evidence that Toguri had bragged about sunken Navy vessels, predicted attacks on Allied troops, gossiped about unfaithful wives and girlfriends to make soldiers and sailors homesick. Forty 10-inch-round acetate discs were stacked on a table next to a phonograph. DeWolfe approached the jury box and promptly deflated the dramatic moment. The prosecution, he told the jurors, would play only six discs, and none of the recordings contained broadcasts related to the eight acts of treason in the indictment. The recordings were presented to establish voice identification only.

"Acetate" is a misnomer; there was no acetate in the discs. The records were actually made of aluminum with a coating of lacquer. Sound quality was poor, and they were extremely fragile. When the jury put on their earphones, they listened to scratchy snatches of broadcast news interspersed with a female voice introducing music. Frequent mention of Orphan Ann and the trademark term for her listeners, "boneheads," did establish that Toguri had made the recordings. But true to DeWolfe's caveat there was not a single word spoken that backed up the government's case.

Typical was the following monologue: "Hello there, you fighting orphans somewhere in that pool of water called the Pacific. This is your playmate, Orphan Ann, taking roll call...." Fifteen minutes of music crackling and fading completed the recording. The poor quality of the recordings, coupled with the incessant attorney bickering, left the jurors bleary eyed. One newspaper account described the presentation as a "dull thud." *Oakland Tribune* reporter Paine Knickerbocker wrote, "It seems to me that the Government has so frail a case that it shows a basic weakness—no evidence exists. Obviously, if there had been damning evidence, it would have been preserved."

DeWolfe concluded his case by calling a dozen veterans to the witness stand. They were the alleged victims of Tokyo Rose propaganda. Who better to make the government's case than those who endured the taunting, insidious transmissions? Under cross-examination the same prosecution bugaboo resurfaced.

Collins continued to bring out contradictions regarding which of the several so-called "Tokyo Rose" broadcasters had said what, and when. His grind-them-down strategy was working, but there was one veteran witness whose testimony Collins could not shake.

Marshall Hoot was a crusty chief petty officer who had served as a boatswain's mate on a P.T. boat in the Gilbert Islands. His testimony was unremarkable until he pulled out a letter he had written to his family after a Japanese raid, in which he described how Tokyo Rose gloated over an upcoming bombing attack. As Rose predicted, the Japanese attacked, and two of Hoot's shipmates were killed. The letter, written by a sailor who didn't know if he was going to live or die, ended with the line, "Honey babies, I hope I dream of you tonight."

Several jurors dabbed tears from their eyes as Hoot concluded his reading. After the trial Judge Roche admitted he too was moved by the dramatic story. As Hoot departed the witness stand, a courtroom reporter turned to a colleague and whispered that the odds for acquittal "broke like the 1929 stock market." On Friday, August 12, the prosecution rested. After six weeks and 500,000 words of testimony, the defense took center stage.

While the government spent over half a million dollars to prosecute their case, the defense had minimal financial resources. Collins was working pro bono. He wrote a memo to the attorney general requesting equal funds for the defense; he was rejected. Due to a lack of resources, the defense had a thin witness list. Cousens, Ince, and Rey were his key witnesses, along with a few GIs and Toguri. No one had more knowledge of what Toguri said or did not say on the air than Cousens, the man who wrote *Zero Hour* scripts. After the war, the Australian government investigated Major Cousens's complicity with the Japanese. No charges were filed, and he returned to radio broadcasting. At his own expense, Cousens traveled to San Francisco to support Toguri.

Collins's strategy was to establish a pattern of duress at Radio Tokyo. The courtroom fell silent as Cousens described Japanese soldiers beating an Australian soldier to death because he stole a can of onions. Weeping silently, the normally stiff-lipped Cousens made it clear that Toguri understood the danger of defying Japanese military orders. DeWolfe sensed his argument that Toguri voluntarily made propaganda broadcasts losing ground.

When Cousens began describing how Toguri smuggled supplies to Bunka prisoners, the prosecution objected. DeWolfe maintained that being a kind-hearted person had nothing to do with whether or not she committed treason. Judge Roche sustained the objection, ruling that risking her life for the POWs was inconsequential to her trial for treason. From that point on whenever a witness testified about Toguri's aid to POWs, DeWolfe objected, and Judge Roche instructed the jury to disregard the remarks. Throughout DeWolfe's withering cross-examination, Cousens was steadfast in defending Toguri's loyalty. DeWolfe closed by asking Cousens if any other Japanese brought him food besides the defendant. Cousens paused and replied, "The defendant is not Japanese. She is an American."

No one had more to risk by testifying for the defense than Major Wallace Ince. He was still on active duty and stationed at the Presidio in San Francisco. Dressed in his summer uniform adorned with campaign ribbons, the tall, red-haired Ince made a strong impression as he walked to the witness stand. According to the *San Francisco Chronicle*, "Ince was a poised and impressive witness in tailored suntans decorated with three unit citations and the ribbons of Corregidor on his Eisenhower jacket." Originally, he had agreed to testify for the prosecution. During their interrogation of him prior to the trial, the FBI had made it clear that they expected his cooperation. As an American officer who worked on *Zero Hour*, he too could be prosecuted for treason. In reality the FBI had decided not to prosecute Ince, but he did not know this. In statements to the FBI, Ince said that, to the best of his knowledge, Toguri freely participated in *Zero Hour*, and no changes had been made to subvert the Orphan Ann scripts

Knowing that Ince would make a devastating government witness, Collins wanted to turn him. Before the trial began, Collins met with Ince and his attorney. He reminded Ince that if he was tried for treason he would need Toguri as a defense witness. Despite a sense of foreboding, Ince changed his mind and agreed to testify on behalf of the defense. Collins asked the major to describe his POW experiences. Ince's composed military bearing dissolved as he described the atrocities at Bunka Camp. In summarizing his experience, Ince said, "We were beaten, starved, and subjected to indignities." Overcome with emotion, Ince buried his head in his hands, his shoulders shaking with sobs. After a few moments, he continued. "It is not so easy.... It is not so easy to talk so matter-of-factly of brutality. It is quite a different thing." Ince insisted that everyone who worked on *Zero Hour* understood the consequences for not cooperating. His emotional testimony did not have the powerful effect Collins hoped it would. The muddled jury had to weigh Ince's comments supporting the defense against prosecution statements he had signed.

Collins had one more Radio Tokyo witness to bring to the witness stand—Norman Reyes. But Collins was unaware that Reyes had undergone intensive FBI interrogation before the trial. The last *Zero Hour* defense witness was the weakest. The son of a Filipino father and an American mother, Reyes was captured by the Japanese when he was 19. Fearful that he too would be prosecuted, he signed several damaging statements against Toguri. Now, as a defense witness, Reyes was on the hot seat, and DeWolfe turned up the heat. How did Reyes, DeWolfe asked, explain the inconsistency between his appearance as a defense witness and statements he signed for the FBI? "I signed to get rid of these people," he said. "I had enough of it. I would sign anything to get out from under. Secondly, I was afraid. I was afraid of these two men, the atmosphere under which the questioning was conducted, and my own status."

De Wolfe drilled Reyes with questions about his character and his mixed racial background. Repeatedly, he hammered away at Reyes's inability to remember details and his shifting of facts. DeWolfe wanted to convince the jury that Reyes was a liar. It was clear to court observers that the naïve Reyes was no match for the wily DeWolfe. To his credit, however, Reyes continued to recant all the statements he signed for the FBI. At the end of his testimony Reyes said, "I would have put my life in her hands."

A parade of GI testimonials favorable to Toguri's defense followed Reyes's testimony. Throughout the trial, whether through cross-examination or its own witnesses, the defense emphasized that Japanese propaganda broadcasts emanated from different places throughout the Pacific, and many included a "Tokyo Rose" type of disc jockey. A Collins witness, Gustave C. Gallagher, was one of hundreds of short-wave listeners who monitored Japanese broadcasts during the war. He estimated that more than 200 broadcasts outlets were managed by Radio Tokyo, and these did not include programs emanating from Manila, Java, or Saigon. Any one of these broadcasts, Collins maintained, could have featured a Tokyo Rose announcer. Sam Stanley, a former baker for the Seabees in the Admiralty Islands, testified that the radio tent could not hold all the GIs who flocked to hear Orphan Ann. Likewise, a warrant officer stationed in Alaska said that a command bulletin recommended listening to Orphan Ann to build troop morale.

On September 7, the 46th day of the trial, Toguri took the stand. The courtroom was hushed as the pale, slender young woman, dressed in the same tan plaid suit she wore throughout the trial, walked to the front of the courtroom, sat in the witness chair, and swore to tell the truth. The *Oakland Tribune* reported that the question uppermost in most people's minds was: "Is this the voice that taunted American GIs in the Pacific as Tokyo Rose?"

Observers expecting to hear a sultry voice were disappointed. Her responses to Collins's questions were clear, brief, and decidedly unsexy. What the jury heard was not the voice of a sensual Tokyo Rose but what Major Cousens once described as a "gin-fog" voice—resonant and crisp, with masculine overtones. Collins asked about claims made by prosecution witnesses. "Did you say, 'Welcome to the First Marine Division, the bloody butchers of Guadalcanal'?"

Toguri replied, "No."

"Did you say, 'Your wives and sweethearts are leaving you because you are overseas too long'?"

"No, I would never say that."

Led by Collins, Toguri waded through each of 41 different accusations, sometimes providing details and growing more emotional as her time on the stand wore on. Then it was the prosecution's turn to cross-examine. For two days DeWolfe battered Toguri's testimony. He tried to create contradictions by wearing her down. One exchange, a double-negative question posed by DeWolfe about her citizenship, produced a mind-numbing series of comments from the judge, Toguri, DeWolfe, and Collins. The *Oakland Tribune* described the verbal exchanges as "a slugging match."

The jury could barely keep track of who was saying what. DeWolfe scored a point when he got Toguri to admit that the duress she felt to broadcast was more psychological than physical. Still, after three days of grueling cross-examination, DeWolfe was unable to get her to admit that she had tried to undermine GI morale.

Finally, after eight days on the stand, Collins used his cross-examination opportunity to review the charges once again. He concluded his question by asking, "Did you ever do anything with intent to betray the United States of America?" In a clear, firm voice Toguri said, "Never." With her last denial echoing through the packed courtroom, Iva Toguri walked to the defense table, sat down, put her head in her hands, and closed her eyes. The trial was over. All that remained was the verdict.

Court reporters were convinced that an acquittal was imminent. The government case rested on a so-called "confession" that in fact had been an interview made on the promise of $2,000 stipend, hearsay testimony from veterans who did not know one "Tokyo Rose" from another, and testimony from two turncoat Nisei who worked for Radio Tokyo. In none of the six Orphan Ann broadcasts introduced as evidence did Toguri do anything other than introduce music and tease her "bonehead of the Pacific" listeners.

Despite the weak prosecution case, Wayne Collins was worried. He understood that anti-Japanese sentiment was the wild card. The all-white grand jury had shown no signs of sympathy toward Toguri despite convincing testimony in her favor from Cousens, Reyes, and Ince. The wily veteran defense lawyer acknowledged that Judge Roche suppressed valuable defense testimony when he instructed the jury to disregard as irrelevant to the case her assistance to POWs. Her insistence on retaining her American citizenship and her detainment in Sugamo Prison for a year without legal counsel were also ruled irrelevant to the case by Judge Roche.

The jury deliberated for 80 hours, and on September 29, 1949, they reached a verdict. Iva Toguri was innocent of seven of the eight charges. She was guilty of charge VI, "That on a day during October 1944, the exact date being to the Jurors unknown, said defendant at Tokyo, Japan, in a broadcasting studio of the Broadcasting Corporation of Japan, did speak into a microphone concerning the loss of ships." The young Nisei who refused to give up her American citizenship was convicted of treason based on the testimony of two Nisei who collaborated with the Japanese.

Judge Roche sentenced Toguri to 10 years in a federal penitentiary, fined her $10,000, and, in a cruel twist of injustice, revoked her American citizenship. Convicted of treason, she was unbowed. On the train ride to the federal penitentiary in

Alderson, West Virginia, she said to the bailiff Herbert Cole, "I will do the ten years, and I will sleep every night of it, but I don't think the same thing will be true for Mitsushio and Oki." Her words would turn out to be prophetic

On January 28, 1956, after serving more than six years of her sentence, Toguri was paroled. She never saw her husband again. The government would not allow him to stay in the United States, and in 1967 they divorced. During and after her incarceration, Wayne Collins attempted to gain several appeals and then pardons, to no avail. After her release Toguri joined her father in Chicago, where she was determined to live out her life in quiet seclusion. For the most part, the media lost interest in the infamous "Tokyo Rose" except for periodic reports of government attempts to have her deported.

However, in 1974 a Chicago reporter once again drew Toguri into the national spotlight. Ron Yates, the Japanese foreign correspondent for the *Chicago Tribune*, was playing golf in Tokyo with a friend, Ken Ishii, who mentioned that he had worked on the radio with "Tokyo Rose." Yates asked Ishii what he thought of Toguri's conviction. Ishii replied, "Well, it's a long story and there are some people involved in it that might not even talk about it." Ishii's cryptic remark triggered Yates's reporter's instinct.

"Ishii's remark set off all sorts of alarm bells in my mind, and I wanted to find out more about it so I began checking and finally, Ken reached these two guys [George] Mitsushio and [Kenchiki] Oki." After a couple meetings between Yates and the Nisei the truth emerged. Yates said, "They didn't want to say very much, and finally the second or third time I talked with them they looked across the table at me and told me what they had done, that they had lied at her trial." When Yates asked why they had lied they said, "Well we were told by the Occupation forces at that time that if we didn't they would arrange a trial for us."

In March of 1976 Yates wrote a series of articles about Toguri's ordeal for the *Chicago Tribune*. A Morley Safer interview on the CBS broadcast *60 Minutes* attracted more sympathetic attention. Antonio Montanair Jr., a San Francisco filmmaker, acquired more than 2,300 government documents about her case through the Freedom of Information Act. After analyzing the documents Montanair revealed that Attorney General Tom Clark, who authorized the trial, knew that there was no such person as Tokyo Rose. In November 1976 Wayne Merrill Collins, the son of defense attorney Wayne Collins, petitioned President Ford for a presidential pardon. On January 19, 1977, in one of his last acts as president, Ford pardoned Toguri and restored her American citizenship.

Iva Toguri is the only American to be pardoned for treason. At the January 2006 celebration at Yoshi's Café, a beaming 89-year-old Toguri looked around the room, the Edward Herlihy Citizenship Award for patriotism draped around her neck. She said, "This is a great honor. I am embarrassed to be able to receive this award, but at the same time I thank you very much. I thank all of the World War II veterans and the World War II Veterans Committee for making this the most memorable day of my life." On September 26, 2006, the 90-year-old American patriot died peacefully. Iva Toguri once said, "I would like to be remembered as confident that one day the truth would be known." She died knowing her wish had come true.

CHAPTER FIVE

Clarence Gideon

The Drifter and the Supreme Court

Photograph by Woody Wisner, courtesy
of the State Archives of Florida

From time to time—with due solemnity, and after much searching of conscience—the [Supreme] Court has overruled its own decisions. Although he did not know it, Clarence Earl Gideon was calling for one of those great occasions in legal history. He was asking the Supreme Court to change its mind.

Anthony Lewis, *Gideon's Trumpet*

*I*t would be hard to find a more unlikely American hero than Clarence Gideon. A four-time felon, Gideon lived on the margins of society. His arrest for burglarizing a pool hall vending machine was an unexceptional event in a town that had more than its share of petty crooks and vagrants. At his trial the judge told the uneducated indigent that he would have to serve as his own counsel. Only in capital offenses, the judge told Gideon, *would the state of Florida provide an attorney to represent him. To no avail Gideon insisted that he had a Constitutional right to a court-appointed defense attorney. His handwritten petition to the Supreme Court from a Florida jail cell set off a chain of events that pitted one of Washington, D.C's most powerful attorneys against a 27-year-old Florida assistant D.A. only two years out of law school. The resulting landmark Supreme Court decision, Gideon v. Wainwright, permanently changed the legal landscape of American courtrooms. Gideon's story is one of grit and determination against incalculable odds, and a saga of resolute belief in the American system of justice.*

On the morning of June 3, 1961, a 51-year-old drifter, Clarence Earl Gideon, sat in a dreary Panama City tavern nursing his breakfast beer. A tap on the shoulder got his attention. It was Panama City deputy sheriff Duell Pitts Jr. The lawman told Gideon to empty his pockets. Accustomed to police shakedowns, Gideon complied: he scooped $25.28 in pennies, nickels, dimes, and quarters from his pants pocket and dumped the change on the bar. Pitts asked him where he got the money. Gideon told him that he had won it in a poker game the previous night.

Pitts didn't buy the alibi. Around 5:30 on the same morning, someone had broken into the Bay Harbor Pool Hall. An eyewitness fingered Gideon as the culprit. Pitts slid the money into a cotton evidence bag, handcuffed Gideon, and charged him with breaking and entering with the intent to commit petty larceny. The insignificant arrest did not merit attention in the daily Panama City newspaper.

In 1961 Elvis was king, John F. Kennedy was president, and cars had fins. Like many other small towns on the Florida Gulf panhandle, Panama City capitalized on its warm waters and sparkling white sands to attract tourists and recreational fishermen. Along the "Redneck Riviera" that stretched from Panama City to Louisiana, an assortment of mom-and-pop motels, efficiencies, and small cottages catered to middle-class white families from Alabama, Mississippi, and Georgia. In Panama City, vacationers toting children mixed with oystermen, shrimpers, and servicemen from nearby Tyndall Air Force Base.

The Panama City boardwalk featured the Hang-Out, a honky-tonk bar where "snowbirds," hustlers, and fisherman sat side by side on barstools swilling cold beer and chomping on fried mullet. At the east end of the boardwalk an amusement park, anchored by a large Ferris wheel, added to the gritty glitz. For the crafty and the energetic there was money to be made. But for Gideon, who preferred poverty in a warm climate to poverty in the cold, the bustling economic oasis of Panama City's tourist attractions shimmered like an enticing mirage—out of reach and unattainable. More scavenger than hunter, he foraged for whatever flotsam of contentment drained into the desolate landscape he roamed.

Gideon lived in Bay Harbor, a bleak assortment of ramshackle buildings and dirt roads adjacent to Panama City. A seedy bar, a pool hall, a flophouse, and a few dilapidated warehouses formed the nucleus of the Bay Harbor landscape. Two massive stacks from an International Paper plant spewed a continuous stench of sulfurous smoke that reeked of chemicals and despair. It was a habitat for losers. The economic engine of Bay Harbor was fueled by cheap drinks and lubricated by quick hustles. Bay Harbor attracted low-life the way an illuminated beer sign attracts moths.

Clarence Earl Gideon peered suspiciously at the world from behind oversized round eyeglasses; he had the worn face of a man 15 years his senior. At the time of his arrest he was sleeping at the six-dollar-a-night Bay Harbor Hotel, just one more loser riding the Bay Harbor treadmill to nowhere. He called Bay Harbor his "Tobacco Road." Gideon's chief survival skill was gambling: he hustled pool and bet on dominoes, but his preferred game was poker. The burglary he was charged with took place at the Bay Harbor Pool Hall, where he frequently ran nickel-ante poker games.

Clarence Gideon grew up in Hannibal, Missouri. His mother and stepfather were strict Baptists. They quarreled frequently, and Gideon was often the object of their wrath. He described his childhood as "miserable." At age 14 he ran away from home and hoboed around the country for a year, traveling as far west as California. When he was 15 he returned to Hannibal and moved in with his uncle. Shortly afterwards his mother had him placed in a detention facility for incorrigible youth. Gideon escaped and roamed the countryside. Homeless and on the lam, young Gideon stole what he needed to survive. A few days after he burglarized a country store for warm clothes, he was apprehended and sentenced to a Missouri juvenile reformatory for three years. It was a cruel place. The whippings the guards administered left him with lifelong scars. Years later Gideon said that, of all the jails and prisons where he did time, the Missouri Reformatory was the worst.

Gideon had ample opportunities to compare penal institutions. From 1928 to 1952 he was incarcerated five times. In 1928, at age 18, he was sentenced to 10 years in the Missouri State Prison for burglary. He was paroled in 1932. Two years later he was convicted of robbing a federal armory and spent more than two years in the Fort Leavenworth, Kansas, prison. From 1937 through 1940 he was in jail again, for burglary. Three years later he escaped and was recaptured after being featured on a "wanted" list in *True Detective* magazine. He was released in 1950 but arrested once again in Orange County, Texas, in 1951. He served 13 months, and was released in early 1953.

A few months later, while working as a cook on a tugboat, the chain-smoking Gideon contracted tuberculosis. The upper lobe of his right lung had to be surgically removed. Between prison stints, he drifted from one menial job to another, drinking and gambling his way through the South and Midwest. He later described himself an "outcast." It was an appropriate sobriquet for a man who lived on the gloomy margins of society.

Gideon married four times. The first three marriages ended in divorce. With his last wife, Ruth Ada Bavineux, he had six children—three of hers plus three of their own. Although unable to provide his children with a stable home, Gideon genuinely cared for his family. During a brief jail stint he served for gambling, his wife took a job working in a local bar; her carousing and drinking led the County Welfare Department to place the children in foster homes. When Gideon was released from jail, he retrieved his kids and joined a Baptist church. In a letter to an attorney several years later Gideon expressed his attempt at a wholesome life:

> I started ever Sunday morning of dressing the children and myself up and going to the Cedar Grove Baptist church at Cedar Grove Florida another of those little municipalities I mention before I believe it is listed as one of the worst speed traps not to be on a major highway by the A.A.A. The people of the church accepted my children with all their heart but me they just tolerated cause they where [sic] mine. My strategy worked my wife decided to go to church with us so I bought her some new clothes and she took a big interest in everything.

A recurrence of tuberculosis required more surgery. While he was in the hospital, his wife quit the church, began drinking again, and moved in with another man. When Gideon was released from the hospital he confronted the two of them, a scene that concluded with yet another arrest, for drunkenness.

After he got out of jail, he left Panama City and took a job in Louisiana cooking on a spud barge. He sent money regularly to his wife. When one of his money orders was returned, he discovered she was in jail for drunken driving and the state had taken his children. When his wife became pregnant by another man, Gideon divorced her. He pleaded with is sister and mother to take in his children, but they refused. He rebuffed the state's child protective service request that he sign release documents so his children could be adopted. Right up to the time he walked into the courtroom on trial for the Bay Harbor Pool Hall burglary, Gideon struggled to reclaim his children. In a rare moment of emotional transparency, he wrote, "Please try to believe that all I want now from my life is the chance for the love of my children, the only real love I have ever had."

At his Panama City arraignment Gideon maintained his innocence. The key prosecution witness, 22-year-old Henry Cook, claimed he saw Gideon burglarizing the pool hall. Cook told police that after a night of carousing with buddies in the nearby town of Apalachicola, he was hanging around the pool hall waiting for it to open. At approximately 5:30 a.m. he heard some noises coming from inside the building. He peered through a window and spotted someone trying to crack open the cigarette machine. Cook identified the intruder as Clarence Gideon.

According to Cook, Gideon pocketed some change, grabbed several bottles of beer, exited the pool hall, and made a call from the corner phone booth. Shortly after, a cab arrived; Gideon hopped in, and it drove away. According to the pool hall owner, Ira Strickland Jr., the burglar stole $65 in change, 12 beers, 12 bottles of Coke, and a bottle of cheap wine.

Gideon did not have funds to post bail. He spent June and July sweltering in a Panama City cell awaiting his trial. The morning of August 4, a handcuffed Gideon entered a plain, windowless courtroom. Facing the bench were two tables—defendant on the right, prosecutor on the left. The jury sat along the wall to the left of the judge's bench, spectators behind a railing that bisected the courtroom. On the day of Gideon's trial, the spectator section was empty. A clerk read the charge: breaking and entering with the intent to commit petty larceny. The crime was a misdemeanor, but Gideon was a four-time felon. If the jury of six found Gideon guilty, the maximum sentence was five years in the state penitentiary.

Judge Robert L. McCrary began by directing Gideon to approach the bench, where he informed him of the charges and asked how he pled. Gideon looked directly at the judge and replied in a firm voice, "Not guilty, Your Honor." Then the judge asked Gideon if he had an attorney. Gideon said that he did not have the money to hire an attorney, and he asked Judge McCrary to appoint counsel to represent him.

Judge McCrary replied, "Mr. Gideon, I am sorry, but I cannot appoint counsel to represent you in this case. Under the laws of the state of Florida, the only time the court can appoint counsel to represent a defendant is when that person is charged with a capital offense. I am sorry, but I will have to deny your request to appoint counsel to defend you in this case."

Gideon looked up at the judge and said, "The United States Supreme Court says I am entitled to be represented by counsel." The judge was unmoved. Again he told Gideon that the state of Florida appointed counsel to indigents only in capital offense cases. Gideon had two choices: plead guilty or defend himself. Dejected, Gideon returned to his seat at the defendant's table.

Despite what Judge McCrary said, Gideon was certain that the Supreme Court guaranteed a poor person the right to an appointed defense counsel. He was wrong. The Sixth Amendment of the Bill of Rights to the Constitution states that the accused shall have "the Assistance of Counsel for his defence [sic]." According to legal authority G.S. Prentzas, "Most states interpreted the right-to-counsel clauses in their state constitutions or state statutes to mean only that defendants had the right to hire a lawyer to argue their case in court." Although the Sixth Amendment provides the right to a defense lawyer, the amendment does not require the government to pay lawyers' fees, just as the Second Amendment guarantees the right to bear arms, but the government does not buy citizens their guns. When Gideon went to trial many states did provide counsel for those who could not afford an attorney, but Florida was not among them.

At the time of Gideon's trial, 7,836 prisoners were incarcerated in Florida. Of those, 5,093 had been tried and sentenced without the benefit of defense counsel. Most were poor. Rather than supporting Gideon's argument that he had a right to a court-appointed attorney, the Supreme Court had ruled just the opposite: in 1942, in *Betts v. Brady*, the Court upheld the practice of states to deny court-appointed counsel for indigent defendants for anything less than a capital crime. In most states, only murder and rape were considered capital offenses; the burglary charge against Gideon didn't qualify. During the 19 years between the *Betts v. Brady* decision and Gideon's trial, the Supreme Court had on several occasions ruled that in "special circumstances," such as a youthful offender or a mentally unstable defendant, states were obliged to provide defense counsel in non-capital cases. But poverty alone as a justification for a court-appointed attorney was not included among those "special circumstances."

Gideon had no option but to try to defend himself. Alone at the defendant's table, with a five-year prison sentence hanging over his head, Gideon tried to piece together his defense. The stress of preparing for trial at a moment's notice must have been overwhelming. In *Gideon's Trumpet* Anthony Lewis described the burden that weighs on a layman forced to defend himself in court: "Probably no one can adequately appreciate the need for a lawyer in a criminal case until he himself is a defendant. The sense of loneliness, the confusion of guilt and outrage, the feeling that one is caught up in a machinery he does not understand—all these emotions well up in a person who finds himself arrested for even a moderately serious traffic offense."

Gideon was hopelessly unqualified to present an adequate defense. A courtroom is no place to sink or swim, and he was in over his head. In 1825 William Rawle, a Philadelphia lawyer, observed, "The most innocent man, pressed by the awful solemnities of public accusation and trial, may be incapable of supporting his own cause. He may be utterly unfit to cross-examine the witnesses against him, to point out the contradictions or defects of their testimony, and to counteract it by properly introducing it applying his own."

Bereft of options or expertise, Gideon forged ahead. He cross-examined the prosecution's key witness, Henry Cook. His inexperience showed when he failed to pursue weaknesses in Cook's testimony. At one point he asked Cook why he was hanging around the pool hall at 5:30 in the morning. Cook replied, "Just come from a dance, down in Apalachicola—stayed out all night."

> Gideon: Do you know positively I was carrying
> a pint of wine?
> Cook: Yes I know you was.
> Gideon: How do you know that?
> Cook: Because I seen it in your hand.
> Gideon: No more questions.

An experienced attorney might have followed up with pointed questions that would cast suspicion on Cook as the culprit, but Gideon dismissed the witness.

He called eight witnesses for his defense. None provided testimony that helped his case. His decision to put Henry Berryhill Jr., the officer who discovered the break-in, and the arresting officer, deputy sheriff Duell Pitts Jr., on the stand as defense witnesses baffled the jury. In his summation Gideon talked for 11 minutes, and prosecutor William Harris for nine minutes. No transcripts for the trial exist to document what either of them said. After a brief deliberation, the jury found Gideon guilty of breaking and entering with the intent to commit petty larceny.

Three weeks later Judge McCrary handed down the maximum sentence: five years to be served in the state penitentiary in Raiford, Florida. Gideon shuffled out of the courtroom in handcuffs. Shoulders slumped and eyes downcast, he looked every bit a beaten man. But he was unbowed in spirit. He still believed the Supreme Court guaranteed him the right to counsel, and he intended to do something about it. The gambler who bet on long shots his entire life had one more to play.

On January 8, 1962, Michael Rodak Jr., an assistant clerk of the U.S. Supreme Court, pulled an 8" x 12" envelope out of the morning mail. The return address was Clarence Earl Gideon, prisoner No. 003826, P.O. Box 221, Raiford, Florida. It was a petition, printed meticulously in pencil on yellow prison stationary. Gideon asked that his Florida conviction be overturned. Before the Supreme Court will hear a case, a petitioner must first follow his state's appeal procedure. A few months earlier Gideon had petitioned the Florida Supreme Court requesting a writ of habeas corpus. He appealed for release from detention because he was unable to hire counsel at his trial. The Florida Supreme Court rejected the request. However, Gideon's habeas corpus appeal fulfilled the Supreme Court requirement that relief must first be sought through the defendant's state legal system.

At the top of his petition Gideon identified H.G. Cochran Jr., Director of Florida Corrections, as the respondent. The appeal began:

> *Petitioner submits that the Supreme Court of the United States has the authority and the jurisdiction to review the final judgement [sic] of the Supreme Court of Florida the highest court of the State under sec. 344 (B) Title 28 U.S.C.A. and because the "due process clause" of the Fourteenth Amendment of the constitution and the fifth and sixth articales [sic] of the Bill of rights has been violated.*

Gideon summed up his appeal with the following statement:

> *When at the time of the petitioner's trial he asked the lower court for the aid of counsel, the court refused this aid. Petitioner told the court that this court had made*

> *a decision to the effect that all citizens tried for a felony*
> *crime should have the aid of counsel. The lower court*
> *ignored this plea.*

Crafting a petition to the U.S. Supreme Court requires legal acumen typically beyond the grasp of an uneducated drifter. It is probable Gideon had help. Soon after his incarceration in Raiford, Gideon met a fellow prisoner, former Palm Beach municipal court judge Joseph Peel. Peel, who once had aspirations to run for governor, was serving a life sentence for the murder of a Florida circuit judge, Curtis E. Chillingsworth, and his wife, Marjorie. Peel killed Chillingsworth because the circuit judge intended to inform the Palm Beach attorney general that Peel and an accomplice, Floyd (Lucky) Holzapfel, were extorting $3,000 a week from gamblers and moonshiners. Holzapfel and Peel abducted the Chillingsworths, tied them up with lead weights, took them four miles out to sea, and dumped them overboard. Neither Gideon nor Peel acknowledged that they collaborated in preparing the petition.

Gideon's *in forma pauperis* petition, which allows a judge to appoint an attorney and waive court fees for an individual unable to pay for counsel, was one of nine such petitions delivered to the Supreme Court on January 8. Gideon's petition was assigned number 890 in the Miscellaneous docket. This category was used primarily for prisoner petitions; 889 Miscellaneous petitions were on file ahead of Gideon's. The Supreme Court received a total of approximately 2500 petitions each year, and, on average, the Court winnowed this number down to 150 for review. The odds did not favor Gideon, but his argument did. Several of the nine judges on the Court believed it was time to overturn the 1942 *Betts v. Brady* decision, but they needed the right case. Gideon's petition served that purpose.

The Supreme Court reviews state laws when there is a legal challenge based on Constitutional principles. Consequently, most state court rulings are never challenged in federal courts. But Gideon based his appeal on the fact that his Constitutional rights were violated—specifically the Sixth and Fourteenth Amendments. It was the Constitutional issue that put Gideon's appeal within the jurisdiction of the Supreme Court. So far, Gideon's petition had smooth sailing, but it still needed to navigate around the shoals of states' rights.

In the summer of 1787, 55 delegates from the 13 states met in Philadelphia to draw up a blueprint for a new nation. George Washington was disinclined to immerse himself in what would surely be a political imbroglio, but he reluctantly agreed to preside. The challenge was immense. The delegates' only democratic model for building a nation was the British system, against which they had just rebelled. After experiencing the oppression of British authority, many Americans wanted a de-centralized system with governmental power residing principally within the individual states. From the very beginning of the convention, any proposal for a strong central government was a lightning rod for debate.

During the convention, conditions inside Independence Hall were insufferable. The summer days were hot and muggy, and swarms of mosquitoes and bluebottle flies forced the delegates to keep the windows shut tight. The only concession to delegate comfort was the dirt spread over nearby cobblestone streets to soften the sounds of passing carriages. Tempers flared often as delegates, entrenched in their positions, debated the fate of the new nation. Cautiously, Washington led them through a minefield of political intrigue and dispute.

Delegates waged a bitter struggle over how much control should reside in the federal government. The Federalists, including James Madison, Alexander Hamilton, and John Adams, advocated a strong centralized government. Federalists argued that the union could not survive without executive, legislative, and judicial powers. Moreover, Federalists maintained that the new nation needed a standing army and navy, a national treasury, a national debt, and federal taxes to pay the bills.

But, having just completed a bloody civil war against British control, the so-called "anti-Federalists" were in no mood to surrender the right of individual states to self-government. Prior to the Constitutional Convention, the states functioned as a confederacy of loosely tied independent provinces. Individual states printed their own money, set tariffs on imports, and established customs duties. Led by Thomas Jefferson, Patrick Henry, Samuel Adams, and James Monroe, the anti-Federalists feared that a strong central government would swallow up the states, destroying the people's right to self-determination. Alexander Hamilton galvanized anti-Federalist opposition when he proposed early in the convention that a chief executive should serve for life and wield absolute veto power. The anti-Federalist position was rock-hard on one point: a powerful centralized government was the ultimate threat to individual liberty. "Government is best which governs least," often attributed to Jefferson, aptly summarized the anti-Federalist position.

On December 15, 1791, three-quarters of the states ratified the final document. A negotiated balance between Federalists and anti-Federalists saved the nation in what some historians describe as the "second American Revolution." The Constitution is actually two documents. The preamble and original seven articles represented the Federalist position, asserting federal power over the states. The seven articles established the executive, legislative, and judicial branches of government; made provision for the common rights of citizens in all the states; and gave guidelines for dealing with treason, statehood, and future amendments.

The Bill of Rights—the first 10 amendments—was added later as a concession to the anti-Federalists, who believed the seven articles of the Constitution were vague and could lead to tyrannical abuse. In an address to the Virginia legislature, Patrick Henry expressed his disdain for the "checks and balances" outlined in the first seven articles: "What can avail your specious, imaginary balances, your rope-dancing, chain-rattling, ridiculous ideal checks and contrivances?" Richard Henry Lee and other anti-Federalists wanted a concise description of limits on federal powers that would infringe on the inalienable rights of citizens. Exchanging the old government for the new without such a bill of rights, Lee argued, would be trading "Scylla for Charybdis."

The Bill of Rights put explicit limits on the power of the federal government. The 10 amendments provided assurance that the federal government could not curb such fundamental rights as freedom of speech, freedom of religion, and freedom of the press—inalienable rights of citizens that were provided for in the constitutions and laws of the individual states. The amendment that pertained to Gideon's case—the Sixth Amendment right to counsel —insured that the accused had the right to be represented by counsel in federal courts. For the next 142 years, in most states, the right to counsel was interpreted to mean the accused had a right to defense counsel *if* he could afford it. Then, in 1932, a Supreme Court decision that began with a fight in a railroad boxcar set off a seismic shift in the legal terrain that separated federal and states' rights.

On March 25, 1931, nine black youths, aged 12 to 19, were riding the rails in a Southern Railway freight car traveling from Chattanooga to Memphis, Tennessee. Hoboing on trains was common during the Depression. Some train jumpers were looking for jobs; others were searching for adventure to offset their bleak lives. The youngsters were hoping to find jobs hauling logs on the Mississippi River. Also in the car were a group of white youths and two young white women returning from Chattanooga after an unsuccessful attempt to land jobs in a cotton mill. A fight broke out when one of the white youths inadvertently stepped on the hand of Haywood Patterson, one of the black youths.

The brawl ended when the train slowed and the blacks tossed all but one of the white boys off the train. The women remained.

The white youths walked to Stevenson, Alabama. They told the Stevenson stationmaster that a gang of blacks had assaulted them. The stationmaster telegraphed ahead to Paint Rock, Alabama. When the train arrived, dozens of armed men apprehended the black youths. The two white women in the freight car, Ruby Bates, aged 17, and Victoria Price, aged 20, claimed they were raped—a capital offense in Alabama.

The posse tied the nine black youths with plow line, threw them on the back of a flatbed truck, and transported them to the jail in Scottsboro. In 1932 a black male accused of raping a white woman in the South might not live long enough to go to trial. A local newspaper headline read: "All Negroes Positively Identified By Girls And One White Boy Who Was Held Prisoner With Pistol And Knives While Nine black Fiends Committed Revolting Crime." The next day an estimated mob of 8,000 swarmed the narrow streets of the town. A lynching seemed imminent. Sheriff Matt Wann called the governor, who in turn ordered the National Guard to Scottsboro. The next day a contingent of 118 Guardsmen, commanded by Major John Stearns, set up a perimeter of six machine guns on the courthouse lawn.

The spectacle of National Guardsmen holding a lynch mob at bay in the Deep South attracted the media like shark to chum. Dubbed the "Scottsboro Boys" by the newspapers, the nine young men became an international sensation. Albert Einstein petitioned for their release. Clarence Darrow volunteered to defend them. A national debate about whether nine black males accused of raping a white woman would get a fair trial in Alabama fueled the controversy.

The Scottsboro Boys were split up and tried in four separate trials over four-and-a-half days. Judge Hawkins asked the Alabama bar to provide counsel for the youth. The only volunteer was 69-year-old Milo Moody, who had not represented a defendant in a criminal case in years. Reluctantly assisting Moody was a Chattanooga attorney and real estate salesman, Stephan Roddy.

Citing the hostile environment, Roddy asked the judge for a change of venue. His request was denied. According to Judge Hawkins, the crowds were neither threatening nor intimidating, merely curious. In a *Stetson Law Review* article, attorney Bruce Jacob described the legal sham:

> Because it was a capital case, the defendants were entitled, under Alabama statutory law, to the appointment of counsel. The trial judge, however, did not appoint a specific lawyer to represent each individual defendant. Instead, the judge appointed "all the members of the bar" of the county to represent the defendants as a group. And since the appointment was indefinite, with no lawyer specifically assigned to provide a defense for any particular defendant, it was easy for the lawyers to do very little. None of the lawyers in the county took responsibility for providing more than a token defense.

One trial followed the other in quick succession. Inflammatory statements like Victoria Price's testimony revved up emotions. "There were six to me and three to her…. It took three of them to hold me. One was holding my legs and the other had a knife to my throat while the other one ravished me." Verdicts and trials overlapped. The jury for one trial was sent out of the courtroom when the jury for the previous trial presented its verdict. The first trial lasted a day and a half. The jury took two hours to deliberate. The first two defendants, Clarence Norris and Charlie Weems, were found guilty and sentenced to the electric chair.

When the crowd outside the courthouse heard the verdict they broke into cheers and sang "There'll Be a Hot Time in the Old Town Tonight." The remaining six defendants, who could neither read nor write, were tried on the following three days.

Each was found guilty and sentenced to electrocution on July 10, 1931, the earliest possible date under Alabama law. Twelve-year-old Roy Wright's trial ended in a mistrial: the verdict was guilty, and seven jurors wanted the death penalty, but the other five argued for life imprisonment because of Wright's age.

In January 1932, an appeal to the Alabama Supreme Court upheld all but one of the eight death sentences. The International Labor Defense Group (the legal name of the American Communist Party) retained attorney Walter Pollak to submit an appeal to the U.S. Supreme Court. On October 10, 1932, the case *Powell v. Alabama* was argued in the Court. In a 7–2 decision, the Supreme Court ruled in favor of the Scottsboro Boys. According to the court, the accused had a fundamental right to counsel for a capital offense. The speed of the trial, the hostile environment, and the ad hoc appointment of counsel violated their due process rights. For the first time in history, the Supreme Court reversed a state criminal conviction because of unfair trial practices. The Court based its decision on the Fourteenth Amendment due process clause. In writing for the majority, Justice Sutherland detailed the Court's reasoning:

> Even the intelligent and educated layman has small and sometimes no skill in the science of law. If charged with crimes, he is incapable, generally, of determining for himself whether the indictment is good or bad. He is unfamiliar with the rules of evidence. Left without aid of counsel he may be put on trial without a proper charge, and convicted upon incompetent evidence....

The Court limited its ruling to capital crimes when the defendant is unable to employ counsel and is unable to present his own defense because of such mitigating factors as feeble-mindedness or illiteracy. However, the Scottsboro decision did not affect either one of the defining characteristics of Gideon's case: *too poor to pay for counsel* and *non-capital offense*. Yet the precedent of the U.S. Supreme Court reversing a state court's decision on Constitutional grounds had been set. Further Supreme Court decisions were needed to nudge the legal pendulum in Gideon's direction. Twenty-two years before Gideon stood before a Florida judge and demanded a lawyer, an itinerant Maryland farm worker made the same plea.

In 1938 a local farmhand was arrested and charged with robbing a drug store on Christmas Eve in Hagerstown, Maryland. Eyewitnesses fingered a man named Smith Betts as the culprit. His take was $51. This was not Betts's first run-in with the law. In 1935 he had been sentenced to two concurrent three-year jail terms for stealing chickens. At the time of his trial he was also under investigation for pilfering six sets of harnesses from a Pennsylvania farmer. Betts requested an attorney, claiming he was too poor to hire one himself. The judge informed Betts that in the state of Maryland the court appointed defense attorneys only for capital offenses such as rape or murder. Betts was forced to defend himself. Predictably, Betts's defense was inadequate, and he was convicted. In view of his prior record (and perhaps because the drug store was owned by a retired state senator), Betts was sentenced to eight years in the state penitentiary.

Betts filed an appeal with the Maryland Court of Appeals. Chief Justice Carroll T. Bond denied it, ruling that the appointment of counsel for crimes in Maryland is not guaranteed by the Constitution. Judge Bond said that only in a case of "peculiar helplessness" or "peculiar urgency" would a Maryland judge appoint free counsel in a non-capital trial. While there might be circumstances such as illiteracy or mental incompetence that would persuade a Maryland judge to provide a defense attorney, Betts did not meet those criteria. In the view of the court he was a man of "ordinary intelligence," and the fact that he could not afford an attorney was not a valid legal argument.

Betts's appeal was rejected, but the principle behind a person's right to a fair trial was too important to go away. With the backing of the American Civil Liberties Union (ACLU), Betts petitioned the Supreme Court. The Court heard his case on April 13, 1942. The ACLU attorneys representing Betts argued that the petitioner was appealing his guilty verdict on the premise that denial of counsel had deprived him of his due process rights under the Fourteenth Amendment, which states:

> No State shall make or enforce any law which shall abridge the Privileges or immunities of the citizens of the United States; nor shall any State deprive any person of life, liberty or property, without due process of law; nor deny to any person within its jurisdiction the equal protection of laws.

In a 6–3 decision the Court ruled that non-capital defendants in state courts did *not* have a right to court-appointed counsel under the due process provision of the Fourteenth Amendment. In writing for the majority, Chief Justice Owen Roberts said:

> [W]hile the want of counsel in a particular case may result in a conviction lacking in such fundamental fairness, we cannot say that the [Fourteenth] Amendment embodies an inexorable command that no trial for any offense, or in any court, can be fairly conducted and justice accorded a defendant who is not represented by counsel.

What Roberts was saying in the inflated prose that seeps into legal reasoning was that, in non-capital cases within state jurisdiction, a defendant is capable of presenting his defense without counsel, and the appointment of counsel is not a fundamental

Constitutional right. Roberts pointed out that Betts had a prior criminal record and that he was familiar with court procedures. Requiring state courts to appoint a defense counsel for everyone who claimed poverty would put an unreasonable burden on the courts. There was more than just the trial to consider; there were indictments, conferences, research, and appeals. Where did one draw the line? If the court provided an attorney for a man arrested for a felony, what about someone arrested for a traffic violation, shoplifting, or any misdemeanor? The Supreme Court decision in *Betts v. Brady* revolved around one key point: the appointment of counsel is not a fundamental right essential to a fair trial.

Associate Justice Hugo Black did not agree. In his dissenting opinion, Justice Black wrote, "Denial to the poor of the request of counsel in proceedings based on charges of serious crime has long been regarded as shocking to 'the universal sense of justice' throughout the country." Dismay over the denial of an attorney for a poor man's defense was not limited to judicial dissent. Writing in the *New York Times*, Benjamin Cohen and Erwin N. Griswold, both noted legal experts, said,

> The decision in *Betts v. Brady* comes at a singularly inopportune time. Throughout the world men are fighting to be free from the fear of political trials and concentration camps. From this struggle men are hoping that a bill of rights will emerge which will guarantee to all men certain fundamental rights.... Most Americans lawyers and laymen alike before the decision in *Betts v. Brady* would have thought that the right of the accused to counsel in a serious criminal case was unquestionably a part of our own Bill of Rights.

While the *Betts v. Brady* decision struck many as patently unfair to those unable to afford counsel, the decision opened the door to a slew of Supreme Court appeals based on the following remark by Chief Justice Roberts in his opinion in *Betts v. Brady*:

> The due process clause of the Fourteenth Amendment does not incorporate, as such, the specific guarantees found in the Sixth Amendment, although a denial by a State of rights or privileges specifically embodied in that and the others of the first eight Amendments may, in certain circumstances, and in the light of other considerations, fall short of such a denial.

For the next 20 years, the Supreme Court grappled with dozens of appeals based on "special circumstances," and in most cases the decisions favored the plaintiff. Special circumstances cited in Supreme Court decisions for plaintiffs included feeble-mindedness, inability to understand the English language, unfamiliarity with court procedures, and illiteracy.

Overarching the Betts decision was the fundamental Constitutional issue of states' rights. In their 6–3 *Betts v. Brady* ruling, the Supreme Court reaffirmed that the Sixth Amendment guaranteed counsel in noncapital crimes only in federal courts. In the minds of many conservatives, to rule otherwise would have exceeded the right of the federal government to meddle in the ways states went about enforcing their criminal laws. Associate Justice Felix Frankfurter expressed the views of many advocates of states' rights when, following the Betts decision, he said, "The federal judiciary has no power to sit in judgment upon a determination of a state court.... Something that thus goes to the very structure of our federal system in its distribution of power between the United States and the state is not a mere bit of red tape to be cut...."

Betts v. Brady reaffirmed the states' rights principle, but the Supreme Court was ready for a change. The plethora of "special circumstances" was adding confusion rather than clarity to court proceedings. Between 1942 and the Gideon decision in 1963, the administration of the "special circumstances" provision had become so cumbersome that, by 1962, the majority of states had put in place provisions for appointed counsel for indigent defendants without the need to prove "special circumstances." Only five states—Alabama, North Carolina, Mississippi, South Carolina, and Florida—still used "special circumstances" as a guideline for determining whether the court should appoint a lawyer to represent a defendant in a felony case. The Supreme Court was ready to overrule *Betts v. Brady*, and Gideon's wildcard petition was the game-changer the justices had been waiting for.

On the afternoon of Monday, January 14, 1962, in the chamber of the United States Supreme Court the Court Crier struck his gavel on a wooden block and announced, "Oyez, oyez, oyez. All persons having business before the Supreme Court of the United States are admonished to draw near and give their attention, for the Court is now sitting. God save the United States and this honorable Court."

The nine justices—Chief Justice Earl Warren and associate judges Arthur Goldberg, Potter Stewart, John Harlan, William Douglas, Hugo Black, Tom Clark, William Brennan, and Byron White—clothed in black judicial robes filed into the chamber. They entered in threes and settled in black leather chairs customized to each judge's size and preference. Chief Justice Warren sat in the center. The associate justices spread out to his left and right; seniority determined their proximity to the Chief Justice. They took their seats behind a gleaming mahogany bench that faced the attorneys' tables and the audience.

The justices gazed out at an impressive sight. Directly across the courtroom, towering mahogany doors provided entry for attorneys and spectators. The ceiling rose 44 feet above a floor of polished Alabama oak. Marble friezes of Hammurabi, Moses, Charlemagne, King John, and John Marshall bordered the chamber. Red tapestries trimmed with gold tassels hung along the walls. At regular intervals 24 stately Ionic marble columns encircled the room.

Attorneys sat at two mahogany tables facing the judicial bench; between them was a single lectern, where each side would stand and present its case. A mahogany railing separated the public seating from the area reserved for court proceedings. During the Gideon appeal two officials sat on either side of the justices' bench. To the left, the Clerk of the Court administered the court dockets. To the right, the Marshall of the Court alternated white and red lights to signal time limits to the attorneys: each had 30 minutes to present his brief.

Because Gideon's petition was *in forma pauperis,* the court appointed Abe Fortas to represent him. Fortas was a successful Washington attorney who would one day become a Supreme Court Justice himself. Representing the state of Florida was a young Florida assistant attorney general, Bruce Jacob. The backgrounds and styles of the two attorneys could not have been more different.

Abe Fortas was a veteran Washington, D.C., insider. Throughout his career he had a knack for befriending the rich and powerful. Shortly after he graduated—second in his class—from Yale Law School in 1933, one his professors, William O. Douglas, helped Fortas gain an appointment as an assistant professor at his alma mater. When Douglas was appointed to head the U.S. Securities and Exchange Commission, he brought Fortas along as an advisor. During the Franklin D. Roosevelt administration, Fortas worked at the Department of the Interior, where the Secretary of the Interior, Harold L. Ickes, introduced him to a young congressman, Lyndon B. Johnson. The two became fast friends, and throughout Johnson's political career Fortas was a key advisor. In 1946 Fortas co-founded the law firm of Arnold, Fortas & Porter, which became one of the largest and most respected within the beltway. Two years after the Gideon hearing, President

Johnson appointed Fortas to the Supreme Court, where he built a reputation as an advocate of children's and students' rights.

Fortas was an accomplished violinist (in Memphis they called him "Fiddlin' Abe"). He had a piercing gaze and an agile legal mind, two important qualities for a courtroom attorney. He was often described as "feisty." According to his biographer Bruce Allen Murphy:

> Nothing in Abe Fortas' physical appearance gave promise of things to come. He was small and slightly built, with hands that struck people as being so delicate that they belonged on a china doll. He always looked younger than his years, with his smooth dark face and deep-set oversized hazel eyes, framed by two huge protruding ears that resembled saucers turned on their edges. People were struck by the young man's temperament. Disarmingly modest, with a rather sticky sweet, quiet sense of politeness, Fortas appeared to be almost too serious. "I wish he'd laugh more," an associate later said. It was not that he didn't have a sense of humor. But he resorted to a dry, puckish wit too sparingly for people to think of him as anything other than businesslike. He seemed to cut through life like a boat that slips through water without leaving a wake, and those ears missed nothing."

The wily Fortas knew that it took more than an incisive legal argument to win a Supreme Court decision; it took votes. But he also believed that a case of this magnitude needed a convincing mandate. Fortas wanted to pitch a shutout—he wanted a unanimous decision in favor of Gideon. Later he explained:

> An advocate usually thinks about winning a case
> and doesn't give a damn whether he wins by
> five-four or some other vote. But in this case—a
> constitutional case of fundamental importance,
> and with political overtones in terms of federal-
> state relations—it seemed to me the responsibility
> was not just to try to win the case but to get as
> many justices as possible to go along with what I
> considered the right result. If you assume *Betts v.*
> *Brady* was going to be overruled, it was right for
> the institution of the Supreme Court, and for the
> law, to have as much unanimity as possible.

Fortas was the right man, at the right place, at the right time. It was 20 years since the "special circumstances" provision in *Betts v. Brady* had generated a veritable cottage industry of Supreme Court appeals. As he weighed his chances of a unanimous decision, Fortas calculated he could count on five votes—Chief Justice Warren and Associate Justices Black, Douglas, Goldberg, and Brennan—and he thought Justice Stewart could be convinced to vote for Gideon. Justices Clark and White were question marks. Clark had written the Court's last dissent in a right-to-counsel case, but later on he had voted to outlaw illegal evidence in a search-and-seizure case—*Mapp v. Ohio*.

The newest justice, Byron "Whizzer" White, an All-American halfback and professional football star, had recently replaced Justice Whittaker; having served only two months as a Justice, he was an unknown quantity. Justice Frankfurter had resigned shortly before the Gideon appeal. In chambers, when the justices discussed whether or not to hear a case, Frankfurter had vigorously opposed Gideon's petition for *certiorari*—a writ or order in which a higher court reviews a decision of a lower court. Frankfurter's departure meant Justice Harlan could be the standard bearer for denying Gideon's petition.

While not as strident a states' rights advocate as Frankfurter, John Harlan, the grandson of a Supreme Court Justice, was a strong believer in judicial restraint. In a 1963 speech he criticized the notion that "all deficiencies in our society which failed of correction by other means should find a cure in the courts." Harlan rarely voted in favor of limiting state criminal procedures. If Harlan anchored the conservative wing of the Court, Fortas's hope for a unanimous decision was unlikely.

While Fortas counted votes in anticipation of victory, his opponent, Bruce Jacob, faced an uphill struggle. Jacob was a tall, blond 26-year-old assistant to the attorney general in Tallahassee. He had been practicing law for only two years when in March 1962, Judge Reeves Bowen, the head of Criminal Appeals asked him to prepare the state's case in Gideon. The selection of such a young and inexperienced assistant district attorney to present Florida's case before the Supreme Court raised some eyebrows, but Jacob saw nothing special in his selection:

> Some have speculated that as the newest and youngest lawyer in the office, I was made the 'fall guy' or 'sacrificial lamb' in an obviously losing cause that no one else wanted to handle. This is not true. One of the possible reasons why Judge Bowen chose me was that he and each of the other lawyers in our office had already briefed and argued cases before the Supreme Court. I was the only one had not done so, and therefore, it was my turn.

Moreover, Judge Bowen had taken an interest in the young Jacob. They spent evenings together discussing cases, and Bowen believed that Jacob had the tools to present a strong brief on behalf of the state of Florida. Jacob had no illusions about his chances of winning the case, but at the same time the opportunity to argue a case before the Supreme Court was an honor in its own right.

Each attorney had 30 days to prepare his brief—the written document an attorney presents to the Court outlining the points and rationale behind his argument. Attorneys exchange briefs before a hearing, giving each an opportunity to argue pre-trial motions. Fortas wanted the transcript of Gideon's trial included in the record presented to the Court, while Jacob contended that it had not been included in his Florida Supreme Court appeal and thus was not part of the official record. In October, the Supreme Court denied Jacob's motion to strike the trial transcript, and Fortas included it in his brief. Jacob had lost the first round, and time was running short. He received the Fortas brief on November 24; he had until Christmas to file his response, and he still had his oral argument to prepare by January 14.

Jacob had a lot to do in a short time, and there were other complications in his life. In June he had accepted a new position with the law firm of Holland, Bevis & Smith, one of the most prestigious in Florida. The attorney general agreed to permit Jacob to continue to represent Florida's case even though he was no longer an assistant attorney general. Jacob promised his new employers that he would do his research on the Gideon case only after hours. From mid-March, assisted by his wife, Ann (they had married in September), Jacob spent evenings preparing his case. He was unable to capitalize on the resources of the attorney general's office in Tallahassee because he and Ann had moved to Bartow, Florida, two hundred and fifty miles away. Jacob was basically on his own:

> During the final three months in 1962, I would leave the law office at 5:00 or 5:30 p.m., and go home for supper. After supper Ann and I would drive to the old county courthouse in the center of Bartow, a block north of our law offices. The

librarian gave me the keys to the main door of
the courthouse and to the county law library on
the east side of the third floor of that historic
building. I would do research there until 11:00
p.m. or 12:00 a.m., and Ann would copy excerpts
from appellate cases onto four-by-six inch cards
in longhand whenever we thought them worthy
of being preserved for later use.

In June, before he left the attorney general's office, Jacob
had sent a letter to attorneys general in other states notifying
them of the upcoming case, and asking them to consider joining
him in a written statement supporting Florida's position (amicus
curiae). Jacob knew that many states had already passed statutes
providing legal counsel for indigents, but he also believed that, if
the Supreme Court ruled in favor of Gideon, the decision could
have serious repercussions for all the states. For instance, if the
Court decided to make the law retroactive, how far back would it
go? Would thousands of prisoners be released? Would defendants
charged with misdemeanors such as traffic violations have the
right to a court-appointed attorney?

Only two states, Alabama and North Carolina, supported
Florida, while 22 states filed amicus briefs in support of Gideon.
Jacob knew that his requests for support were a long shot, but
he took offense when some suggested that the letters were a
misguided strategy:

> It certainly would have been pleasing if more
> than two states had joined in an amicus brief in
> our behalf, but for anyone to suggest that our
> 'strategy' had backfired missed the point. I was
> neither thinking in terms of a 'strategy,' nor was
> I trying to 'win' the case when the letter to the
> other Attorneys General was sent. My goal was

221

to make sure the other states knew what was happening and what was at stake in Gideon, and that they were given an opportunity to become involved if they wished to do so. In my view, 'strategy' has no place before the Supreme Court in a case as important as Gideon. The job of the lawyer in such a case was not to prevail through strategy, but instead to prepare the case honestly and thoroughly and to help the Court reach the best possible result for everyone.

While Jacob spent his evenings crisscrossing Florida searching for documentation to support his brief, Fortas had the luxury of utilizing the resources of his prestigious law firm. John Hart Ely, a summer associate from Yale Law School, worked on the case for two months. Ely pored over law reviews searching for opinions and case histories that would buttress the Gideon appeal. He found that the Florida courts almost always used the Betts decision to turn down defendant requests for counsel. On the other hand, in four cases since 1959 the Supreme Court had reversed the Florida decisions upon appeal. In his report he wrote: "The fact that the United States Supreme Court has reversed the Florida Supreme Court in four right-to-counsel cases suggests that the two courts have different ideas as to how the factors should be balanced."

Ely concluded that the discrepancy in interpretation of "special circumstances" was based on the multitude of ways that the Supreme Court defined the term. The plethora of different circumstances put the burden on a trial judge to determine who should get a court-appointed attorney and who should not. The constant review of state court decisions by the Supreme Court strained the resources at both the state and federal levels. It was time for the Supreme Court to stop applying bandages to a failing patient. Betts needed to be euthanized.

Although compelling as an argument, the "special circumstances" mélange did not give Fortas the knock-out punch he needed for a unanimous decision. He wanted a constitutional victory, not simply one more link added to a chain of "special circumstances" that stretched back two decades. The Betts decision affirmed that the Fourteenth Amendment's due process provision would apply to non-capital crimes only if special circumstances warranted an appointed counsel. In writing for the majority, Justice Owen Roberts had said that rights under the Fourteenth Amendment were more fluid and less stringent than under the Sixth Amendment right to counsel, and that "appointment of counsel is not a fundamental right essential for a fair trial." Fortas wanted to persuade all nine Supreme Court Justices that Chief Justice Roberts had been wrong.

On Saturday, January 12, 1963, Bruce and Ann Jacob took a red-eye flight to Washington. Oral arguments for *Gideon v. Wainwright* were scheduled for the next day. (Louie L. Wainwright represented Florida because he had taken Cochran's place as director of corrections.) It was a bumpy ride in an old prop plane, and Jacob got airsick. Still in preparation mode for his big day before the Supreme Court, he lugged 35 case-books along with their personal baggage. At the hotel, Jacob had a final meeting with George Mentz, the Alabama assistant attorney general who would deliver an amicus brief before the Court. The next morning Jacob, his wife, and Mentz walked into the marbled chamber of the U.S. Supreme Court. Bruce Jacob, the young attorney, licensed for only three years, was about to have the experience of a lifetime.

What he encountered was entirely unexpected. The judges sat in their black leather chairs perched above the courtroom floor. The chair for Justice White, the ex-football star, was enormous; the diminutive Justice Black sat in a chair only half its size. The justices were in the midst of reading opinions for previous cases. It was clear that the presentation of oral arguments in the Gideon case was going to be delayed until the next day. The justices briefly discontinued their monologues to allow Chief Justice Warren to swear Jacob in as a member of the Bar of the Supreme Court. Then the opinion readings resumed and continued for the rest of the day. The air of informality astonished the young attorney.

> [T]he Justices would send notes to court pages, and the pages would would come in and out of the court delivering messages or carrying books to the Justices. Sometimes, a Justice would get up from his chair and leave. At one point, Justice White whirled around and faced away from the audience. Justice Douglas wrote feverishly for some time and, when he finished, he began licking envelopes and pounding the envelopes shut with his fist…. Justice Potter Stewart looked out into the audience and began combing his hair with his fingers, looking straight ahead as if looking into a mirror.

Jacob had expected to see Fortas in the courtroom, but he was absent. Evidently the veteran attorney knew that the Court would not be hearing their arguments that day. The next day, Tuesday, the Court had two cases before them—*White Motor Company v. United States* and *Gideon v. Wainwright*.

Meanwhile, 700 miles south of the majestic courtroom, Gideon sat in a prison cell and waited. His successful Supreme Court petition had elevated his status among both prisoners and prison officials. The fact that a Gideon victory might spark the release of hundreds if not thousands of fellow prisoners was fine with the assistant warden, who said, "Our feeling is: Boys, if you can get out of here legal, we're with you."

Gideon's petition was big news. Anticipating a landmark Supreme Court decision, Pulitzer Prize-winning author Anthony

Lewis traveled to Raiford for an interview. The prison was not altogether an unpleasant place. Trusty prisoners, Gideon included, dressed in white fatigues and, when not in their cells were free to move around manicured green lawns bordered by shrubs and flowers. During the interview Lewis and Gideon sat at a long table in a plainly furnished prisoner "office." While he rolled cigarettes with nicotine-stained fingers, Gideon discussed his role as jailhouse lawyer

> There's no real lawyers in here now. I guess I know more than most, and I help out. I have one boy in here that can't read or write. I wrote a letter to the Supreme Court of Florida for him asking them to appoint an attorney to write him a petition for habeas corpus. They accepted the letter as a petition and denied it without a hearing, so I wrote the whole thing over and sent it to the Supreme Court of the U.S.

Gideon felt a great deal of satisfaction about his Supreme Court appeal. When Lewis asked him why he persevered in his fight to obtain a defense attorney, he replied:

> I knew that was my only chance.... I don't know if you've ever been in one of those courtrooms, but the prejudice is obvious. In this state—except for Dade County [Miami], in Dade County they go by the books—they just run over people who have nothing. I've never taken the witness stand in this case, nobody knows what I'd say. Without a lawyer, with the criminal record I had, what I'd have said they'd never have paid attention to.

Gideon's determined belief that a poor man had a right to an attorney earned him his day before the Supreme Court; now it was up to Abe Fortas to prove him right.

On the morning of January 15, 1963, Fortas stood before the lectern and addressed the nine judges. In measured sentences tinged with a Southern drawl, Fortas outlined the case. His key point was simple and direct: *Betts v. Brady* needed to be overturned because no layman can be expected to conduct a trial in his own defense. Fortas pointed out that Clarence Darrow, considered by many to be the most talented attorney in American jurisprudence history, hired a lawyer when he faced charges of jury tampering.

Almost immediately Fortas encountered his first hurdle— Justice Harlan. Fortas was not surprised. Harlan was the most likely of the judges to raise objections based on the principle that states had the right to set their own legal guidelines for conducting criminal trials. Fortas was prepared to handle this objection by arguing that the Fourteenth Amendment requires a fair trial, and you cannot have a fair trial without adequate defense counsel.

In the quirky world of political terminology "federalism" had morphed from a belief in a strong central government to the opposite—a belief that the federal government, particularly the judicial branch, should be limited in its power to influence state laws. When preparing his brief, Fortas commented to his research assistant, John Ely, that he wished he could bring the justices into a courtroom to watch a defendant try to represent his own case. Now he used Harlan's probing about federalism as an opportunity to introduce the human element into an otherwise abstract legal discussion. Fortas said:

> I may be wrong about this, but I do believe that
> in some of this Court's decisions there has been a
> tendency from time to time, because of the pull
> of federalism…, to forget the realities of what
> happens downstairs, of what happens to these poor,

indigent people when they are arrested and they are brought into the jail and they are questioned and later on they are brought in these strange and awesome circumstances before a magistrate, and told, 'Clarence Earl Gideon, defend yourself'.... But I think that in some of the Court's opinions, if I may say so, Mr. Justice Harlan, this element, this failure to remember what happens downstairs, has crept in.... I don't think that the argument of federalism here is either correct or soundly founded or stands the test of experience, and that's what I want to come to.

Next Fortas uncorked a curve ball. He argued that, rather than safeguarding states' rights, *Betts v. Brady* actually undermined state sovereignty. It was a clever ploy:

...I should like to restate that very simply and very plainly, Your Honors: I believe that Betts against Brady does not incorporate a proper regard for federalism. I believe that Betts against Brady, laying down as it does the principle of case-by-case supervision by the Federal courts of State criminal proceedings, is antithetical to federalism. Federalism requires, in my judgment, if Your Honors please, that the Federal courts should refrain so far as possible from intervention in State criminal proceedings.

Fortas went on to point out that in the past 20 years many Supreme Court decisions had reversed state court decisions that denied a court-appointed attorney. Each Supreme Court reversal introduced a new "special circumstance." Fortas maintained that this litany of reversals was a consistent intrusion into the states' right to self-government. And unless the Supreme Court reversed Betts, this intrusion would continue because the notion that a trial judge could make the correct call on a defendant's need for a court-appointed attorney was wrong.

Fortas continued:

> A defendant is arraigned. How can a judge, looking at the defendant, decide whether there are special circumstances in his case? Does the judge look at this defendant and say: You look stupid; you look as if you're a moron? Does he have a mental examination of him at the time?

Fortas reminded the judges that 37 states had taken matters into their own hands and passed legislation requiring court-appointed attorneys for indigents. The justices quizzed Fortas about whether or not he was advocating court-appointed counsel for felony cases only or for misdemeanor, traffic, and civil cases as well. Fortas maintained that he was not arguing for civil cases. This must have been good news to Jacob, sitting at the table on the other side of the lectern.

Fortas weaved his way through a number of thorny questions regarding the relationship between the Sixth Amendment right to counsel, due process, and equal protection. He was not about to lose momentum on the shoals of complicated Constitutional issues. He summed up his presentation by stating that he wasn't making an argument that the Fourteenth Amendment incorporates the Sixth Amendment, but he added that Justice Black had often made an eloquent argument to that point in previous cases. His flattery was not lost on the justices, who chuckled at Fortas's smooth escape from a complicated Constitutional question. Then Fortas turned the lectern over to Lee Rankin.

Rankin, who was arguing an amicus on behalf of the ACLU, continued the Fortas argument that a layman was not capable of weaving his way through the technicalities of a criminal case. To reinforce his point, he used the familiar adage that an individual who represents himself has a fool for a counsel. After a rambling soliloquy about habeas corpus and prisoners' right to a retrial, Rankin concluded by urging the judges to overturn *Betts v. Brady*, and to make the decision retroactive.

After Rankin returned to the plaintiff's table, Chief Justice Warren invited Bruce Jacob to approach the lectern. Jacob might have hoped that the chummy atmosphere during the conclusion to the Fortas presentation would carry over to his. It didn't. Jacob felt more like he was standing in a foxhole than at a lectern.

> My first impression was that I was in a pit. The Justices were very close to the speaker's lectern, and they were seated high above me and were spread out far to my left and to my right.... The lectern had lights on it. There was a green light, a yellow light, and a red light to indicate when the speaker was supposed to stop... I began to make my prepared argument, but there were questions almost immediately.... There was no reverence for established rules.... A total of ninety-two questions, comments, or interruptions took place during my argument, and most of these came during the first half hour or so.

The justices hurled questions at him. While he tried to answer one, another would come flying at him. Jacob was sinking, and there were no lifelines. Searching for solid ground, he tried to explain to the Court why Florida did not provide the Court with Gideon's trial transcript, contending that state judicial transcripts that don't constitute a judgment are outside the Supreme Court's jurisdiction to review, but the justices kept shooting him down:

> Justice Harlan: Why do you have to waste time on that? Because Mr. Fortas is not contending…, as I understand him, that if the Betts and Brady rule is adhered to, that this case should be reversed.

> Mr. Jacob: Okay, Your Honor, I was—I wanted to be sure that the Court did not rule upon the transcript as it appears in this—

> Justice Harlan: His position is that we are faced in this case really either affirming, adhering to Betts against Brady or overruling it. And that's the only premise he's argued his case on.

> Mr. Jacob: Okay, Your Honor, I'll proceed with our argument—

> Justice White: Well, I take it you're not raising any questions at all about this being, the judgment that's here for review, being a final judgment—

> Mr. Jacob: No, Your Honor.

> Justice White: And there is no question of our appellate jurisdiction here?

> Mr. Jacob: No, Your Honor.

As the hearing proceeded, it became clear that Jacob's script was unconvincing. His insistence that a judgment overturning *Betts v. Brady* would intrude on the right of the states to their own criminal procedures seemed, more than anything else, to annoy. Jacob's argument lost traction when Justice Brennan pointed out that *Betts v. Brady* actually interfered with states' rights by keeping criminal courts guessing about which of their decisions would be overturned by another Supreme Court-identified special circumstance (the argument Fortas had made earlier). A prolonged discussion about whether or not it was possible to get a fair trial without counsel went nowhere.

Then the Court returned to the reality that 5,200 prisoners who had been found guilty with no representation by defense counsel were incarcerated in Florida jails. As the justices homed in on this issue, the prospect that these prisoners would have to be retried or be released spurred Jacob to take a new tack. Citing several Supreme Court decisions, he argued that due process was a relative rather than an absolute rule. He seemed to gain some ground with this statement: "So, historically, under the definition of due process as it's been formulated by the Court, due process cannot be an absolute requirement. We cannot have an absolute rule requiring appointment of counsel in these cases and not in those cases. We cannot draw an inflexible dividing line anywhere."

A prolonged question-and-answer session about right-to-counsel for capital and noncapital cases had Jacob's head spinning. Later he described his experience as being "caught in a crossfire," and went on:

> It was difficult to know which question to take next and difficult to respond with so many questions coming from so many different directions.... Not aware that one would have had to remember several rapid-fire questions at a time, I neglected to bring a pad and pencil to the lectern that could have perhaps helped in answering.

Justice Stewart asked Jacob if it was possible for a layperson such as Gideon to provide adequate counsel to a defendant. It was a tricky question. If Jacob said "no" he would undercut his position that Gideon was capable of defending himself; a "yes" answer implied that a layperson could represent a defendant as adequately as a trained attorney. Jacob tried to finesse the situation. He said that a judge could choose whatever system he thought was fair. For example, he could choose not to have a prosecutor. This exaggeration brought a warning from Justice Harlan: "Don't go too far now," followed by chuckles from the bench. Embarrassed, Jacob made an effort to explain himself. He said that state legal systems should not be discouraged from experimenting with different trial options. If a defendant asked Gideon to serve as his lawyer, he didn't think a judge would object. This prompted Justice Black to ask, "Wouldn't Gideon maybe get into trouble for practicing law without a license?" This question was greeted with more laughter. Jacob's red-faced apology for his "stupid answer" was followed by more laughter.

Jacob summarized his position by arguing the dangers of overruling *Betts v. Brady*. Constitutionally, the states have the right to set rules of procedure in their courts. Changing this standard would infringe on states' rights and due process encoded in the Fourteenth Amendment. If the Court did reverse *Betts v. Brady*, Jacob implored the justices not to make the reversal retroactive, and to limit the decision to felony cases only.

No doubt vastly relieved to be out of the line of fire Jacob returned to his seat, and George Mentz, assistant attorney general of Alabama, walked to the lectern. Mentz was one of the four state amicus curiae that supported the state of Florida's fight. After witnessing Jacob's ordeal, Mentz was not about to endure a similar grilling. "Regrettably," he told the Court, "my presentation will in many areas duplicate that of Mr. Jacob, but fortunately, I'll be brief." Mentz then summarized his amicus position.

> We contend that the Sixth Amendment providing
> for representation by counsel in criminal
> prosecutions operates only on the Federal
> Government; that State appointment, in and of
> itself, is not an essential to a fair trial; that an
> asserted denial of due process should be tested by
> an appraisal of the facts in a given case; and that
> the Fourteenth Amendment's due process clause
> does not make the Sixth Amendment applicable
> to the States.

Then Mentz proceeded to plow through the argument that it can favor an indigent not to have an attorney. According to Mentz, trial judges are more lenient and jurors more sympathetic to a defendant who cannot afford counsel. It was evident to everyone in the Courtroom that, rather than cultivating a convincing argument, Mentz had dug himself a hole, when Justice Douglas commented, "Maybe we should have some new constitutional limits. Maybe if these laymen are so good at defending themselves as you say, maybe we should get the Sixth Amendment repealed." The comment was followed by sardonic chuckles.

From that point on, Mentz had nowhere to go. When his time was up Justice Harlan asked him if he really thought he had a chance to win this case. Mentz replied, "Well, as I say, we—it's the old situation of hope springs eternal, I guess. We hope to win this one." His comment prompted another laugh from the justices. The Broadway composer George M. Cohan wrote a song titled, "Always Leave Them Laughing When You Say Goodbye." In that, Mentz succeeded.

Later, in the hall outside the Court Chamber, Fortas approached Jacob and his wife. They shook hands, and Fortas said, "You know you have a wonderful way before the Court." For Jacob this praise was the high point of his day. After the hearing, the participants resumed their regular lives. Certain of victory,

Fortas returned to his prosperous Washington law practice. Jacob, equally certain of defeat, but still hoping a decision favorable to Gideon would not be retroactive, settled into married life and his private practice.

The Supreme Court does not announce deadlines for their decision. Fortas, Jacob, and Gideon could only wait. The lonely vigil must have been excruciating for Gideon. He might have been a "used-up man," as Anthony Lewis described him, but Gideon still believed every man had a Constitutional right to an attorney. Life might have taken away his hopes but not his sense of justice. Lewis described Gideon's state of mind as he awaited the Supreme Court decision:

> The idea of prejudice on the part of Florida officials against the poor and unfortunate was a fixation with Gideon. He spoke again and again about the welfare authorities and what he called their attempt to take his children from him. He spoke bitterly of the Florida Supreme Court and its refusal to do anything about counsel for the poor.... "They think it's perfectly all right to take a man into a courtroom and deny him all his rights."

Whatever bitterness Gideon felt, it did not diminish his fervor. In a letter to Abe Fortas, he wrote, "I have no illusions about law and courts and the people who are involved in them. I believe that each era finds an improvement in law. Each year brings something for the benefit of mankind. Maybe this will be one of those small steps forward."

On March 18, 1963, the Supreme Court ruled in favor of Gideon and reversed *Betts v. Brady*. The decision was unanimous. Almost two years had passed since Gideon stood before a judge in a Florida courtroom and insisted he had the right to defense counsel. Now the Supreme Court of the United States agreed.

The Court's ruling made the Sixth Amendment right-to-counsel provision mandatory in all state felony cases. Never again would a poor person be found guilty of a crime without benefit of counsel. In courtrooms across the nation, the public defender would become as much a fixture as judge, jury, and prosecutor.

The Supreme Court is the only branch of the Federal Government that explains the reasons for its decisions. In writing the Court's opinion in *Gideon v. Wainwright,* Justice Hugo Black said:

> The right of one charged with crime to counsel may not be deemed fundamental and essential to fair trials in some countries but it is in ours. From the very beginning, our state and national constitutions and laws have laid great emphasis on procedural and substantive safeguards designed to assure fair trials before impartial tribunals in which every defendant stands equal before the law. This noble ideal cannot be realized if the poor man charged with crime has to face his accusers without a lawyer to assist him.

On August 5, 1963, Gideon was retried in the same courtroom in front of the same judge, but this time he was represented by defense counsel Fred W. Turner, a wily local attorney. Turner shot holes through the testimony of star prosecution witness Henry Cook. It took the jury 65 minutes to acquit Gideon. Tears streaming down his face, Gideon told supporters "This is the happiest day of my life."

A free man, Gideon went back to the only life he knew—odd jobs and gambling. He did manage to avoid trouble with the law, except for a vagrancy arrest a few years later. At his arraignment the judge asked Gideon if he was pleading guilty or not guilty. Gideon replied that, before they went any further, the judge might want to read a book, and he handed the judge a copy of

Anthony Lewis's *Gideon's Trumpet*. The judge took the book, and Gideon spent the night in lockup.

The next day the judge told him that the book was interesting, and he was honored to have such a noteworthy person in his courtroom. But, the judge added, free counsel is only a guaranteed right for felonies, and Gideon was charged with a misdemeanor. He would have to plead guilty or pay for a defense counsel. Gideon pled guilty, and the judge let him go.

Gideon walked out of the courtroom and into obscurity. On January 18, 1972, he died as he lived— a down-and-out indigent. But the name Gideon and his struggle for justice is a lasting reminder that the Constitution of the United States applies to all citizens regardless of income or social status.

Acknowledgements

H e said his name was "Frenchy." It sounded like a moniker invented to impress Bourbon Street tourists, but he had a deft touch with Bananas Foster, and a lyrical cadence to his voice added a dollop of credibility to his claim. While Frenchy flambéd, I gazed at a mural that covered the wall opposite my table. In splashy colors it depicted a dashing, sword-wielding character leading a charge against 19th-century British soldiers. Several skirmishes, some on land and others at sea, provided an action-packed backdrop to the painting. "Who's the guy in the mural?" I asked. To his credit, Frenchy didn't roll his eyes, but his smile was tinged with a bit of wryness. "That's Jean Lafitte, the Robin Hood of New Orleans."

I knew Lafitte was a pirate and the hero of the Battle of New Orleans, but the Robin Hood comment was an intriguing angle. After dessert Frenchy served brandy, coffee, and tales of the city's most beloved scoundrel. He told me that Lafitte shared his booty with the less fortunate denizens of the French Quarter. He never attacked American ships, and, when the governor of Louisiana offered a $500 reward for his arrest, Lafitte offered a $1500 reward for the arrest of the governor. How could you not like a rogue like that?

Over the following months I thought about Lafitte and wondered about other notable miscreants whose actions defied their infamous labels. On a trip to Lake Champlain in Upstate New York I discovered that the traitor Benedict Arnold was a Revolutionary War figure of epic proportions. Gradually the notion of a history book about scoundrels who made America great began to take shape. Over the ensuing months many names appeared and disappeared from my list of candidates. Unfortunately, Jean Lafitte did not make the final cut. His heroic participation in the Battle of New Orleans took place at the same time the United States and Britain were signing a peace treaty at Ghent. But his absence from the pages does not lessen his influence. Lafitte's heroic spirit is the inspiration for this book.

Researching *Scoundrels* was an adventure. I cruised Valcour Island Bay guided by 19th-century nautical maps, hiked Benedict Arnold's escape route to the British frigate *Vulcan*, and stood at arm's length from the freight wagon that had transported John Brown to the gallows. I've roamed George Washington's headquarters during the siege of Boston, shaken the hand of Pulitzer Prize-winner Anthony Lewis, and wandered the ramparts of Fort Ticonderoga.

During each step of my literary pilgrimage an astonishing group of historians, journalists, and academics assisted me. I owe a huge debt of gratitude to my copy editor, Kitty Burns Florey, who like a vampire hunter, drove a stake through misplaced commas, periods, and grammatical miscues that sucked substance from my sentences. I owe immeasurable thanks to Anthony Lewis, David Glenn, Ron Yates, Barbara Trembley, Michal Rozbicki, David Fox, Fred Close, Bruce Jacobs, Phil Zampini, and Douglas Perks for both their professional expertise and their personal enthusiasm. I am especially indebted to the historical novelist William Martin; his support bolstered me during the many times my task seemed too big.

Many thanks to Nicholas Long, Sandy Berkowitz, Patricia Montagna, Maggie Henley, Edward Shea, Gillian Voight, and Carol Weis for reviewing and offering helpful comments on early drafts. I am indebted to the rangers and administrators at the National Park Service historical sites at Saratoga, New York; Fort Ticonderoga, New York; Harpers Ferry, West Virginia; Longfellow House, Cambridge, Massachusetts; and North Elba, New York for their enthusiastic and insightful comments. The Historical Park Service is truly a national treasure.

I owe thanks to the librarians at Lake Placid, New York; Boston, Massachusetts; and Westfield, Massachusetts. I am grateful to the curators at the Springfield, Massachusetts, Museum for the many times they sought out and organized historical documents on John Brown for me. Many thanks to diligent map-maker Karen Kleinerman. And I am especially grateful to my cousin Jan Klapetzky, who fixed last-minute resolution problems with photos and maps.

Writing is lonely work, so the opportunity to hobnob with experienced writers, agents, and publishers provided welcome and informative interludes. The Write Angles, Backspace, Random House, River Teeth, and Bay Path College conferences helped me clarify both my writing and publishing goals—a valuable service for someone writing his first book of history. And thank-you to literary agent Jon Sternfeld, who, after reading my query five years ago, said, "This is fascinating." That meant the world to me then, and it still does.

Bibliography

Introduction

Lehrer, Tom. "Wernher Von Braun" in *An Evening Wasted with Tom Lehrer:* Reprise Records, 1959.

Neufeld, J. Michael. *Von Braun: Dreamer of Space, Engineer of War.* New York: Vintage, 2008.

Chapter One
Anne Hutchinson
Books

Carnes, Mark C. and Winship, Michael P. *The Trial of Anne Hutchinson: Liberty, Law and Intolerance in Puritan New England* (2nd ed.). New York: Pearson, 2005.

Hall, David D. (ed.). *The Antinomian Controversy, 1636–1638: A Documentary History.* Durham, N.C., and London: Duke University Press, 1990.

Hall, Timothy D. *Anne Hutchinson: Puritan Prophet.* In the *Library of American Biography* series (Mark C. Carnes, ed.). Upper Saddle River, N.J.: Pearson Education, 2009.

LaPlante, Eve. *American Jezebel: The Uncommon Life of Anne Hutchinson, the Woman Who Defied the Puritans.* New York: HarperCollins, 2004.

Ranlet, P. *Enemies of the Bay Colony: Puritan Massachusetts and Its Foes* (2nd ed.). Lanham, Md.: University Press of America, 2006.

Winship, Michael P. *The Times and Trials of Anne Hutchinson: Puritans Divided.* In *Landmark Law Cases and American Society*

(Peter Charles Hoffer and N.E.H. Hull, eds.). Lawrence, Kans.: University Press of Kansas, 2005.

Winship, Michael P. (ed.). *Making Heretics: Militant Protestantism and Free Grace in Massachusetts 1636–1641.* Princeton, N.J.: Princeton University Press, 2002.

Primary Sources

John Underhill account of attack on Pequot village, June 5, 1637; retrieved Dec. 8, 2014: http://www.mashantucket.com/pequotwar.aspx

The trial and interrogation of Anne Hutchinson (1637); retrieved Nov. 13, 2014: http://www.swarthmore.edu/SocSci/bdorsey1/41docs/30-hut.html.

Ditmore, Michael G. "A Prophetess in Her Own Country: An Exegesis of Anne Hutchinson's 'Immediate Revelation.'" *William and Mary Quarterly* 57 (2): 349–392 (2000).

Web Sites

Statue of Anne Hutchinson, Massachusetts State House: www.dcmemorials.com/index_indiv0008064.htm

Anne Hutchinson murder: www.nytimes.com/1990/10/07/nyregion/anne-hutchinson-puritan-rebel-and-westchester-pioneer.html

National Women's History Museum: www.nwhm.org

Trial and interrogation of Anne Hutchinson: www.swarthmore.edu/SocSci/bdorsey1/41docs/30-hut.html

Anne Hutchinson trial transcript: http://www.constitution.org/primarysources/hutchinson.html

Pequot massacre: www.mashantucket.com/pequotwar.aspx

Chapter Two
Benedict Arnold
Books

Allen, Thomas B. *Tories: Fighting for the King in America's First Civil War.* New York: Harper, 2010.

Bellico, Russell P. *Sails and Streams in the Mountains: A Maritime and Military History of Lake George and Lake Champlain* (revised ed.). Fleischmanns, N.Y.: Purple Mountain Press, 2001.

Boylan, Richard B. *Benedict Arnold: The Dark Eagle.* New York: W.W. Norton & Co., 1973.

Cohen, Eliot A. *Conquered into Liberty: Two Centuries of Battles along the Great Warpath That Made the American Way of Life.* New York: Free Press, 2011.

Ellis, Joseph P. *Founding Brothers: The Revolutionary Generation.* New York: Vintage Books, 2000.

Kelly, Jack. *Band of Giants: The Amateur Soldiers Who Won America's Independence.* New York: Palgrave Macmillan, 2014.

Klimeade, Brian and Don Yaeger. *George Washington's Secret Six: The Spy Ring that Saved the American Revolution.* New York: Sentinel, 2013.

Ketchum, Richard M. *Saratoga: Turning Point of America's Revolutionary War.* New York: Henry Holt and Co., 1997.

Langguth, A. J. *Patriots: The Men Who Started the American Revolution.* New York: Simon and Schuster Paperbacks, 1988.

Luzader, John F. *Saratoga: A Military History of the Decisive Campaign of the American Revolution.* New York: Savas Beatie, 2008.

Martin, James Kirby. *Benedict Arnold, Revolutionary War Hero: An American War Hero Reconsidered.* New York: New York University Press, 1997.

McCullough, David. *1776.* New York: Simon and Schuster, 2005.

Murphy, Jim. *The Real Benedict Arnold.* New York: Clarion Books, 2007.

Palmer, Dave R. *George Washington and Benedict Arnold: A Tale of Two Patriots.* Washington, D.C.: Regnery Publications, 2006.

Randal, Willard Sterne. *Benedict Arnold: Patriot and Traitor.* New York: William Morrow and Co., 1990.

Roberts, Kenneth. *Rabble in Arms.* New York: Doubleday, 1933.

Stimson, F.J. *My Story: Being the Memoirs of Benedict Arnold: Late Major-General in the Continental Army and Brigadier-General in that of His Britannic Majesty.* New York: Charles Scribner's Sons, 1917.

Young, Alfred E., Gary Nash, and R. Raphael (eds.). *Revolutionary Founders: Rebels, Radicals, and Reformers in the Making of the Nation.* New York: Alfred A. Knopf, 2011.

Primary Sources

Benedict Arnold to George Washington, on board the *Vulture*, September 25, 1780. *The Papers of Alexander Hamilton*—27 vols. (Harold C. Syrett et al., eds.). New York, 1961–1987), 2: 439–440.

Benedict Arnold to B. Douglas, St. George's Key, June 9. 1770. *Historical Magazine*, 1857: 119.

General Gates's Instructions to General Arnold, Aug. 7, 1776. *American Archives*, ser. 5, Vol. I, 836.

Maguire, J. Robert. *Dr. Robert Knox's Account of the Battle of Valcour: October 11–16, 1776.* Montpelier, Vt. Reprinted from *Vermont History*, 141–150 (1978).

Darley, Stephen. *Voices from a Wilderness Expedition: The Journals and Men of Benedict Arnold's Expedition to Quebec in 1775.* Bloomington, Ind.: AuthorHouse, 2011.

Darley, Stephen. *The Battle of Valcour Island: The Participants and Vessels of Benedict Arnold's 1776 Defense of Lake Champlain.* ©Stephen Darley, 2013.

Washington's orders regarding expedition led by Arnold to Quebec. W.W. Abbott, Philander D. Chase, and Dorothy Twohig (eds.). *Instructions to Nathaniel Tracy,* September 2, 1775, in *Papers of George Washington, Revolutionary War Series,* Vols. I–VIII. Charlottesville, Va.: University Press of Virginia, 1985–1998, 405.

Arnold letters regarding Canadian expedition. Maine Historical Society Collections. Vol. 1, 341-416, Portland, Maine, 1831.

U.S. Navy records. *Naval Documents of the American Revolution,* Clark, William Bell and Morgan, William (eds.). Washington, D.C.: Naval History Division. Department of the Navy, 1964: Vol. 6. (Aug. 1–Oct. 31, 1776).

Oct 12, 1776. Letter from Arnold to General Gates. Naval Documents of the American Revolution, V.6, P1235.

Instructions to Arnold from Gates prior to Valcour Island Battle. "Orders and Instructions," Ticonderoga, Aug. 7, 1776, AA, ser. 5, 1:826–27.

Steward, Jahiel. First-person account of Battle of Valcour Island by American seaman. *Journal,* Oct. 11, 1775: vermonthistory. org/journal/misc/StewartJahiel.pdf

Wells, Bayze. First-person account of Battle of Valcour Island by American seaman. *Journal,* Oct. 11–13, 1776. *Collections of the Connecticut Historical Society,* 7 (1899): 283–284.

Schuyler, Phillip, Horatio Gates, and Benedict Arnold: letters. *Bulletin of Fort Ticonderoga Museum,* Vol. 4, No 7, July 1938: Vol. 4, No. 1, January 1939.

Web Sites

Lake Champlain Maritime Museum, Vt.; includes Battle of Valcour Island exhibit: www.lcmm.org

Lake Champlain and Lake George historical site: www. historiclakes.org/Valcour/valcour_battle.htm

For detailed bibliography of V.I. Battle see: www.historiclakes. org/biblio.html

Fort Ticonderoga, N.Y.: www.fortticonderoga.org/

Saratoga National Park, N.Y.: www.nps.gov/sara/index.htm

Longfellow House/Washington's Headquarters, Cambridge, Mass.: www.nps.gov/long/index.htm

Chapter Three
John Brown
Books

Benfey, Christopher. "Terrorist or Martyr?" in *The Tribunal: Responses to John Brown and the Harpers Ferry Raid*. John Stauffer and Zoe Trodd (eds.). Cambridge, Mass.: Belknap Press/Harvard University Press, 2012.

Brown, G.W. *Reminiscences of Old John Brown—Thrilling Incidents of Border Life in Kansas*. Rockford, Ill.: printed by Abraham E. Smith, 1880.

Carton, Evan. *Patriotic Treason: John Brown and the Soul of America*. New York: Free Press, 2006.

Horwitz, Tony. *Midnight Rising: John Brown and the Raid that Sparked the Civil War*. New York: Henry Holt and Co., 2011.

McGlone, Robert E. *John Brown's War Against Slavery*. New York: Cambridge University Press, 2009.

Harpers Ferry Historical Association. *John Brown's Raid*. National Park Service History Series. Harpers Ferry: The Donning Co. Publishers, n.d.

Oates, Stephen B. *To Purge This Land With Blood: A Biography of John Brown* (2nd ed.). Amherst, Mass.: University of Massachusetts Press, 1980.

Quarles, Benjamin. *Allies for Freedom and Blacks on John Brown*. Jackson, Tenn.: Da Capo Press, n.d.

Articles

Bordewich, Fergus M. "Day of Reckoning." *Smithsonian*, October 2009, 62–69.

Horowitz, Tony. "Why John Brown Still Scares Us." *American History*, December 2011, 39–45.

Wright, Harry Andrew. "John Brown in Springfield." *New England Magazine,* May 1894.

Primary Sources

Magazine of the Jefferson County Historical Society. *John Brown Raid Issue.* Vol. LXXXV, October 2009.

Earle, Jonathan. *John Brown's Raid on Harpers Ferry: A Brief History with Documents.* The Bedford Series in History and Culture. Boston: Bedford/St. Martin's, 2008.

Barry, Joseph. *The Strange Story of Harper's Ferry with Legends of the Surrounding Country* (14th printing). The Woman's Club of Harpers Ferry District, 2013.

Leech, S.V. *The Raid of John Brown at Harper's Ferry as I Saw It.* Miami, Fla.: HardPress Publishing, n.d.

Townsley, James. "The Pottawatomie Killings: It Is Established Beyond Controversy that John Brown Was the Leader." http://www.kansashistory.us/pottamassacre.html

Springfield, Mass. Historical Archives.

Springfield Daily Republican. "The Execution of John Brown." December 3, 1859.

Letter from John Brown to Rufus Chapman asking Chapman to serve as his defense counsel. October 21, 1859. Chapman did not reply.

Letter from John Brown to Reverend Luther Humphrey, November 19, 1859. Justifying his actions in the cause of freedom.

Lee, Egbert. First-hand account of life as a slave in Georgia, n.d.
Letter from Salmon Brown to F.B. Sanborn describing the Pottawatomie raid, with notes by Sanborn. November 17, 1911.

Web Sites

Harpers Ferry National Historic Park (U.S. National Park Service): www.nps.gov/hafe/
University of Virginia, John Brown homepage: http://www2.iath.virginia.edu/jbrown/master.html
University of Missouri–Kansas City. "The Life and Trial of John Brown: A Commentary": http://law2.umkc.edu/faculty/projects/ftrials/johnbrown/brownaccount.html
John Brown's Farm–State Historic Site: http://parks.ny.gov/historic-sites/29/details.aspx

Chapter Four
"Tokyo Rose"
Books

Close, Frederick. *Tokyo Rose: An American Patriot.* Lanham, Md.: Scarecrow Press, 2010.
Duss, Masayo. *Tokyo Rose: Orphan of the Pacific* (2nd ed.). New York: Harper and Row, 1983.
Pfau, Ann Elizabeth, *Miss Yourlovin: GIs, Gender, and Domesticity during WWII.* Chapter 5, "The Legend of Tokyo Rose." New York: Columbia University Press, 2009.
Gunn, Rex. *They Called Her Tokyo Rose* (revised ed.). Bateman, Brent, 2007: www.booksurge.com

Articles

Coleman, Joseph, "1945 Firebombing Left Legacy of Terror, Pain." *Associated Press,* March 10, 2005; retrieved February 2, 2011: http://www.commondreams.org/headlines05/0310-08.htm

Yates, Ron, "Tokyo Rose Accusers Claim U.S. Forced Them to Lie." *Chicago Tribune,* March 22, 1976.

O'Brien, Keith, "They Call Her Tokyo Rose." Retrieved November 18, 2010: http://www.weeklywire.com/ww/01-20-98/chicago_cover.html

Holbert, Tim G. W. "Convicting a Myth: Debunking the Legend of Tokyo Rose and the Real Woman Who Took the Blame." *World War II Chronicles,* Issue XXVII, Winter 2004–2005; retrieved September 10, 2010: http://www.americanveterancenter.org/magazine/wwiichronicle

HistoryNet Staff, "Tokyo Rose: They Called Her a Traitor." *American History.* Retrieved accessed November 11, 2010: http://www.historynet.com/tokyo-rose-they-called-her-a-traitor.

Sherrer, Hans. "'Tokyo Rose' Was Innocent!" *Justice Denied,* Issue 28, Spring 2005, 22–25; retrieved September 27, 2010: http://forejustice.org/wc/tr/tokyo_rose_040503.htm

Primary Sources

Dunn, Eldon J. "Synopsis of the criminal trial of Iva Ikuko Toguri D'Aquino (aka "Tokyo Rose")." Federal Bureau of Investigation, 07/05/1949–10/06/1949; retrieved November 3, 2010: http://arcweb.archives.gov/,

Web Sites

Radio Propaganda Page, EarthStation 1: "Orphan Ann" ("Tokyo Rose"). Includes excerpts from Iva Toguri *Zero Hour* broadcasts: http://www.earthstation1.com/Tokyo_Rose. html

National Japanese American Historical Society: http://www. njahs.org/research/references/ja_women.php

Eyewitness to History. "The Tokyo Fire Raids." http:// eyewitnesstohistory.com/tokyo.h

Chapter Five
Clarence Gideon
Books

Lewis, Anthony. *Gideon's Trumpet*. New York: Vintage, 1964.

Murphy, Bruce Allen. *Fortas: The Rise and Ruin of a Supreme Court Justice*. New York: William Morrow and Co., 1988.

Prentzas, G.S. *Gideon v. Wainwright: The Right to Free Legal Counsel*. (Tim McNeese, consulting ed.). New York: Chelsea House, 2007.

Monographs

Jacob, Bruce R. "Memories of and Reflections about Gideon v. Wainwright," in *Stetson Law Review*, Volume XXXIII, No 1, Fall 2003.

Primary Documents

The Constitution of the United States with the Declaration of Independence and the Articles of Confederation. Introduction by R.B. Bernstein. New York: Fall River Press.

Petition for a Writ of Certiorari from Clarence Gideon to the Supreme Court of the United States. National Archives; retrieved March 11, 2013: http://research.gov/id/597554

Oral arguments before the Supreme Court *Gideon v. Wainwright.* January 15, 1963; retrieved February 26, 2013: http://www.oyez.org/cases/1960-1969/1962/1962_155

Web Sites

The U.S. Constitution: http://www.archives.gov/national-archives-experience/charters/constitution.html

U.S. Supreme Court rules: http://www.supremecourt.gov/ctrules/2013RulesoftheCourt.pdf

"Scottsboro Boys" trial: http://law2.umkc.edu/faculty/projects/ftrials/scottsboro/scottsb.htm

Betts v. Baker: https://www.law.cornell.edu/supremecourt/text/316/455

Index

About the Author

Martin Henley is a retired professor emeritus from Westfield State University, Westfield, Massachusetts. He was graduated from the State University at Oswego, New York with a B.A. in history. He earned his M.Ed. and Ph.D. in special education at Syracuse University. Henley is the author of four books and dozens of articles on teaching at-risk youth. He is a Navy veteran and he served in Viet Nam on an ammunition ship, the U.S.S. Maun Loa. His daughter Margaret is a social worker in western Massachusetts where Henley lives with his partner for life Patricia Montagna. "Scoundrels Who Made America Great", combines his love of American history with his fondness for the underdog. For information regarding presentations, comments or questions contact the author at mhenley21@comcast.net